United We Stand

The Role of Polish Workers in the
New York Mills Textile Strikes, 1912 and 1916

by

James S. Pula & Eugene E. Dziedzic

EAST EUROPEAN MONOGRAPHS
DISTRIBUTED BY COLUMBIA UNIVERSITY PRESS, NEW YORK

1990

EAST EUROPEAN MONOGRAPHS, NO. CCLXXXVI

Dedicated to

St. Mary, Our Lady of Częstochowa,

and to

The Men and Women of

Local 753, United Textile Workers of America,

Who Took a Stand for Justice and Equality.

Contents

Contents

Acknowledgements

The authors are indebted to a number of people and institutions who assisted in various ways in the research without which this study could not have been completed. Michael Dziedzic proved to be a limitless source of information and suggestions, in addition to which he also provided translations of some important documents and lent invaluable assistance in arranging interviews. Stella Furgal not only agreed to be interviewed herself but provided us with access to interviews that she had conducted, shared with us other information that she had gathered, and provided translations of the early anniversary books of St. Mary's Church. Kathleen Jacklin of the Olin Library at Cornell University located and provided access to the W. Pierrepont White Papers which were crucial in determining the company's attitude and efforts during the period in question. L. Louise Rozwell contributed tireless efforts in translating a great volume of important articles from *Słowo Polskie*.

There were many institutions which offered access to their facilities and collections, and many helpful individuals employed in those institutions who went out of their way to offer assistance. These included the Immigration History Research Center at the University of Minnesota; Carol Clemente of the Interlibrary Loan Office at the State University of New York at Binghamton; Katharine Vogel of the George Meany Memorial Archives; the Labor Archives at New York University; the Labor Studies Archives at Cornell University; Florence Kowal and Ann Harris of the New York Mills Public Library; Daniel Lorello and William Evans of the New York State Archives in Albany; the Olin Library at Cornell University; Douglas Preston, Michael Kenneally and the staff at the Oneida County Historical Society; Rev. Peter Gleba , Rev. John Drozdzal, Helen Gadziala, and Stella Jachim of St. Mary's, Our Lady of Częstochowa Parish in New York Mills; Mayor Stephen Zurek and Hazel Topor of the New York Mills village offices; Robert C. Dinwiddie and Leslie S. Hough of the Southern Labor Archives at Georgia State University; the State Historical Society of Wisconsin; Town Justice Ann A. Murray and Town Clerk Gail Wolanin of the Town of New Hartford; Justice Stanley Wolanin and Court Clerk Marianne Buttenschon of the Town of Whitestown; and Barbara Brookes and Robert Quist of the Utica Public Library.

Special appreciation is due all of those individuals who agreed to provide their own personal recollections through interviews. They include: Cecilia Powroznik Chrabas, Zenon Chrabas, Michael Dziedzic,

Stella Furgal, Mary Jones, Peter Kogut, Bertha Nowicki Kozak, Stanley Krawiec, Josephine Kupiec, Stanley Kupiec, Pauline Kozak Madey, Leonard Motyka, Sadie Nassif, Stephanie Nowicki, Joseph Piszcz, John Rogowski, Richard Rosinski, William Silcox, Sophie Szczych, Stanley Zima, and Stephen Zurek.

We are especially indebted to those who assisted by translating materials into English. In this category, special appreciation is due L. Louise Rozwell who translated a great many articles from *Słowo Polskie*. Others who rendered valuable translation assistance were: M. B. Biskupski, Serafina Clarke, Helen Dziedzic, Michael Dziedzic, Stella Furgal, John Kubiniec, and Piotr Mizia.

In addition to the above, but no less important, were a number of people who shared papers, photographs and other materials, or offered valuable suggestions and other assistance. These included Stanley Babiarz, Matthew Bielaska, Sr., Ian Booth, Thomas Calogero, Barbara Crane, Ann Dziedzic, Nancy Dziedzic, Rose Smola Gates, Rev. Peter Gleba, Thomas Hagerty, Joseph Kielbasa, Mark Kulikowski, Edward Kwiecinski, Richard Kwiecinski, Anita L. Merritt, Raymond Motyka, Dr. Eugene Nassar, Stephanie Nowicki, Nellie and Edward Palczynski, Martin Pezdek, Stella Pilawa, Alfred Piszcz, Louise and Andrew Przybyla, Cheryl A. Pula, Winifred Pula, Frances and Ronald Pytko, William Samel, Bertha Solnica, Richard Thomas, Gladys Trzepacz, Hon. John J. Walsh, Edwin Waskiewicz, Esq., Wayne Wright, Joseph Wolak, Stanley Wolak, and Marcia Wolter.

Preface

Quite often people take the area they live in for granted; its advantages, its history, and its way of life are overlooked or considered of little importance. This is particularly true when one grows up in an area. One reads of other times and places, sees exciting or exotic scenes on television, or dreams of opportunities and adventures that lay beyond the boundaries of everyday life. Next to these idealized images, the familiar routine of daily life, the passing reminiscences of family and friends, and the occasional recollection of an event in local history seem unexciting, or mundane.

Growing up in New York Mills, we lived in a comfortable environment. The community was safe and friendly, families were stable, and life was good. We never lacked the necessities of life, and there were many social and recreational opportunities. Sometimes the older residents of the village alluded to times when people were poor and life was hard, but that seemed like ancient history, and certainly unimportant. After all, our ancestors were poor immigrants who worked hard, had few material comforts, and enjoyed few opportunities beyond the confines of the factory system. True, there were occasional rumors of labor strikes in the distant past, vague references to the National Guard occupying the village, and some haunting old photographs in the village library that showed people standing along the roadsides, their worldly possessions piled about them. But how important could all of this be? Surely, we thought, these old stories could not be very important — let alone exciting.

It was only much later, long after high school, college, and years of teaching that we began to wonder exactly what *had* happened in this small town three-quarters of a century earlier. Perhaps, we thought, there might be enough information to write an article, or a brief booklet. After finally deciding to look into the matter, we were astounded by the amount of information and material available on these seemingly insignificant events. Local newspapers carried detailed accounts of the strikes, older residents remembered early village life, university libraries contained theses and personal papers, state archives housed labor and national guard reports, and labor archives preserved correspondence and organization reports. Soon, the brief article took on far greater proportions as our thin file folder of information grew first to a cardboard box, and eventually to several boxes and a file cabinet, enough so that we soon decided, once the current work was complete, to write a second book on the general history of the community. All of these finds further sparked our curiosity, as did the hitherto unknown revelation that each of us had ancestors involved as leaders in the history we were trying to recover.

After nearly three years of research and writing, this book is our attempt to tell the story of the mysterious "strikes" we first heard about in our youth. As historians, we attempted to preserve our objectivity and to avoid any over-glorification of what turned out to be a very significant time in the history of central New York. Every event described in this book, every interpretation that we offer, is supported by written documentation or by the recollection of two or more interviewees.

The purposes of this book are to describe the events that took place in New York Mills between 1910 and 1916, and to offer interpretations of their significance to the village and to the greater perspective of "History." This is *not* intended to be a work of historical theory; rather, it is a narrative history. The noted historian Carl Becker once observed in an address before the American Historical Association that the essence of all history "is story, in aim always a true story; a story that employs all the devices of literary art ... to present the succession of events in the life of man, and from the succession of events thus presented to derive a satisfactory meaning."[1] That is what this work is intended to be — a story with a meaning.

We set the stage for the story by describing the founding and development of the textile mills and the company town that quickly grew up around them. We then describe the coming of the Poles, the mutual uncertainty that divided the village into two communities, the conditions of life in the Polish settlement, and the conditions that existed in the mills. This serves as prologue to the major focus of the work — chapters four through eight — the strikes of 1912 and 1916. We believe that these descriptions provide an insight into the anatomy of the strikes as few other works have, examining the attitudes and strategies of the owners, the hopes and activities of the workers, and the various external forces that shaped the constant turn of events as the strikes unfolded. An epilogue provides a summary of what transpired in the community in succeeding years, much of which can be linked as long-term affects of the earlier period considered in this book. Finally, the concluding chapter offers our interpretation of the short and long-term results of the strikes locally, and the place they hold in the greater historical perspective.

In the end, though, as Carl Becker said, this is a story. We hope that it is an interesting and informative one.

Chapter 1

Rise of a Company Town

The early rays of dawn gradually crept westward along the Mohawk Valley, illuminating one small, sleepy village after another until they finally reached the textile mills of the A. D. Juilliard Company lying at the western edge of the valley in the suburbs of Utica. It was a cool, crisp April morning in 1912 and people were just beginning to stir. Mary Jones rose early, as was her custom, and made her way to the kitchen to begin preparing breakfast for her family. A sudden noise drew her attention out the kitchen window where her eyes were greeted with the surprising sight of armed men in uniform roaming about her backyard. Startled, she quickly called to her husband Sam who immediately finished dressing and went outside to find out what was happening. There, to his absolute amazement, he found himself faced with an encampment of troops from the New York State National Guard. Approaching them, he asked why they were there, on his property. Rather than an answer, he was immediately arrested for trespassing on a government encampment![1]

What was the national guard doing in this small, peaceful mill town? What awful calamity occurred to cause the forced occupation of the village by several companies of armed soldiers?

Once alive with the fifes and drums of marching armies during the French and Indian War and the American Revolution, the Mohawk Valley had since become a peaceful land of farmers and small towns, a tranquil place where life passed slowly and people hunted and fished to supplement what they grew in their gardens or purchased from local farmers. Commercial industry was nonexistent in the Valley during colonial times, and commerce was generally restricted to the movement of crops to market and the importation of finished goods along the Mohawk and Hudson River routes that linked the area with the outside world through the port of New York.

It was not long after the Revolution, however, that the seeds for economic change were sown when Amos Wetmore, John Beard and

Hugh White, the latter a native of Middletown, Connecticut, for whom the Town of Whitestown would be named, erected Wetmore's Mill, the first commercial mill in Oneida County, along the banks of Sauquoit Creek in 1788.[2] In the years that followed, the growth of an extensive dairy farming industry in the area led to a great demand for cheese cloth to package dairy products for market. Sensing an opportunity to profit from this emerging demand, Dr. Seth Capron formed a new business partnership on February 2, 1808, and soon finalized the purchase of land and water rights necessary to establish a textile mill. Although he had become familiar with textile operations in Rhode Island before moving to the Mohawk Valley, Capron could boast little direct manufacturing experience himself. Consequently, he invited Benjamin Stuart Walcott to become a member of the business to superintend construction of the buildings and organization of manufacturing operations.[3]

Born in Rhode Island in 1755, Walcott possessed extensive business expertise and was then the proprietor of textile mills in Cumberland, Rehoboth, and Central Falls, Rhode Island, the latter of which he personally managed. He arrived in the Utica area in May of 1808. On October 31 of that year he formalized a joint partnership with the sale of ten shares of stock at $1,500 per share: two each to Benjamin S. Walcott, Jr., and Newton Mann; one each to Capron, Asher Wetmore, William M. Cheever, and Benjamin S. Walcott, Sr.; and two being jointly held by lawyers Thomas Gold and Theodore Sill. This partnership, formally known as "Walcott & Company," resulted in the erection, in the following year, of the first cotton and woolen mills in New York State at a site along Sauquoit Creek about a mile from where it flowed into the Mohawk River. This site offered the advantages of a stable, swift-running stream which dropped 1,014 feet in 17 miles and could readily be tapped for water power to operate the mill, and easy access to the Mohawk River for purposes of shipping and receiving. The first water-powered spinning equipment west of New England began producing cotton yarn there in the same year, with some eighty people employed in spinning and carding operations at what later came to be known as the "Lower Mills." The finished yarn was sent to the homes of local farmers who wove it on hand looms into "a coarse cotton cloth about three-fourths of a yard wide."[4]

Benjamin Walcott, Sr., returned to Rhode Island in 1809 to look after his other interests, leaving his son, Benjamin, Jr., to act as superintendent of the new mill. Under the junior Walcott's leadership the venture prospered, while relations with the state authorities developed to the point where Walcott succeeded in inducing the state legislature to pass a law exempting his mill employees from jury duty. In March of 1810 an act of the New York State legislature incorporated the growing business as the "Oneida Manufacturing Society" with a capital of some

$200,000. By this time the original shares, purchased for $1,500 each just two years previously, had increased in value to about $7,500 each. A handsome profit indeed![5]

But the younger Walcott was not satisfied with the early successes of the enterprise. Always seeking ways to improve operations, he determined to bring the weaving process into the mills to eliminate the expensive and time-consuming practice of consigning the yarn to individual hand weavers some distance from the mills. Consequently, in 1812 he hired Ezra Wood, a professional weaver, who he charged with training and supervising a staff of on-site weavers. Soon thereafter Walcott, in partnership with General George Doolittle, organized the "Whitestown Cotton and Woolen Manufacturing Society" and purchased an old wooden grist mill about a mile south of the Oneida Manufacturing Society. The property was at that time known as the "Buhr-stone mill" because it employed the first French buhr-stones to be used in New York. On this site Walcott constructed a large building outfitted with hand looms run by "expert weavers ... introduced from England and Scotland." Once this facility became operational, Walcott sent William B. Copley, a mechanic employed in the Oneida Manufacturing Society, to Rhode Island to learn about the construction and operation of the new power looms. Copley secured employment as an operator to learn how to run the machinery, while at the same time secretly taking measurements of its various parts. After obtaining all of the information he needed, he returned to New York where Walcott used the information that Copley had gained to build the first water-powered loom west of the Hudson. With the construction of these power looms there was no longer a need to have the thread woven in private homes. The entire manufacturing process could be done in the mills, and the speed and accuracy of the machines soon allowed Walcott to surpass all of the other cotton manufacturers in the United States in the production of "sheeting, shirting and muslins," as well as "the finer grades of corduroy, denims, hatistes, plush and the finer fabrics." By 1828 the plant facilities included 1,600 spindles, 48 power looms and 90 employees with an annual production of 312,000 yards of shirting.[6]

In 1824, seeking further expansion, Walcott succeeded in obtaining the financial backing of Benjamin Marshall, a wealthy New York City merchant. This new capital allowed him to purchase 89 acres of land midway between the Oneida Manufacturing Society and the Whitestown Cotton and Woolen Manufacturing Society, in an area later called the "Middle Mills," to construct a dam on Sauquoit Creek and an accompanying system of dikes to maintain a constant supply of water power, and to erect a large five-story brick mill that significantly increased both the amount and variety of production. The new factory, later known as Mill "Number 2," was a large masonry structure in Federalist design,

120 feet long by twenty feet wide. Styling themselves the "New York Mills Company," Walcott and Marshall began operation on November 15, 1827 and were soon able to boast the finest grades of cotton sheeting.[7] Indeed, *Lamb's Sectional Histories of New York State* noted that the New York Mills "had the reputation of producing cotton cloth superior in quality to any other made in the United States."[8] Seconding this, Simon Dixon, a resident of nearby Oriskany, testified before the U. S. House of Representatives' Committee on Manufactures in 1828 that he "knew of no other factory in the United States weaving cottons as fine as those of the New York Mills. Their cloth was said to be the standard for fine fabrics wherever produced."[9]

The increase in operations also required an increase in employees, leading to a need for housing. Thus, by 1825 twenty-two company-owned houses had been constructed for rental to factory workers, and two boarding houses were in operation: one catering to men and the other to women. These first company houses were one and one-half story white frame structures made of clapboards with shingle roofs and rubble foundations. Containing four rooms on each floor and designed to house two families, they initially rented for $17.50 per year. A community-spirited philanthropist, Walcott made a genuine effort to provide for the needs of the new community developing around the factories. He provided financial backing for the construction of a Presbyterian Church in 1818, assisted with the formation of a school district in 1826, provided company funds for the maintenance of company houses, financed community athletic teams, and donated large sums to other worthy community projects.[10] One observer reported that "Nowhere in the United States can there be found a factory village which excels the New York Mills in the beauty of its natural surroundings, the neatness and comfort of the operatives' homes, the excellence of its schools, the prosperity of its churches, or the contented intelligence of its people."[11] Further, a study of the community conducted by the New York Folklore Society some 150 years later concluded that:

> "The village's appearance soon attested to a sense of order and stability, which the company fostered in its dual attempt to draw workers and promote public favor. Both workers and proprietors lived near the mills: the workers clustered in company housing; the owners lived in finer homes, set somewhat apart by expansive lawns, but still close at hand. The workers' dwellings were brick or frame row houses and duplexes of simple but sturdy construction. Frequently the cottages were built on a four-room New England plan, with sheds added in saltbox style. Churches and proprietors' homes displayed a full range of

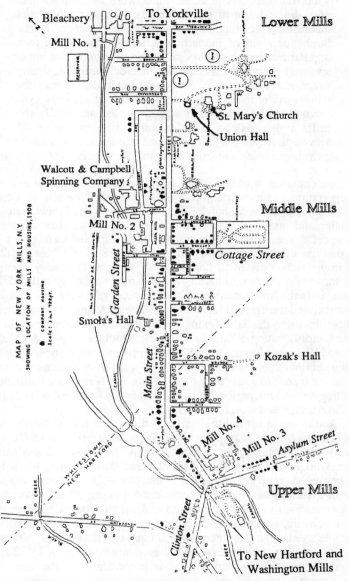

A map of New York Mills ca. 1915 adapted from Jareckie
and the atlases noted in the bibliography.

Victorian fashions, and the mills were kept up to date with the addition of stylish details such as cupolas and mansard roofs, which further reflected their owners' tastes. Such treatment of industrial buildings gave voice to a popular nineteenth-century philanthropic notion that home and work atmospheres could be rendered one in a company town, provided tasteful design be incorporated into the work environment. Of course, popular taste was synonymous with the owner's preferences, and while the mills and mansions received embellishment, workers' homes displayed only an occasional fan light over the door or a simple brick and stone design in the facade."[12]

The completion of the Erie Canal in 1825 provided an excellent transportation facility running past the north end of the village, considerably closer than the Mohawk River located only a mile away, making it easier and less costly to ship completed merchandise to market. Transportation improved even more with the establishment of the first railroad line connecting Albany with Utica in 1836. Each of the factories in the New York Mills had its own siding, and the easy, inexpensive movement of raw materials and finished goods by rail provided further impetus for expansion of operations. Following a fire in 1828 that destroyed the original factory of the Oneida Manufacturing Society, Walcott invested the $13,000 insurance payoff in the construction of a stone factory costing $70,000. This new structure housed 2,500 spindles and 96 power looms. By 1831 the mills operating under Walcott's various partnerships produced 1,800,000 yards of cloth annually, virtually all of it sent to New York City. Thus, the New York Mills began reaching beyond the regional economic network to compete for the first time in national and world markets.[13]

Continuing in his bid to develop and improve his operations, Walcott brought Samuel Campbell to the New York Mills in 1831. Born in 1809 in Tarbolton, Ayrshire, Scotland, Campbell was a mechanical expert who possessed "an inventive mind and manufacturing know-how, and instituted many improvements in machinery."[14] Characterized as "a man of great physical power, of tremendous energy," he "entered into his business with a determination to make it successful."[15] Beginning as a mechanic, Campbell soon rose to foreman and, over a period of time, began managing an increasing amount of the business. Under his care the company grew and prospered even more, becoming by 1838 the largest cotton manufacturing operation in the United States outside of New England. In 1840 he built another new stone structure in the Upper Mills, known as Mill "Number 3," bringing total employment in the village to 325 operatives who produced 25,000 yards of fine sheeting per week utilizing modern Arkwright machinery. The continuing success of these operations led to Campbell's acceptance into partnership in January, 1847, when Benjamin Marshall sold his interest in the company. With this the company became known officially as "Walcott & Campbell." Under this name, the partners were "very successful in selling their goods as American goods, while other manufacturers had given goods manufactured in this country a foreign label in order to sell them."[16]

Campbell, like Walcott, displayed a special interest in philanthropy and public service. An admirer of Henry Clay, he gravitated toward the Whig Party before becoming an active supporter of the infant Republican Party when it first organized in the 1850s. During the Civil War he was instrumental in the success enjoyed by the Oneida County War Committee, served a term as Supervisor of the Town of Whitestown in 1863-64, and was a delegate to the 1864 Republican National Convention in Baltimore. Following the war he was responsible for the erection of the first Civil War monument in Oneida County, and served as an officer and member of the Boards of Directors of such volunteer community organizations as the New York State Lunatic Asylum, the New York State Agricultural Society, and the Central New York Farmers' Club. Continuing his interest in politics, gained election to the New York State Senate in 1865 and 1867 where, not surprisingly, he proved to be a staunch believer in, and supporter of the protection of American industry. He capped this dimension of his career by serving as a Presidential Elector in 1872.[17]

By 1851 the village numbered nearly 2,000 residents, with Methodist and Presbyterian churches, its "full share of merchants and mechanics, and a temperance tavern."[18] A bleachery opened in 1860, and during the Civil War the New York Mills produced substantial amounts of cloth to meet the needs of the Northern armies. Many village residents saw military service during the conflict, and Walcott, who "reported an annual income of $100,000 each year," the largest in central New York, donated liberally to both religious and charitable causes, and to the aid of veterans and their families.[19]

Profits from the Civil War period, combined with better transportation and growing domestic and foreign markets, led to a rapid rise in production during the 1870s. In 1870, "Mill Number 4," a massive four-story brick structure measuring 250 feet by 70 feet was erected in the Upper Mills. By 1878 steam nearly replaced water as the source of power for the mills, which then employed some 1,000 workers. To meet the need for additional labor, the original English, Welsh and Scottish residents were joined by French Canadians who sought opportunity in the rapidly expanding industry experienced male weavers earned $1.00 per day, with women and children making from $.50 to

$1.75 per week. The northern and central portions of the village, generally referred to as the Lower and Middle Mills, boasted "seven stores of various kinds, one blacksmith shop, a tailor-shop, two district school buildings, three churches, [and] two physicians."[20] An observer wrote that "New York Mills is very attractive in summer, it is one of the places in Oneida County which strangers go to see. The houses of the operatives are neat, convenient, and healthy; most of them standing back from the road, with yard in front, garden in rear, and half-hidden by foliage. The good standing of New York Mills is due to the character of the employees, which has always been high, and to the regulations and example of the employers."[21]

In 1884 the Walcott & Campbell Company reorganized to consolidate all of the partners' various holdings in the village under the single name of the "New York Mills Corporation." President of the enterprise was William D. Walcott and the treasurer was Samuel Campbell, with their sons, William Stuart Walcott and Samuel R. Campbell, serving as secretaries. The new corporation boasted $1,000,000 in capital with 1,000 shares of stock valued at $1,000 per share. This later increased through the issuance of $400,000 in preferred stock. By 1888 this new consolidated company operated 1,600 looms to produce some 7,000,000 yards of cloth annually.[22]

As the need for new labor increased, the New York Mills Corporation began to advertise for workers in the New England textile communities. During the final decades of the nineteenth century, as the need for labor continued to rise, "the company sent agents to Europe in order to encourage workers to immigrate and take jobs in the mills. The company paid transportation costs for the first immigrants, and the workers repaid the company by a series of wage deductions. As the immigrants became established in the mills many sent for relatives and friends to follow them."[23] Naturally, the influx of new workers caused the size of the village to increase, forcing the construction of additional company housing to supplement the structures built prior to 1856. The new residences were brick buildings containing two-stories and an attic, and designed to accommodate two families.[24] By this time there were three company-owned boarding houses where Evelyn Morgan Evans recalled that meals were "all home cooking and it was served family style in a large dining room."[25] People who did not reside in the boarding houses, but wished to take their meals there, could do so at a reasonable fee. In addition to the boarding houses and the company-owned homes, there was also a company store where employees could purchase food and other necessities on credit with payment being deducted from the succeeding week's wages.

The Walcotts and the Campbells ruled their small fiefdom with a very strict code of conduct that all employees and residents were obliged to observe. The driving force behind this was Benjamin Walcott. Always fastidious in his own personal life, Walcott apparently underwent a conversion at the hands of the revivalist Rev. Charles G. Finney who convinced him that merely living a good life was not sufficient, it was his responsibility to ensure that others observed a strict moral code as well. The use of profanity or alcoholic beverages were strictly forbidden, while the sabbath was to be properly observed by all. Failure to observe any of these rules could result in loss of employment and expulsion from the village. Curfew bells rang out from the larger mills at 6:00 a.m. to signal the people to leave for work, at 12:45 p.m. to indicate the time when they were to return from lunch, and at 9:00 p.m. "as a warning to all mill workers that they should be at home, to insure proper rest for the next day's work." Two night watchmen patrolled the streets after nightfall to be sure all lights were out by 10:00 p.m. Any violation, aside from sickness or one of the very few other acceptable reasons, was cause for a warning from the mill offices, while two such unwarranted offenses were cause for possible dismissal.[26] The bells also tolled for fires because there was no fire department and the "millworkers often left their jobs to battle village blazes utilizing a hand-drawn, hand-pumped apparatus which was owned by the mill."[27]

At the insistence of the Walcotts and the Campbells, the village prohibited the sale of alcoholic beverages, and there were many other regulations which the owners imposed upon their workers as a condition of employment and residence in the village. Looking back upon this era in 1915, a Utica newspaper explained:

> "For know ye that there were rules and regulations about New York Mills in the early days as rigid as the blue laws of Connecticut. Along with their ingenuity, their industry, their enterprise, and frugality, the early settlers along the Sauquoit brought with them from New England deep religious convictions. No family could find employ in the great stone mill without a commendation from the minister. No family could continue in the employ that disregarded public worship, that was addicted to alcoholic habits, that failed to restrain its children properly, that ran into debt, that did or did not do a number of things to conform with the strict ideas of the founders."[28]

Thus, as the beginning of the twentieth century loomed on the horizon, the development of the New York Mills as a company town was complete. The New York Mills Corporation and the surrounding village were so intertwined as to be indistinguishable. The Corporation

Mill No. 1 in the "Lower Mills."

Mill No. 2 in the "Middle Mills" in the background,
with the company offices in the foreground to the right center.

Mills No. 3 (right) and No. 4 (left) in the "Upper Mills."

This brick building on Main Street originally housed company offices,
a company store, company-owned lodgings, and a post office.

was the village. Virtually every family had at least one member who worked in the mills, or in the various service and subsidiary businesses the factories supported. The Corporation exercised direct control over some essential facets of life, such as employment, and indirect control over virtually all of the important social, economic and political activities of the village.

Although there were occasional neighborhood disputes, dissatisfaction with wages, threats of strikes, and the inevitable complaints regarding the excessively restrictive paternalism of the Walcotts and the Campbells, the village remained a quiet, tranquil place where business thrived, employment was generally secure and visitors marveled at the well-kept homes of the operatives and the more elegant residences of the employers.

Yet, as the new century dawned, its first decade witnessed developments that eventually brought the state militia into the community and lead to profound changes that permanently altered the social, economic and political character of the village and its people.

Chapter 2

New People,
New Perspectives

As the industrial revolution continued to gain momentum in the United States, American factory owners began to look increasingly to Europe to satisfy their growing need for inexpensive labor. The New York Mills Corporation followed a similar pattern, first sending recruiting agents to the textile communities of Massachusetts, Connecticut and Rhode Island, then to Europe. As early as the 1890s, the previous influx of French Canadian workers began to be supplemented by the arrival of the first Polish people in the mills. Initially they came from New England where they originally settled upon arrival in the United States, but gradually, as the demand for more labor in the village increased, they began to arrive directly from Poland.

Once a powerful force in European affairs, Poland had a long tradition of democratic development which rivaled the more familiar aspects of English democracy. As early as the fourteenth century Poland established an elective monarchy. In 1425 the Polish *Sejm* [Parliament] passed a law guaranteeing personal liberty to all citizens, and in 1430 further legislation proclaimed that the state could not imprison anyone without a lawful verdict of the courts. Shortly thereafter, religious freedom became a legislative guarantee within the Polish domains. In the sixteenth century, when religious warfare tore Europe asunder, Poland continued to reject the imposition of specific religious creeds upon its populace. Indeed, her king, Sigismund Augustus, once commented that "I am the king of the people, not the judge of their consciences." In 1683 armies under the leadership of King Jan III Sobieski saved Europe from Ottoman invasion at the Siege of Vienna, and Poland played an leading role in the commerce and diplomacy of Europe well into the eighteenth century. Finally, as the *Sejm* further democratized the nation, providing religious liberty and equal legal protection to all, her more autocratic neighbors became alarmed and conspired against her. As a result, Poland lost its independence in a series of partitions by Russia, Prussia and Austria in 1772, 1793, and 1795. Each of the occupying powers, to a greater or lesser degree, suppressed Polish culture, discriminated against Poles in economic and social affairs, and otherwise tried to enforce assimilation with the dominant group. The result was that many Poles, especially in the rural areas of Russian and Austrian occupied Poland, lived in a state of economic poverty that engendered in them a sense of fatalism, much like that observed in the Irish peasants suffering under British rule during the dire economic conditions of the 1830s.

By the time that Walcott and Campbell began to recruit Poles to work in its mills, Poland was an occupied nation for an entire century. Most of the Poles came from the Russian or Austrian controlled areas, particularly from Galicia in the Austrian-ruled portion of Poland, in the area stretching east from the city of Kraków through the Carpathian Mountains and into the agricultural plains beyond, an area which included mountain villages like Nowy Targ, Nowy Sącz and Jasło, as well as cities like Rzeszów, Tarnów, Lwów and Przemyśl. There, during the final two decades of the nineteenth century, a dramatic increase in population, coupled with the lack of sufficient non-agricultural employment, produced a large pool of labor seeking better economic and social opportunity. Most of those who migrated were poor, and many had never had the opportunity to learn to read and write. "They didn't have much to eat," Walenty Zima would later tell his son Stanley. "If you had a pair of shoes you didn't wear them all the time. You wore them when you got into the church. You walked barefooted until you got to the church to save them from wearing out."[1] Given their poverty, most brought few material goods with them when they arrived at Castle Garden or Ellis Island. "The Polish people had nothing when they arrived in America," recalled Kazimierz Dziedzic. "All that most of them brought when they came was ten fingers, a strong back, a willingness to work hard and a strong faith in God."[2] This spirit was summarized succinctly by Zenon ["Zeke"] Chrabas who reflected upon the arrival of his parents in New York Mills: "They thought that America was the land of opportunity. They came here to make a new life."[3]

The first Poles arrived in the area around 1870, generally settling along Lincoln Avenue in the western section of nearby Utica. Soon, a small ethnic community developed with its own distinctive stores and homes. Between 1898 and 1906 the Polish population of West Utica increased rapidly from 100 families to 400, with a total population of over 4,000. Many of these people worked in the New York Mills, commuting there on foot or on the new carriage line that connected Utica with its smaller neighbor some two miles away. In 1898, for example, Mary Kamickski [probably Marya Kamiński] and Julia Roskiloski [?] appeared on the payroll list of Mill No. 2, with the latter

receiving $2.26 for 62 hours of work per week. A review of the exist-
ing company records indicates that the Polish workers received wages
comparable to what other employees received in similar positions at
that time.[4]

The success of the New York Mills Corporation's efforts to solicit
new workers directly from Europe can be seen in the dramatic increase
in Polish names on the company payroll lists beginning in 1904. Between February and April of that year, for example, the number of
recognizably Polish names listed for one department of Mill No. 2 rose
from two to at least thirteen.[5] As these dramatic increases continued,
the Polish population of the village grew to 500 people by 1906 when
the *Utica Saturday Globe* noted that "The prominent trait of the Pole is
his industry. He is thrifty and frugal and his most cherished ambition
is to own a little home. With this end in view he has saved on the
smallest of wages, and in a few years is a property owner. A good
index to the character of the Polish people in this city is their gener-
osity toward the church."[6]

Not everyone shared this view of the newcomers. Both locally and
nationally, many "old stock" Americans, whose ancestors had arrived in
the United States from northern and western European countries before
1890, seemed to view the "new immigrants," who arrived in record
numbers from southern and eastern Europe, as a national menace.
"Respectable" anthropologists, sociologists and psychologists compiled
statistics and wrote books to "prove" that the new arrivals were cultur-
ally and intellectually inferior to people of Anglo-Saxon descent.
Madison Grant, for example, published an argument for Anglo-Saxon
racial purity in *The Passing of the Great Race in America*. Such sentiments even entered the halls of Congress where Senator Henry Cabot
Lodge was quoted in the *Congressional Record* on March 16, 1896, as
favoring a literacy test as a qualification for immigration because it
"will bear most heavily upon the Italians, Russians, Poles ... and very
lightly, or not at all, upon English-speaking emigrants.... Statistics
show that the change in the racial character of our immigration has been
accompanied by a corresponding decline in its quality.... If a lower race
mixes with a higher in sufficient numbers, history teaches us that the
lower will prevail...."[7]

The acceptance of these racial stereotypes eventually became so
widespread that in 1907 Congress formed the United States Immigration
Commission to examine the effects of unlimited immigration. Comprised of politicians and "experts" such as Senators Henry Cabot Lodge
of Massachusetts and William P. Dillingham of Vermont, nearly all of
whom had previously made public statements in favor of immigration
restriction, it is little wonder that the Commission's findings, published in forty-two volumes between 1912 and 1914, concluded that the

new immigration from southern and eastern Europe was a detriment to American society, could not be readily assimilated, and ought to be greatly restricted.[8]

Given this widespread attitude toward the "new immigration," it is not surprising that similar sentiments should surface with the dramatic increase in the number of Poles arriving in the Utica area. During the Fourth of July celebrations in 1907, when a tragically fatal fight occurred among several Poles, various Utica newspapers took advantage of the occasion to paint a derogatory stereotype of Poles in general. Commentaries such as the following had a tremendous effect on readers, contributing significantly to the development of prejudices in the collective mind of the general populace. With obvious allusion to Sir Thomas Campbell's popular poem *Pleasures of Hope*, written in 1799, which contains the line "And Freedom shrieked as Kosciuszko fell," the *Utica Herald-Dispatch* reported that:

"When Pole meets Pole, then comes bloodshed.

While freedom was shrieking in an eerie sort of way on the early morn of Independence Day, sons of Kosciusco [*sic*] battled to the death on the bank of the canal in Yorkville, two of their number taking a free pass to the bourne from which no traveler returns to make endless visit with that distinguished Polish patriot who took the journey so long before....

New York Mills and Yorkville are reaping a heavy harvest of woe from the seeds sown when the mill company some years ago, in the interests of economy in labor, imported foreigners to do the work of the mills which had been previously performed by a class of citizens that had made those communities models of ideal factory settlements.

When the company began importing labor, Poles of the very lowest type of civilization found employment in the mills and domiciles in the company's houses. As this element in the population increased in number trouble grew apace and the standing which New York Mills and Yorkville had previously enjoyed departed, never to return until it is made desirable to this class of foreigners to move elsewhere."[9]

Covering the same story, the *Utica Saturday Globe*, under the heading "POLISH FACTIONS FIGHT" castigated the Poles in even stronger terms:

"Once more is attention drawn to that turbulent, undesirable class of Poles who live and work in New York Mills by Thursday morning's sanguinary fight between opposing factions of that race in which two men were killed and a third frightfully injured. Fierce and bloody fights between Polish residents of New York Mills are of almost weekly occurrence, and the county authorities seem well-nigh powerless to cope with these brutal foreigners, the majority of whom have little or no respect for law or order. For a number of years past Poles have been superseding the employees of other nationalities in the large factories and now they form the bulk of the working population of that village. The greater part of these Poles in the mills have come from Russia and Galicia and are among the most illiterate of the lower order of immigrants who seek our shores. ... At best the Poles in the village are a surly, sullen lot, even when sober; intoxicated, they are savage and dangerous."[10]

The *Utica Daily Press* added in its coverage the following barbs about both Poles and their surnames:

"By some the fight is also attributed to an ancient feud between the Russian Poles and the Austrian or Galician Poles. These factions love each other with all the aversion a tramp has for work and every little while they get a chance to pay off some old score, always taking care that like the serial story it is not ended too soon. 'To be continued in our next,' is the motto on which they scrap; but they are wise enough not to make it like a southern feud, a war of extermination, for then there would be no more to fight. The knowing ones say the fight of Wednesday night is not a marker to what there will be when a return engagement is played in this tragedy.

Here is hoping that when next they get together they cut each other's names down to ordinary proportions and excise some of the ski's and scz's which look well on paper but are difficult to pronounce."[11]

Nor were these expressions of disgust and disapproval limited to the popular press. The rapid influx of new people into the village presented the older inhabitants with a very real threat of competition for jobs, housing and the other necessities of life. The fact that these new residents possessed a different and seemingly strange culture, which often violated the long-accepted norms of the company town, and an unknown language, only served to heighten the fear and hostility which developed between the newcomers and the earlier settlers. Mary Jones remembered that when the Poles first began to arrive the residents of the village tried to bridge the language barrier by placing pictures of open Bibles on the fronts of churches so that the newcomers would know what they were, but in general the Poles were looked upon as a strange people, "crude greenhorns" who did not understand the ways of the village and could not assimilate into its society. Given this climate, misunderstandings between the Poles and the earlier Anglo-Saxon residents of the village were bound to occur. In 1907, for example, members of the Society of St. Stanislaus, a Polish religious group, planned a picnic to honor the birthday of their new homeland. At the appointed hour on July 4 some 350 Poles gathered at a hall owned by Jan Kozak, a Polish string band played Polish and American patriotic songs, and everyone began to enjoy themselves on a rare day of rest. But, the sight of such a gathering, particularly one at which alcoholic beverages were present, caused many of the Anglo-Saxon residents to fear the outbreak of violence. No sooner had the celebration began than Sheriff Gilmore, Attorney Douglas and four deputies, acting on orders from Justice of the Peace Daymont and Rev. Corbin, arrived to confiscate all of the beer and liquor, and break up the gathering. "The prompt action of the authorities is highly commended by law-abiding citizens," the *Utica Herald-Dispatch* noted with satisfaction.[12]

Bertha Nowicki Kozak was one of the earlier Poles to move to New York Mills. Born in Massachusetts of immigrant parents, she came to the village as a child with her family in February of 1900. More than three-quarters of a century later she still vividly recalled the treatment that she received as an impressionable young child in her new surroundings.

"I remember when we lived on Garden Street and I was the only Polish child going to school where the firehouse is. There used to be a school there — a grammar school and then the high school on the second floor. I remember when we first came I'd be walking up the street and the other children would gather and they'd yell 'Oh, here comes that Polak!', and everybody was running to see the Polak because I was the only one walking up the hill to the main street. I walked up — I was afraid of the kids — so I walked straight to the school because the door was opened. I walked in and sat down where the seats were and then the other children came in and took their seats. The teacher put me in one of the seats there and a girl was sitting in there — there were two in one seat -- so she stood up and she said, 'I don't want to sit with a Polak!' So the teacher called me over and she had me sit in front, all alone, right near her desk because this girl didn't want to sit with me. I was the only Polish student in the whole school."[13]

Stella Furgał had similar memories of her childhood:

>"When I was walking to [St. Mary's] school ... I had to go by Elm Street and those Welsh kids would be walking to their school. They would spit on us and call us Polaks. I remember being pushed around and I remember being spat at. I was old enough then so that I remember it distinctly."[14]

In the winter some of the Anglo-Saxon children armed themselves with snowballs and lay in wait for Polish children on the way to school. Stephanie Nowicki recalled how "Sometimes, when we were going to school, they would follow us and call us Polaks. I remember that. My sister Julie, ... she was lame. We would walk together. She would have her arm around my neck and I had my arm around her waist. I'd be walking her to school. They would throw snowballs at us."[15] Other children climbed on roofs with shovels and when a Polish man or woman came walking by they shoveled snow onto them. Bertha Kozak's father drove a horse-drawn wagon for the company, transporting cloth from one mill to another as it proceeded through the manufacturing process. Frequently, as he drove from Number 2 to Number 3 where the finishing stage took place,

>"this boy made a hard snowball and he'd always watch out for him and he'd throw the snowball. He hit him in the face so my father thought he's got to do something about that. So he came home and the following day he took a stick with him and as he was going to work this boy started throwing snowballs. My father took the stick from under his coat and he ran after the boy and the boy ran in the house with my father right after him. Of course the mother was so frightened and she was yelling and my father shook the stick and he said: 'He's not going to hit me anymore.'"[16]

Stephanie Nowicki   Józef Powroźnik

Bertha Kozak   Stella Furgał

The whole experience left Kozak with unpleasant memories that would last a lifetime. "You felt as if you were just nothing in their eyes," she sighed.[17]

Stanley Krawiec spoke of how, as a child, his family's neighbors always used expressions such as "God damn Polak" and "dumb Polak." He recalled how he used to carry coffee to his father in the mills in a large pail. His family had boarders staying with them, and occasionally these people would borrow his pail to go and get some beer. "One time, I remember they came back beat up pretty bad." They had been intercepted by a group of Anglo-Saxons who attacked them and spilled all of their beer. "There was a lot of discrimination," he concluded.[18]

When Józef and Zofia Powroźnik arrived at Ellis Island, the immigration officials pinned labels on them and put them on the train for Utica. They ended up in New York Mills where they stayed at a boarding house owned by a relative. Józef went to night school to learn English and become a citizen. He worked as part of a group operating a workers' co-operative store selling groceries and dry goods. Later, he and his wife opened a small store where they catered to the village's Polish residents. Their daughter Cecilia also harbored indelible impressions of the reception that they received in the village.

"We lived in an area where there were more Welsh people than Polish people. There were a great many Welsh people and they resented the Polish people terribly. They just thought that we were all dumb and uneducated because we children spoke the Polish language [and] they wanted us to use the English language. ... They didn't play with us, they just called us 'squareheads' and 'dumb Polaks' and all this stuff."[19]

Cecilia eventually married Zeke Chrabas, who observed correctly that where one lived in the village generally determined the level of discrimination. "We lived on the Lower Mills," he noted, "and it was predominantly Polish. Where she lived on the other end there were a lot of Welsh people and she was more subjected to some of the snide remarks and things because they just didn't like the Polish people."[20]

Nor was all of the discrimination physical or verbal. Bertha Kozak recalled that when she and her husband attempted to purchase property to open a store they had difficulty doing so because no one wanted to sell to "Polaks." There were sometimes conditions written into the actual property deeds precluding them from being sold to Poles. As late as 1946 one such deed carried the stipulation that the seller "dose herby sell this land under the following condition, that this land should not be sold to any Jews. Pollocks. Negros or Italian. and in case is sold to any

This Indenture

Made the   Twenty-Fourth   day of   June   in the year One Thousand
nine hundred and   Forty-Six.

Return   Glendon A Rulcever of 301 Riverside Ave. Scotia. N.Y.

part y of the first part, and   Samuel Decker and John N Eckert. of

Middletown. Orange County. N.Y.

parties of the second part,

Witnesseth, That the said part y of the first part, for and in consideration of

the sum of One Dollar——————————————— Dollars

($ I.00) lawful money of the United States,

paid by the said part y of the second part, do

hereby grant and release unto the said party heirs and

assigns forever,

All that Tract or Parcel of Land, situate in the   Town.

of   Forestport.   County of   Oneida.   and State of New York,

being a part of great Lot 13. Woodhull Tract. and more Particul-
ary Bounded and Decribed as Follows.

Designated on a Map made and File in the Clerks.Office.June 29th
1926 and which said Map showing said Lots being Lot 139 and 140

this being the same portion of Land conveyed to Elizabeth A App
by Jerry App. and wife by deed dated Sept 12th 1894 end recorded
in the Oneida County Clerks Office Nov 19th 1894 and in Book of
Deeds 514 at page 252 the name of Elizabeth A.App.now being
Elizabeth A App. Turk.

the said Elizabeth A App. Turk does herby sell this land under
the following condition, that this land should not be sold to
any Jews. Pollocks.Negros or Itslian. and in case is sold to any
of above menshion people. then this deed revert back to the part
of first part.

The above deed contains a restrictive covenant prohibiting
the sale of the property to Jews, Poles, Blacks or Italians.

of the above menshion people, then this deed revert back to the party of the first part [*sic*]." The Kozaks finally secured the aid of a non-Polish friend who purchased land for them, removed the offending stipulations, and then transferred the deed over to them.[21]

Despite this often hostile reception, the Poles continued to move into New York Mills in an attempt to find employment and an opportunity for a better life. Much like the refugees from the Irish potato famine of the 1840s, they came "*za chlebem*," for bread. When they first arrived, many people stayed at the company boarding houses, or at private boarding houses that sprang up to accommodate the increasing population. Some stayed as boarders in private homes, or sub-let space from tenants of company-owned homes where the pressure of economic necessity forced the residents to accept boarders, or where relatives in need of a place to stay were accommodated. Although it was not a preferred lifestyle, opening the home to boarders was one means of acquiring additional income, especially for those families with young children at home. "In the early days mom worked in the shop," Stanley Zima recalled. "But she didn't work in the shop for long. When the children came she didn't go back to work. We lived in a company house on Garden Street ... and we had four or five boarders in the house and so she had a lot of work." Bertha Kozak remembered that "In some homes they had more boarders than they had room for so those that worked nights would sleep and when those who worked days came home the ones who worked nights would get out of bed and make room for them." The boarders would all take their meals in common, usually cooked by the wife of the owner, and it was not uncommon for each boarder to have his own loaf of bread into which he carved his initials or other identifying mark. Usually the owner's wife, or the landlady, also did the boarder's laundry, mended worn clothing, and performed other similar tasks to earn a few extra cents per week.[22]

The United States Census of 1910 provides many examples of how the Polish people lived in extended family households that also included boarders. Typical of these were the Hałat residence at 438½ Main Street, which accommodated fourteen people in space originally meant for less than half that number, and the Samon residence at 102 Sauquoit Street which housed eighteen people. Rented by Marek and Zofia Hałat, the Main Street home included Andrzej, Johanna, Włodzimierz and Józef Dziedzic, and Rozalia Hałat, all of whom were relatives, as well as Tomasz and Andrzej Dudek, Józef and Marya Luranc, Zofia Uszczak, Franciszek Biś and Marya Hodek. The Sauquoit Street building, the residence of Michał and Katarzyna Samoń, also provided shelter for sons Józef, Jan and Piotr, relatives Józef, Michał, Julia and Aniela Samoń, Piotr and Marya Czechowicz, and Stanisław Bednarz and board-

The Walcott Mansion

The Campbell Mansion

These brick houses, each accommodating two residences,
were reserved for management officials.

A typical company house occupied by the workers.

ers including Stanisław and Marya Chrabąszcz, Józef Gadziała, Józef and Marcin Jachym, and Sobiestyn Łachut.[23]

By the time that the Poles began arriving in the village most of the company-owned housing was between half and three-quarters of a century old. Never built as sturdily as the mills or the mansions of the owners, the wear-and-tear of use and age was already apparent on these humble structures. The streets were simple dirt paths, and cisterns were used for gathering water for washing clothing and dishes. On Cottage and Garden Streets, where the newer company houses were located, there was a well in the center of the road and all of the families that lived on those streets had to pump their own cooking and drinking water into pails. Behind each home was an out-house that the company cleaned once per year. Each house usually had a half-barrel that served as a tub for bathing and for washing clothes on a scrub board. Bathing water was be heated on a coal stove, and boiling water was used to wash white clothing and sheets so that they would look clean. The clothing and sheeting were stirred and removed with a stick to avoid being scalded.[24]

The normal diet consisted of *chleb* [bread], *ziemniak* [potatoes], *kapusta* [cabbage], *groch* [peas or beans] and *słanina* [fatback]. A standing joke among the Poles was that for lunch they had *kapusta i groch* and for dinner *groch i kapusta*. Some people would buy a piece of *słanina*, slice it into little squares, fry it, and place it between two slices of bread as a sandwich. Others would chop it into little pieces, sauté it, and then spread it onto the bread. Still others made *polewka* [soup or gruel], a concoction of hominy mixed with sour milk. "I pray that I never have to have that again," Stella Furgał grimaced over a half-century later.[25]

"They used to call the people in New York Mills farmers!" one resident recalled, "because that's how they survived."[26] Almost everyone planted a garden to raise vegetables, some kept chickens, and occasionally one would have a pig or a cow. They made their own *kiełbasa* [sausage], *pierógi* [stuffed dumplings], *czelsosón* [head cheese] and *kiszka* [bloodwurst] by hand, and the tantalizing smell of *babka* [sweet bread] baking in the oven would waft aromatically through the air each morning.[27] "I can remember that we would buy sixty heads of cabbage," recalled Peter Kogut,

> "and process it and we would have it all winter. Potatoes — we would have anywhere from sixteen to twenty bushels put aside in the cold cellar. ... On Sunday we would have hamburg made out of eggs and bread crumbs, and it was a little bit on the fatty side because it was made

out of pork. We had mushroom stew once in a while on Sunday. During the week we had *kapusta*, we had vegetable soup, we had *rosół* [broth] from the chicken, we had chicken soup that had a lot of fat globules that shone [in the light]. ... We had our own garden, we raised potatoes for winter and we raised vegetables.... In the summertime we had buttermilk with boiled potatoes mixed in. It was delicious and very cooling."[28]

Some people supplemented these staples with domestic chickens, rabbits or pigs, or by hunting for pheasants, partridges, raccoon or deer. As a sweet, children took a slice of rye bread, sprinkled it with water and dunked it in sugar. "That was a treat," recalled Zeke Chrabas with obvious delight.[29]

When he first arrived in New York Mills, Józef Powroźnik became a member of a cooperative store. His responsibilities included delivering groceries by horse-drawn wagon in the summer, and by sleigh in the winter. "My father would go in the morning," his daughter Cecilia recounted. In the winter "it would be bitter cold and he used to have boots up to his knees. When he'd come home at night we children would try to help take them off. They were ice crusted on the inside. It was so bitter cold."[30]

Eventually, Powroźnik opened a small store of his own. His daughter recalled how people would come in to charge groceries until the next pay day. "*Na książka*," they would say, "on the book." Sometimes people had a bill of ten dollars. They would come in and pay two dollars on their account, but then buy three dollars more "*na książka*."[31] Cecilia described her typical day as follows:

"I would dust all the shelves and dust the showcases so that it was spotless. Then I opened the store to the people who were coming to [work at] the mill. They would start at six o'clock in the morning. They would bring with them a couple of slices of bread and usually they would ask to have a couple of slices of ham or a couple of slices of veal loaf and they made their sandwich right there on the counter. The biggest seller of tobacco was Bull Durham. Then they would go to work. I would run to school, the high school. The mills would let out at four o'clock at that time. We'd get out [of school] at five minutes to four and I ran the three blocks [to the store] and I was there when the first customer arrived. We had the store open until ten o'clock and I did my homework right at the store. I'd be kind of tired sometimes, but that's how we did it."[32]

It was a difficult life, devoid of any of the material goods and plentiful foods that have since come to be accepted as staples of life in the village. Hard work was the rule, but there were also times when work and austerity were ignored to celebrate special occasions. One of these was the announcement of a wedding. In Poland there were many prescribed stages leading up to the wedding and the festive occasion itself might last the better part of a week; but in New York Mills, the demands of work dictated that the wedding ceremonies begin on Saturday and end by Sunday evening so that the guests could return to work on Monday morning. The wedding preparations began with a *zarȩczyny*, an engagement party. Following this, there was the obligatory *zmówiny*, a pairing-off party, which also served as a planning session for the wedding ceremony. The proper pairing-off of the ushers and bridesmaids was considered a very important task, with each couple matched for height and looks. This done, those involved would plan parties for the bride and groom, and discuss issues such as the proper clothes and colors to be worn for the bride, the groom, the bridesmaids, the ushers, and everyone else involved in the wedding. Finally, after a shower for the bride and a party for the groom, the wedding day arrived.[33]

A typical wedding picture. Front row (l. to r.) Franciszek Gołąb, Stanisław Pluta, Katarzyna Gołąb (bride), Kazimierz Dziedzic (groom), Zofia Dziedzic, Andrzej Dziedzic. Back row (l. to r.), unknown, Katarzyna Kosmider, Józef Tobiczyk, Rozalia Mieszczak, unknown, Aleksandra Dziedzic, Stanisław Puła, Waleryja Rey. The groom was treasurer of Local 753 during the 1916 strike.

Following the actual wedding ceremony was a *wesele* where friends, relatives and neighbors enjoyed an opportunity to sing, dance, and partake of food and drink in both a variety and quantity not normally seen in the more austere daily life. One observer described the *wesele* as "a period of relative license for people who, in their daily lives, fought against poverty and need."[34] It lasted well into the evening, and was followed on the next day by a *poprawny*, a "straightening-out" party characterized by more music and dancing and consumption of the remaining food and drink from the previous day. The newlyweds could not go on a honeymoon, since work began again on Monday morning, so they normally attended both the *wesele* and the *poprawny* where they were the subject of much of the song and not a little joking.[35]

These diversions aside, life was demanding for mill workers in the textile industry at the beginning of the twentieth century. To strengthen their resolve, most relied to a great extent on the religious beliefs which they brought with them from Poland. In *Stary Kraj*, the Old Country, the Poles inherited from their ancestors a very deep faith in Catholicism that sustained them through droughts and famines, and through the ravages of a host of invading Austrians, Germans, Russians, Swedes, Tartars, and Turks. Their faith became even stronger after the infamous partitions erased Poland from the map of Europe in 1795. During a century of occupation by foreign powers, Poles came to rely upon the Catholic Church as a haven where they could speak their own native language, celebrate their national holidays and customs, and teach their children about their own heritage in the face of attempts by the partitioning powers to stamp out any vestige of Polish nationality. It is no coincidence, then, that faced with the difficulties of adjusting to life in a new country with all of its linguistic, cultural and social differences, the Poles sought comfort and support in the one organization which offered some hope of familiarity and continuity in their lives, the Catholic Church. Thus, the focus of these early Polish communities in the United States revolved around the parish, which acted as a bond for both religious and secular life.

The first Poles in New York Mills commuted to Utica to attend services at St. Joseph's Church on Columbia Street, but soon became dissatisfied by the lack of Polish religious customs in a predominantly German parish. They wanted to be able to say Confession in Polish and to be able to celebrate the holidays and customs of their own native land, rather than those of St. Joseph's German parishioners. When their number proved sufficient, they purchased a small house on Lincoln Avenue in 1896 and Rev. Szymon Pniak, a native of Galician Poland, arrived that December to celebrate before an overflow crowd of some 800 people the first Polish Mass ever heard in Utica. The new church was dedicated on June 11, 1899, and Holy Trinity Parish immediately became the center of religious and social life for the growing Polish colony.[36] Not only did people worship there, they attended social functions, held meetings, went to school, and relished in the intangible warmth of their extended families. In fact, aside from weddings, family celebrations, and patriotic occasions, most of the immirants' social life outside of the mundane existence of the factory system focused on religious celebrations. The Poles transposed religious festivals and celebrations from the Old Country to America where they not only provided diversion from the daily routine, but also served as a psychological link to the homeland and a common bond that helped to preserve community unity in the face of an unfamiliar and often hostile environment. To these Polish immigrants, faith was not something to be exhibited only on the Sabbath, but to be lived each day. Their everyday lives were filled with religious allusions, as, for example, when they went to visit friends.

"Niech będzie pochwalony Jezus Chrystus," the guest would say upon stepping through the doorway, "May the name of Jesus Christ be praised."

"Teraz i na wieki, wieków," would be the reply from the host, "Now and for eternity."

"Idź z Bogiem," each would say to the other when departing, "God be with you."

"It was beautiful," recalled Cecilia Chrabas. Her husband Zeke observed that "Nobody thought anything of it. It was accepted any time you went visiting. It was the proper thing to do. It was a way of life."[37]

One of the more important religious holidays was Easter, which began with forty days of fasting during Lent. On Palm Sunday the faithful obtained palms in Church that were blessed by the priest, after which they were taken home and placed behind a picture of Our Lady of Częstochowa, the "Queen of Poland," to retain this symbolic presence until the following year. During the next week families decorated *pisanki*, the colorful and elaborately painted Easter eggs that adorned the home during the holiday season. The egg, the symbol of life, also had a particular significance when it was broken and shared with family and friends. The week preceding Easter was filled with daily religious observances and processions, while at home everyone remained busy preparing food for the *Święcone*, the blessing of the Easter food by the priest. On Holy Saturday, the day before Easter, the priest went from door to door greeting his parishioners and blessing the food they prepared for Easter dinner. The Lenten season ended with the Mass of the Resurrection on Easter Sunday morning, followed by joyful festivities and feasting at an Easter table decorated with the colorful *pisanki* and a traditional Easter lamb made of butter.[38]

Similar religious celebrations took place regularly throughout the year, culminating in the Christmas season. In Poland, Christmas Eve was a time reserved for family gatherings. The appearance of the *Gwiazdka*, the first star in the Christmas Eve sky, signaled the beginning of an elaborate meatless supper of ethnic delicacies, the *Wigilia*, during which tradition required the setting of an empty place for any family members who were absent, or for passers-by who might stop in to visit. The *opłatek*, a Christmas wafer similar to the unleavened wafer used in Catholic religious ceremonies, was broken and shared with each of those gathered, to the accompaniment of good wishes for peace and happiness. The traditional meatless supper was followed by the singing of Christmas carols, after which everyone adjourned to attend midnight Mass where they offered further greetings to their friends and neighbors. On Christmas Day, some people visited friends and relatives, some went caroling, and the children received treats that might include oranges, sweets, or a small gift.[39]

Given the economic uncertainties of their everyday lives, the Poles in New York Mills, much as immigrants in other communities throughout America, decided to organize themselves for mutual support. Under the leadership of Józef Smoła, one of their first actions was to form the *Towarzystwa Święty Stanisława, Biskupa i Męczennika* [Society of St. Stanislaus, Bishop and Martyr]. At a meeting held on June 25, 1905, they formed an organization and began making plans for the collection of funds to construct a church in the village and to provide mutual assistance including moral and financial help in times of sickness and death. The latter was particularly important in the immigrant community for a death in the family could cause serious economic hardship. At that time it was customary for friends and neighbors to take up a collection to assist the bereaved family with funeral and burial expenses, thus the early emphasis among Polish American organizations on financial death benefits. The first officers of this new society, the first voluntary self-help organization to be founded in the village, were: Antoni Gondek (president), Jan Robak (vice president), Jan Wętka (recording secretary), Józef Smoła (financial secretary), Józef Nowicki and Stanisław Solnica (comptrollers), Jan Sliski (director of the sick), and Bronisław Śliski and Sylwester Bartosz (marshals). Organized along military lines, the society purchased uniforms which its members were required to wear on special occasions under pain of fine for non-compliance. Fund-raising for the new church began on September 6 when the raffle of a ton of coal, valued at $1.00, netted $10.30, a goodly profit when one considers that an average week's wage at that time was only about $3.00.   Progress was slow, initially inhibited by flagging spirits and internal bickering, but gradually the society took shape, and in 1908 it grew rapidly in both membership and accomplishments.   Prayer services were held in several places around the village, members provided solace and financial benefits in time of sickness or death, and organized efforts were made to raise funds for a church and to lobby with the Bishop of Syracuse for the creation of a Catholic parish in the village.[40]

These efforts bore fruit in 1909 when the Bishop answered persistent requests with the appointment of Rev. Stefan Płaza, a native of the Warsaw area of Poland, to organize a parish in the village. In the following year the Most Rev. Patrick Ludden, Bishop of the Diocese of Syracuse, formally established the Parish of St. Mary, Our Lady of Częstochowa. It was named for Our Lady of Częstochowa, the Patron Saint of Poland credited with intervening in Polish history through the performance of a miracle.[41]

In 1655, invading Swedish armies conquered nearly all of Poland and its people were demoralized and dispirited. The situation appeared hopeless when a Swedish army some 10,000 strong laid siege to the small monastery of Jasna Góra, defended only by some 160 Polish knights, 70 Paulite monks and a few hundred townspeople and peasants. Yet, after the Poles offered prayer to the icon of the Virgin Mary located in the monastery, the Swedish assaults were repulsed and all of Poland became revitalized to throw out the invader. Because of this, Częstochowa is considered to be the most sacred shrine in Poland. Thus the Poles in New York Mills, seeking for their endeavors the divine assistance of St. Mary, named their parish in her honor. Eventually they built their church upon a hill which caught the first morning rays of the sun, an act further symbolizing their Old World heritage in that the parish's namesake shrine in Poland stood on a small hill named Jasna Góra, which can be translated as "bright mountain."[42]

Soon after the formal recognition of the parish, the Society of St. Stanislaus was joined by another voluntary association, Group 459 of the *Zjednoczenie Polskie Rzymsko-Katolickie pod wezwaniem Najświętszej Rodziny*, the Polish Roman Catholic Union named in honor of the Holy Family. Formed under the leadership of Michał Tuman and Jerzy Kozakiewicz, assisted by Jan Augustyn, Jan Puła, Andrzej Kobielski, Stanisław Komurek, S. Jerominek, Franciszek Szot, Jan Wdowiak, A. Walus, and Jakób, Józef and Wiktoria Urbaś, this local chapter of the nationally organized Polish Roman Catholic Union was created to provide spiritual assistance to the faithful, perform service functions for the new parish, undertake educational work and offer financial benefits in times of misfortune. Its first officers, installed on

The Church of St. Mary, Our Lady of Częstochowa, in 1910.
The inset in the upper right is Father Stefan Płaza,
the first pastor of the parish.

December 19, 1909, included Rev. Stefan Płaza (chaplain), Jakób Urbaś (president), Antoni Walus (vice president), Józef Urbaś (recording secretary), Jerzy Kozakiewicz (financial secretary), Michał Tuman (treasurer), Andrzej Kobielski and Franciszek Szot (trustees), Józef Wadas (marshal), and Jan Puła (sergeant-at-arms). During the coming years Group 459 raised funds for church projects, and provided substantial financial aid to the sick, to widows and children, and to the parish school. Together, these two societies labored diligently for the further development of St. Mary's parish.[43]

The first Mass in New York Mills was celebrated in a hall on Main Street owned by Jan Pezdek and Stanisław Boduch. Soon, a fund raising drive began for the purpose of purchasing land and building a permanent church. Many individuals and organizations contributed their hard-earned money to make the dream a reality, and the New York Mills Corporation assisted by contributing a small parcel of land to be sold at auction for cash to fund the new church. Members of the parish committee searched for suitable property for a permanent church, but few would sell to the Poles. Finally they were successful in purchasing a large barn owned by Margaret C. Warner, a former riding stable on a hill next to the Campbell estate, under the pretense of using it as a farm. Once purchased, the property was quickly converted into a church. "When that happened," Michael Dziedzic recalled, "those people up there were so upset about it that they built a great big wall out of brick" to separate the Polish church from the Campbell estate. "They talk about the Berlin Wall," Dziedzic continued, "we had that happen right here."[44]

The structure was blessed on August 14, 1910, and the first Mass celebrated there on Sunday, January 3, 1911. With the establishment of St. Mary's parish, the Polish residents of New York Mills had the focal point necessary for the development of a strong, unified community. It was not long before additional religious and civic organizations, all of which were based within the parish, rose to provide an infrastructure of spiritual and material support. In October, 1911, an organization comprised primarily of women, the *Towarzystwo Najsłodszego Serca Pana Jezusa* [Sacred Heart of Jesus Society] was formed under its first president, Karolina Pietruszka, to gather donations for the purchase of a statue for St. Mary's church, a statue of Kazimierz Pułaski on the Parkway in Utica, and to send aid to orphans in Poland. In December, 1911, the *Towarzystwo Dzieci Maryi* [Society of the Children of Mary] was organized for young ladies of the parish. It's purpose was to provide spiritual assistance, to participate in Church activities and to raise funds for the purchase of appropriate religious statues and other items to outfit the new church. Under its first president, Zofia Trzepacz, it held monthly devotional meetings, gathered to march in funeral processions in honor deceased members, and worked "for the betterment and improvement of St. Mary's parish."[45]

To break the monotony of factory life, the Poles organized frequent Sunday afternoon picnics during the summer. In November, 1911, the *Towarzystwie Św. Cecylii* [Society of St. Cecilia], the St. Mary's parish choir, held its first concert in Smoła's hall, with people from throughout the area attending to hear solos by Helena Jankiewicz, Wanda Jagłowska and Mrs. Sakowska, and the ever-popular duet featuring Mrs. Wasilewska and Mrs. Kowalska. From that time on, concerts and theatrical productions at Smoła's hall became a regular feature of village social and cultural life.[46]

The same year also saw the creation, in a more secular vein, of the *Towarzystw Krakusów Polskich Pod opieką św. Kazimierza* [St. Casimir's Polish Men's Society] and Nest 320 of the *Związek Sokołów Polskich* [Polish Falcons Alliance]. The former, organized under the leadership of Gabrjel Ruchwa and Józef Wdowiak, was, like the Society of St. Stanislaus, devoted primarily to the promotion of "brotherly love" and the provision of spiritual and material assistance to members in times of need. Its constitution specified that it engage in charitable work and assist members in case of sickness, accident, or upon the death of either husband or wife. The latter, a branch of the national Polish Falcon movement, was organized on March 3, 1912, with the following officers: Piotr Kozak (president), Jerzy Kozakiewicz (vice-president), Piotr Karpiński (recording secretary), Jan Czyżycki (financial secretary), Jan Wętka (treasurer), Jan Czyżycki (manager), and Walenty Mądry and Antoni Sokal (trustees). Not unlike the German *Turnverein* or the Y.M.C.A., the Falcons promoted moral development and physical exercise, while at the same time also supporting political activities to promote the unification and independence of the homeland from foreign domination.[47]

Thus, soon after the founding of St. Mary's Parish, the Polish community succeeded in establishing an infrastructure of several organizations to minister to its primary needs. The Church cared for its moral and spiritual well being, providing strength and purpose as it had in Poland. The various societies provided both the moral support of fraternal bonds and the financial support so necessary in times of sickness, death or other emergency. The Polish Falcons provided physical training and a political outlet for the undying ideal of Polish national independence.

They arrived as "greenhorns," unaccustomed to the language, the culture or the ways of their adopted land. They met with discrimination, and at times open hostility. Their life was not easy, yet by the end of their first decade in "the Mills" they became a permanent fixture of village life, a community within a community where customs and traditions from *Stary Kra*j were adapted to fit their new surroundings. Initially a movement of individuals and single families often overwhelmed by their isolation in a sea of Anglo-Saxon peoples, they became a community with businesses and stores, schools and organizations — and at the hub of this activity was the Parish of St. Mary, Our Lady of Częstochowa.

By 1910 the village of New York Mills consisted of two villages. Though living in close proximity in the same geographic area, the social and cultural distance between the two groups imposed a greater barrier than spatial considerations could ever erect. The Anglo-Saxon community predominated in the Upper and Middle Mills, while the Polish community was more populace in the Lower Mills, extending somewhat into small sections of the Middle and Upper Mills. They worked in the same factories, but shopped in separate stores, socialized in separate clubs, and worshiped in separate churches. The Anglo-Saxons attended the Presbyterian, Methodist, or Welsh churches, enjoyed their ice cream socials, tea parties, bicycling and community athletics, and subscribed to a traditional regimen that deplored the use of alcoholic beverages and the use of the sabbath for anything save worship. The Poles attended St. Mary's, celebrated festivals associated with Catholic beliefs and Polish nationalism, joined in the community and social activities of the Society of St. Stanislaus or the other religious and secular ethnic organizations, were not averse to using beer and liquor, and traditionally celebrated the sabbath not only with Mass, but with public Sunday afternoon picnics. By the end of the first decade of the twentieth century, the coming of the Poles permanently changed the landscape and environment of the community; but another change was about to take place that would set the two communities on a collision course.

Seeds of Dissension

W. Stuart Walcott passed away on September 4, 1905. His death brought an end to the vigorous and paternalistic management of the Walcott and Campbell holdings. W. S. Walcott's heirs found themselves in a very precarious business position. With debts mounting from necessary modernization and from various ventures into new fabrics which did not return the profits anticipated, Walcott & Campbell sought a loan from their selling agent, the A. D. Juilliard Company of New York City. When Walcott & Campbell could not meet its repayment schedule, A. D. Juilliard foreclosed, paying local investors who held Walcott & Campbell securities only about six cents on the dollar. Thus, by 1908, one hundred years after the original founding of Walcott and Company, the Walcotts and the Campbells no longer owned the controlling interest in the New York Mills Corporation, retaining only the small, separately operated Walcott & Campbell Spinning Company on Sauquoit Street. With the passing of the Walcotts and the Campbells from the helm of the New York Mills Corporation, much that characterized the village of New York Mills and the employer-employee relations within the company that dominated the small town underwent subtle, but nonetheless dramatic change.[1]

Life in the textile industry was never particularly enjoyable. Work was often unpredictable, with frequent layoffs and shut-downs in times of economic decline. In prosperous times, people rose early and worked long hours with only a brief thirty to forty-five minute break for lunch. The average work week for employees in 1908, for example, was between fifty-eight and sixty-three hours. "It was dark when they went to work and dark when they came back home," recalled Stanley Krawiec.[2] And the fast pace of the work left little time for relaxation. Each weaver tended at least eight looms, depending upon the type of loom and the cloth being woven, being constantly engaged in "checking the quality of the cloth, keeping bobbins full, adjusting heddles and harnesses, and marking defects."[3] In the words of one employee,

"it was more than eight hours and you'd be on your feet
constantly. Sometimes you'd have to run fast to go to
the toilet. Sometimes we were working eight hours
straight, no lunch time. You just put your sandwich on
the machine, where the cloth was, and underneath was the
roll. It was weaving, rolling slowly. You'd put your
sandwich in, fill up the shuttle, walk down a little further
... it was hard."[4]

When asked to identify the worst jobs within the mills, Richard
Rosinski, a long-time labor activist who worked there in a later era after
federal regulations had improved some of the worst of the conditions,
observed:

"Well, there is an element of danger no matter where you
work around machinery. But if I had to take my druthers,
it would be the weave shop, for one, with that constant
clattering, and the carding room, because, my God you
would have to see it to believe it, this is where they originally processed the product. So, you had this lint in the
air continually. I don't know how many people died because of it. In those days who ever looked at it? Now-a-
days, my God, they'd shut the place down."[5]

The noise in the weaving rooms was as overwhelming as it was
continual, much like the graphic scenes in the movie *Norma Rae*.
Shuttles flew back and forth at a furious pace, banging and clanging as
they drew the thread first one way and then another. Thousands of
shuttles at once, each at its own pace, led to a thunderous roar that re-
verberated throughout the plant. "I couldn't hear anything," recalled
Stephanie Nowicki. "The clattering went on all day long. It was terrible."[6] The constant movement of thousands of shuttles actually made
the weaving rooms vibrate, one had to shout to be heard over the noise,
and those employed there for any length of time inevitably became hard
of hearing. "The people who worked in the weave shop had their own
language," Stanley Zima explained. "It was a hand or sign language.
You learned lip reading ... [and in] talking to one another I would put
my chin on your shoulder and I would talk to you. Chin to shoulder,
that's how you would do it." Some weavers scraped the lint from their
machines, rolled it into little balls, and used it as an earplug to reduce
the noise.[7]

Weavers were also exposed to high concentrations of dampness because of the moisture used to prevent the thread from becoming too
brittle, and to large amounts of ever present dust and cotton fibers that

irritated throats and lungs and caused innumerable cases of chronic laryngitis. An unidentified New York Mills weaver interviewed by the New York State Bureau of Labor Statistics testified that "the temperature is high and the rooms are moist; they have a spray running all the time which I think is injurious; the temperature is hard to regulate and the floor is wet, and the girls feet are wet very often; this morning the heat was somewhere about ninety, and the spray pump was broken."[8] In the carding rooms, where the cloth was combed and its nap raised by brushing, cotton fibers were so thick that they formed a perpetual haze and often made it difficult to breath. In fact, the New York State Factory Investigating Commission, which held hearings throughout the state in 1911, concluded that textile mills in the Utica area posed a danger to health through "the presence of cotton and woolen dust in the air, which is particularly objectionable in the napping [carding] room." The same Factory Investigating Commission, commenting specifically on the mills located in the Utica area, noted that textile knitting "is classed among the dusty trades, and consumption is common among employees of knitting mills. The fact that the women and child operators, all on piece-work, are compelled to work eight and ten hours a day, according to age, on machines geared up to make as many as forty thousand stitches a minute would seem to constitute an even greater danger. Moreover, the continuous standing necessary for women winders, knitters, inspectors and folders is in the highest degree destructive of health."[9]

In later years Richard Rosinski recalled how one of the first jobs he was offered by the company required working in the carding room. "I walked through one door and right the hell out of the other door. I wouldn't work in there ... because you were breathing in all the cotton."[10] Eventually, workers employed in the carding rooms were as easily recognizable by their persistent coughs as those who worked in the weaving rooms were by their hearing disabilities. Although it is impossible to tell the rate of lung diseases in New York Mills because no records were kept and people were less aware of the long-range causes of illness and death than they later became, it is indicative of the problem that a sanatorium was built at Broad Acres, in nearby Deerfield, to treat the many varied throat and lung diseases. In fact, a report on the textile industry prepared by the United States Bureau of Labor Statistics in 1919 concluded that the likelihood of a textile worker between the ages of 15 and 44 dying of tuberculosis was "100 per cent greater than among the general population."[11]

In the dye house workers routinely handled bleaches, dyes, fixing agents, and cleaning fluids that are today labeled as hazardous, if not in fact carcinogenic. Their skin was exposed to concentrated liquid chemicals, while their lungs breathed in fumes from dozens of large open vats. "Paris green," for example, was a dye used in the textile industry which was later shown to be particularly hazardous to the health, causing the New York State Department of Labor and the State Industrial Commission to issue a warning in 1917 that "Paris green" was a dangerous poison that should be neither breathed nor allowed to come in contact with the skin. Still, in the room where the colors were mixed, liquids routinely spilled on the floor and temperatures were kept so high that there was always steam in the atmosphere, causing workers to suffer from chronic colds, rheumatism and coughing. In a study of the textile industry conducted by the Workers' Health Bureau of the United States Department of Labor, researchers investigating dye room employees concluded that "Eight out of every ten workers complained of severe irritation of the eyes, nose or throat. Over one-third were no longer able to digest their food, complaining of belching, cramps, nausea and frequent vomiting. Over a third had constant headaches, and almost as many were suffering from rheumatism or muscular pains." Nor were the effects of the dye room limited to those who toiled within its walls. Wastes from the dye house discharged directly into Sauquoit Creek where children went to swim. Many were the times when these unsuspecting victims returned home with a green, blue or red hue![12]

Further dangers lay in the equipment. In the weaving rooms each machine was equipped with numerous shuttles, each measuring seventeen inches long, weighing in excess of one pound and equipped with a steel point on each end. These potentially deadly weapons occasionally came loose and flew across the room like shortened javelins. Stephanie Nowicki remembered standing by one of her machines near the window one day when a shuttle came loose and "shot right by me and through the window and landed outside. It went right through the window. On its ends it had those steel points. It could kill you. People used to get hurt by them."[13] Many people were injured by flying shuttles. Stella Furgał recalled seeing a young Pole hurt in just such a fashion: "He lost his eye when a shuttle flew out of the loom and went right into his eye. They called the doctor but he wouldn't let them touch that eye until the pastor from a Polish church came. He came and they took him to the hospital."[14] Bertha Kozak recounted how a man named Kowalski suffered a different misfortune when "one of the gears took his hand right off and the poor man didn't work for months ... he couldn't work."[15]

Nor were there any worker protection or compensation programs. The federal and state governments had a long history of favoring business over labor, with organized labor still in the process of fighting to obtain an opportunity to so much as discuss its case at the state and national levels. As a result, there were no coffee breaks, no paid vacations, and when the mills closed for holidays such as Christmas or

The Walcott & Campbell Spinning Company on Sauquoit Street.

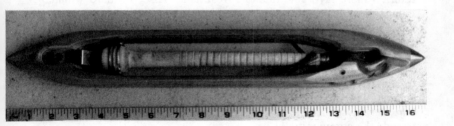

A typical shuttle illustrating its length in inches.
Note the metal tips clearly visible on the ends.

Thanksgiving the workers were not paid for the time that they did not work. Those who went home sick were not paid during their absence. If injured on the job, there was no medical plan, no worker compensation, and pay stopped at the time of the accident, not to be resumed until the injured party returned to work.[16]

With the death of W. Stuart Walcott and the subsequent sale of the New York Mills Corporation to the A. D. Juilliard Company, conditions in the mills, and in the surrounding community, appeared to worsen. The familiar personal contact between employer and employee under the Walcotts and Campbells, though perhaps more imagined than real, had a stabilizing influence on the community and its people. The strict control of the Walcotts and Campbells was tempered with a religious paternalism characterized by a moral and philanthropic concern for the welfare of the workers. As Ernest J. Savoie concluded in his study of managerial attitudes and practices in the New York Mills Corporation, when the A. D. Juilliard Company replaced the Walcotts and Campbells, "the paternalistic structure of the mill village no longer denoted primarily a genuine solicitude for the workers, but instead came to be used as a method of labor control and exploitation."[17]

In place of the omnipresent rule of the Walcotts and the Campbells, and what remained of their paternalistic interest in the community, came the leadership of Augustus D. Juilliard, the noted merchant, capitalist and philanthropist whose many public charitable activities included endowing the famous Juilliard School of Music. Under Juilliard's absentee ownership, with its reliance on hired superintendents to run its enterprise for maximum profit, any pretense of paternalistic care for employees disappeared. As a result of the economic panic in 1907, the following two years saw wages reduced by ten percent in order to return a more favorable rate of investment. Also, Juilliard's management styles, designed to return the highest possible profits, were completely different from those of the Walcotts and the Campbells, differences which only served to magnify the other issues that increasingly separated employer from employee. The employers no longer lived in the community, they could no longer be seen on the streets or spoken to directly when difficulties arose. The funds which Walcott and Campbell made available for the upkeep of company homes decreased considerably under the new management, while company profits went outside the community.[18]

Within a few years of the A. D. Juilliard takeover, the *Utica Saturday Globe* noted the more obvious of these changes when it informed its readers that:

> "At one time New York Mills was regarded and with
> justice as one of the neatest industrial towns in the coun-

try. Its dwellings were well kept. Its lawns were carefully tended. A paternalistic spirit ruled the place and its
streets after 9 o'clock at night were almost as quiet as a
cow pasture.
     ... But New York Mills has changed. ... The general
appearance of the village has altered for the worse. It still
has beautiful places, but many of the houses have a
weather beaten look — different far from the time when
William D. Walcott and after him his son W. Stuart Walcott ruled the destinies of the New York Mills Corporation.
     Yet the fault is not that of the present employees of
the village. These employees are industrious, frugal, ambitious, desirous of steeping their souls in the American
spirit of pluck and energy and anxious to leave to their
children an education denied themselves. The spirit of the
Polish people is to be seen in the handsome church and
school they maintain and in the sacrifices they are prepared
to make both for education and religion."[19]

Nor were the changes in the village and the mills only cosmetic.
By 1910 Chester A. Braman, a leading stockholder and member of the
Board of Directors of the A. D. Juilliard Company, became increasingly
concerned that Robert Campbell, master mechanic for the New York
Mills Corporation, and other persons held over from the Walcott and
Campbell years were purposely making it difficult to implement
changes desired by the Juilliard Board of Directors. As a consequence,
in the same year the master mechanic was dismissed and Samuel R.
Campbell, who stayed on as president of the New York Mills Corporation after the transfer of control to A. D. Juilliard, was asked to resign.
At the same time, J. P. Campbell was asked to resign as vice president,
and Juilliard officials acted to terminate or demote assistant treasurer E.
M. Coughlin, agent Timothy Mooney and others whom they suspected
of being either too close to the community or not sufficiently concerned
with company profits. Samuel R. Campbell was replaced as president
by William Pierrepont White, a Utica attorney, banker and descendant
of community founder Hugh White, whom Juilliard officials felt would
be better able to promote their interest in cutting costs and maximizing
profits. The services of George Fish were retained as vice president and
general manager. In a letter to White, Braman sought to clarify the role
the company expected the new president to play, emphasizing that the
company wanted "someone there in whom we have faith and who will
carry out our instructions intelligently, and with an eye singly only to
the interests of the company."[20]

To the Poles, it appeared that the new managers employed by A. D. Juilliard were not only unsympathetic to their needs as employees, but biased against them as people. Under the new management, weavers were "stretched-out," that is, they were assigned an increased number of machines to operate, and they were assessed fines for any imperfections in the cloth they produced regardless of whether these were caused by the worker or by faulty equipment. Fines and the necessity of spending more money on upkeep of the home once company funding was withdrawn cut deeply into the workers' actual take home pay. In addition, when new spinning and weaving equipment was installed Juilliard's Board of Directors decided to lower wages to compensate for the increase in worker productivity. "Now is the time to make the proposed changes in pay," Braman wrote to the company's agent, "while help is plentiful, and not wait until next summer."[21]

Worse still was the attitude of the employers. To the Poles, it appeared as if they never had an opportunity for the better jobs in the mills, only the low-level operative positions. Verbal abuse, ridicule and even physical mistreatment took place.[22] Bertha Kozak recalled how "They were physically pushed around and of course everything was 'Polak.' They were treated with contempt and as inferiors. ... I used to see once in a while when they'd pass by a Pole standing by his machine they would spit on him."[23]

Faced with these conditions, the Polish workers, who by 1911 constituted approximately one-half of the employees in New York Mills, decided that something must be done to improve their lot. They saw how their collective action in the Society of St. Stanislaus and the Polish Roman Catholic Union led to the establishment of St. Mary's Parish. They saw how these organizations, together with the Society of St. Casimir and the Polish Falcons, provided for their further spiritual and financial support. They saw that organization worked to better their community and their lives, so they determined to use the same means to achieve better working conditions. Once again, they planned to organize — this time it would be a labor union.

At that time in American history, organized labor was not very popular. Despite a century of long hours, low pay, poor health and safety conditions, and other abuses, both popular sentiments and the powers of government were consistently arrayed on the side of management rather than labor. Federal injunctions prevented work stoppages, federal courts halted labor initiatives, and federal troops broke strikes and protected the property of business owners. Indeed, the mere formation of labor unions was illegal in every state prior to a Massachusetts Supreme Court decision in 1842 giving workers, at least in that one state, the right to organize. Still, even after 1842 the right to organize spread slowly, with union formation still slower. Employers, supported by state and federal authorities, combined to control the labor market so that those suspected of agitating for organized labor were fired and "blacklisted," while new employees were forced to sign "yellow dog" contracts as a condition of their employment. The "blacklist" was a listing of union agitators circulated among employers so that known activists would not be rehired, while the "yellow dog" contract required that the worker pledge not to join a union after being hired.[24]

Organized labor made sporadic gains throughout the nineteenth century, often accompanied by serious violent disorders and bloodshed. In 1875 attempts to organize workers in the coal mining districts of Pennsylvania and West Virginia led to a virtual reign of terror, the conclusion of which saw twenty-four workers convicted of inciting violence, ten of whom were hanged, and public opinion turned even more against organized labor. The great railroad strike of 1877 resulted in a pitched battle in Pittsburgh between striking workers and the Pennsylvania State Militia that left twenty-four dead. The Haymarket riot in Chicago in 1886 killed seven and injured over seventy, resulting in the execution of four anarchists who were, at least in the public mind, linked with the violence they believed to be inherent in organized labor. This event led to the demise of the Knights of Labor, the first promising attempt at forming a national union. During a strike against Carnegie Steel in 1892 the Homestead Massacre took the lives of three Pinkerton detectives, hired by the company to protect its property, and ten strikers. Thus, the movement to create organized labor unions was viewed by both government and the general public as a very dangerous activity and received little support from either.

It was not until 1886 that the American Federation of Labor was formed as the first permanently successful national labor organization. But the A.F. of L. was at that time a skilled craft union that did not enroll unskilled workers. Although there were industrial unions such as the United Mine Workers within the A.F. of L., they were the exception rather than the rule. In keeping with its disdain of unskilled factory labor, the A.F. of L. also opposed immigration, which it characterized as a detriment to the economic status of labor.[25] During its first decade of existence the A.F. of L. publicly called for a restriction of immigration, proposing that this be accomplished by a literacy test as a qualification for those who desired to enter the country. On March 21, 1906, the A.F. of L. presented a Bill of Grievances to the United States Congress which included a call for the restriction of immigration. The A.F. of L. supported government controls to restrict the number of workers coming into the country in the belief that a more limited pool of labor would increase its scarcity, and hence its value, thus resulting in a rise in wages. This position was explained in an article on "The Un-Americanization of America" by A. A. Graham, published in the *American Federationist*, the official organ of the A.F. of L., in 1910. In it, Graham lamented what he characterized as the "foreignization" of the American work force and called upon corporations to cease their practice of hiring immigrants as a "national and patriotic solution to this question."[26] Similar articles appeared in the *American Federationist* with regularity throughout the pre-World War I era, including two pieces authored by A.F. of L. president Samuel Gompers in 1916 and 1917 which renewed the call for immigration restriction.[27]

Under Samuel Gompers, the A.F. of L.'s rather limited early goals included obtaining the right to collective bargaining, higher wages, and an eight-hour work day. It was only after 1900, under the presidential administration of Theodore Roosevelt, that the federal government began to place some minimal restrictions on business, and to adopt an attitude which, though still favoring employer over employee, emphasized an attempt at amicable settlement of disputes through negotiation.[28]

Although membership in the A.F. of L. increased from approximately 548,000 in 1900 to about 1,500,000 by 1910,[29] the general atmosphere for labor organization was still not good and strikes were normally both feared and opposed by employers, government, and the general public alike. It was amidst this foreboding atmosphere that the Poles in New York Mills decided to organize. Their task was particularly difficult because of differences separating the workers themselves into sometimes hostile factions. Animosities and distrust served to separate the Poles from the other workers of various nationalities and, along with the language barrier, to mitigate against joint action. There were also divisions between the various classes of workers. Weavers and spinners, for example, worked on a piece rate but depended upon skilled loom fixers, who received an hourly rate, to keep their equipment running smoothly. The loom fixers had no incentive to hurry, while the weavers and spinners lost money with each passing minute that the loom was not running, thus resulting in many hard feelings. Within the Polish community, there were rivalries and jealousies based on the section of partitioned Poland where each originated. Those from Galicia referred to their compatriots from the sections of Poland occupied by Russia and Prussia with the disparaging terms *"Moskali,"* and *"Prusaki,"* while they themselves were considered *"Galicjaki"* by the others. Then too, given the physical separation of the Lower, Middle and Upper Mills, families tended to identify with their place of employment and residence, and not to mix very much except at church services.[30]

As rumors of unionism spread throughout the mills, they quickly reached the ears of management. On January 27, 1911, Braman wrote to White urging him to "follow up the Polish organization matter and endeavor to get fully posted on this situation, and if any steps are necessary in order to prevent trouble see that they are adopted." This letter was soon followed on February 6 by more specific instructions on how to handle the move toward unionization. "The Poles are going ahead and forming a union," he wrote. "I have advised Mr. Fish to find out who the ringleaders are and discharge them. I understand that they hold their meetings in the gin mill of one of their countrymen, named Kozak. This man is a notorious breaker of the law and sells liquor on Sunday, and has been convicted and fined once for this offense, and yet he is carrying on the business the same as ever. The two things to do are, to put this man out of business, and get rid of the ringleaders, as above indicated."[31] Thus, the immediate short-term policy of the A. D. Juilliard management was one of threat, intimidation and dismissal. In subsequent letters, Braman determined to implement a long-range policy of eliminating the Poles altogether. On March 23, for example, he wrote to White to share with him his understanding that

"we are not re-engaging any Poles at the New York Mills now that have been discharged, and they are taking great care in this respect. I think that the general superintendent has got a system now by which they can be kept out of the mills in almost all cases. Of course, once in a while there is an exception and a man gets back through some misunderstanding, but as a general thing I think that these people that have been discharged for cause are being kept pretty well out of the mills, and I believe that it is agreed with the mill management that it is desirable to get rid of several hundred Poles and replace them with workers of other nationalities with as little delay as possible."[32]

To implement the short-range plan, those suspected of being active in the movement were to be fired, while others were pressured to become informants. Braman also took a specific interest in Jan and Piotr Kozak whose hall at the end of Porter Street was used as a meeting place by union activists and whom he consequently suspected of being ringleaders in the union movement. Indeed, Braman's correspondence throughout this period illustrated a strong fixation on eliminating the Kozaks' business and running them out of town. On February 21 he authorized White to hire Pinkerton detectives to obtain evidence of union activity and to "work in conjunction with you against the saloon keepers there." In doing so, however, Braman urged caution in the belief that "These men would not hesitate a moment to kill a man who might inform against them." He maintained a constant interest in the

Kozaks, displaying on several occasions an apparent frustration that they remained in business. On February 18 he complained to White that "It is incomprehensible to us why some of you there do not close up some of these Polish saloons. ... Please outline to me, if convenient, exactly what evidence is necessary and if there is nobody there who could get it, perhaps I can steer the thing from this end. The New York Mills has suffered tremendously from the fact that there are no local stockholders there who are willing to go to any trouble in a matter of this kind, which just now is very vital, because the Union is being formed and run in and from these gin mills. ... If we can put Kozak out of business there would be no meeting place in New York Mills for them, and in my judgment there is no time to be lost." On March 23 Braman asked White why the case against the Kozaks "was not prosecuted," while as late as May 8 he lamented: "I fear that your efforts to give us relief from this man have been like the Dead Sea fruit."[33]

As difficulties intensified, the workers held a meeting on the hill at the end of Porter Street in Kozak's hall on February 11, 1911. The meeting was attended by Charles A. Miles, a labor organizer for the United Textile Workers of America whose home was in Paterson, New Jersey, and by Michał Kostor, an officer in a Utica textile union, who served as interpreter for Miles. Following a speech on the benefits of union affiliation, Miles answered questions from those in attendance and urged them to join the union movement. By the end of this historic meeting, thirty-six people signed their names as members of a new union known as Local 753, United Textile Workers of America. Its first president was Michał Tuman. Born in Poland in 1883, Tuman was a well-known community activist who earlier played a leading part in the formation of the Society of St. Stanislaus and the local chapter of the Polish Roman Catholic Union. Elected with him as officers were Michał Wolak (vice president), Jan Czyżycki (recording secretary), Ludwik Krupa (financial secretary), Tomasz Osika (treasurer), Jan Solnica (marshal), and Michał Smoła (trustee). Stanisław Pluta, Wojciech Ryczek and Jan Wolak were elected the first "collectors," the people entrusted with recruitment and collection of dues.[34]

The United Textile Workers of America came into existence in Washington, D.C., on November 19, 1901, as a national organization to enlist workers in the textile industry under the sponsorship of the American Federation of Labor. Its' success since its inception was minimal due to strong opposition by employers, infighting among union officials, and a vacillating economic situation in the industry. Indeed, prior to World War I it never enrolled more than ten percent of all textile workers.[35]

Jan Kozak   Piotr Kozak

This hall, owned by the Kozaks, served as a meeting place
for union activists. Standing with hands on hips is Jan Kozak.

With the formation of Local 753, tensions rose in the village, and newspapers openly speculated on the probable beginning of a strike. On April 14 the *Utica Observer* noted that Sheriff Becker was preparing to call out his entire force of deputies "to protect life, liberty and the pursuit of happiness" should a strike break out. The paper also speculated on the cause of the unrest, which it attributed to poor wages.[36] Such public accounts of the union activities were not at all compatible with the interests of the A. D. Juilliard Company. Consequently, Braman wrote to White on April 11 cautioning him "against having either written or verbal communication with any of the union officers. I should acknowledge no letters, or permit any interviews, except with our own employees who are actually working for us at the time the request for an interview is made. This is a time for fortitude and for a display of good judgment ... by talking to a man like Miles the present agony will only be prolonged because, as you must know, there is no middle ground with the union officers; it is unconditional surrender or strike. The way to break this union idea is to discharge the agitators and especially the officers of the union as soon as they become known, and throw them out of our houses without the slightest hesitation. Let them get the idea that we ask for no quarter and shall give none."[37] There was to be no compromise with unionism.

On April 17 Braman again wrote to White to urge further action not only against the Kozaks, but against Józef Smoła, another union activist, and against the *Utica Observer* for running the story about Sheriff Becker's preparations for a possible strike. This interesting letter, which clearly illustrates the "no quarter" mentality of Braman and his associates, read as follows:

> "Your letter of the 15th inst. is at hand, and the outcome of the Kozak cases is as I feared. I hope you will see to it that the judge does not suspend the fines of these men. They are villains of the worst type, and would not hesitate to commit murder if necessary, and there will be no peace in New York Mills while they live there and can sell liquor in defiance of law. However, let us keep right after these fellows until we get rid of them.
>
> There is a fellow by the name of Smoly [*sic*], a saloon keeper, who sells liquor every Sunday at his home, which is next door to his saloon, and he makes speeches at every meeting of the union. This man's case should be taken hold of immediately. Mr. Fish can give you information regarding him.
>
> Referring to the enclosed article from the 'Utica Observer' of the 14th inst. This is all wrong, and I wish you

A. D. JUILLIARD & CO.

70 & 72 WORTH & 23 & 25 THOMAS STS.

P.O. BOX 446.

NEW YORK. April 11th, 1911

Dear Mr. White:

  I strongly advise against having either written or verbal communication with any of the union officers. I should acknowledge no letters, or permit any interviews, except with our own employees who are actually working for us at the time the request for an interview is made. This is a time for fortitude and for a display of good judgment, and much consideration should be given to the present condition of the cotton industry, and full force to the fact that a great many mills have shut down and most of the others are working on short time. If all the mills in that community stand together it will make the establishment of a textile union there impossible. Of this you may be sure, and by talking to a man like Miles the present agony will only be prolonged because, as you must know, there is no middle ground with the union officers; it is unconditional surrender or a strike. The way to break this union idea is to discharge the agitators and especially the officers of the union as soon as they become known, and throw them out of our houses without the slightest hesitation. Let them get the idea that we ask for no quarter and shall give none. Urge Mr. Fish on your own responsibility, i. e. without mentioning my name, to pursue this course relentlessly.

  I am just in receipt of the following telegram from our friend at Albany; "Have devised a modus-operandi after a conference here."

    Very truly yours,

Wm. Pierrepont White, Esq.,
Utica, N.Y.

A letter from Chester A. Braman to W. Pierrepont White, April 11, 1911, instructing White to avoid communication with the union and to discharge and evict union activists.

could exert sufficient influence with the publishers of this
paper to stop them from publishing articles which can
only be injurious to us. If the newspapers will only keep
out of it, we will have no strike. Miles is about to take
his departure with the probabilities of his not returning,
and we are slowly but surely winning out. Can you do
anything in this respect.[38]

Acting under Braman's firm instructions, White, Fish and the other
top executives of the New York Mills Corporation began to put Juilliard's policies into effect by firing union activists and attempting to
close down the union's meeting places in Kozak's and Smoła's halls.
Relying upon spies to identify union activists, and detectives hired by
A. D. Juilliard officials to manufacture evidence against the Kozaks,
White and Fish were able to fire those who were speaking in favor of
unionization and to convince the local courts to levy fines upon the
Kozak brothers. Their combined efforts, however, proved less than satisfactory to their superiors in New York. "Referring to your letter of
yesterday," Braman wrote to White on April 19, "I see that Kozak had
to pay his fine, but has his license been revoked. This last ought to go
with his conviction. It is reported to me that saloon-keeper Smolla
[sic] is a big factor in the union at present. Competition between he
and the Kozaks is so keen that Smolla became an agitator so as to draw
custom [sic] for his saloon. He makes a speech at every meeting and is
filling the Poles with all kinds of 'hot air'; that the business men will
help to defeat the company when a strike occurs. I believe it very necessary that we should get this man, if possible."[39]

```
#94a reports:-


                                          Sunday, April 30, 1911.



        Michael Zladuk, 37 years of age, 5 feet 9 inches, 175
pounds, red hair and mustache, works at nights on the cars, said
that he is ready to go out on strike at any time, and that the
company cannot do him any harm, as he intends to move from the
company's house.

        Charles Przybyla, working on the cars daytime, 40 years
of age, 5 feet 11 inches, 185 pounds, light brown hair, tan com-
plexion, big light brown mustache, and a union man, said that the
bosses of the W. & C. Co. should be given a good beating because
they are asking girls and young boys too many questions about the
union; that the Poles should not hold off too long, but that they
should get together and fight while they have the chance.
```

A detective's report.

Another problem that bothered Braman was an apparent weakening of resolve among the officials at the neighboring Walcott & Campbell Spinning Company. Not only did Braman have information that Walcott & Campbell had hired the union activists terminated by A. D. Juilliard, but at the beginning of May it considered offering its employees a ten percent increase in wages. As soon as he became aware of these moves, Braman immediately acted to force the smaller Walcott & Campbell into line behind his hardline policies. In a letter to White dated March 16 Braman complained that he found Walcott & Campbell explanations of the hirings unsatisfactory, "and it is inexplicable to me why he should now, under the circumstances, start in to reemploy this class, and especially those who have been dismissed by the New York Mills as agitators. After he has fought out the battle and paid part of the cost at least, it does seem to me an insane way to proceed. He ought to make it a hard and fast rule, until all danger of strike is past, not to engage any Poles, either male or female, and he clearly told me when he was last here that it was his intention not to do so."[40]

Similarly, when he found out about the proposed increase in wages to be offered by Walcott & Campbell, Braman took steps to pressure that company into rescinding its proposed new salary schedule. "Under no circumstances should the W. & C. Co. make such a step as this," he stated emphatically, "as it would be very injurious to the New York Mills, and will not help them in the least. I hope they will not show any weakness in dealing with the present situation. Conditions are improving all the time, and there will be no strike, in my judgment, if we maintain our present attitude."[41]

Faced with these concerted attempts to disrupt and defeat its activities, and the many other factors which divided the workers, the new U.T.W.A. local grew slowly. But moral support for the Polish organizers soon appeared. In early 1912 Ludwik Leśnicki began publishing *Młotek Duchowny* [The Spiritual Hammer], a militant labor-oriented Polish-language newspaper that viciously attacked all capitalists as exploiters of the working class, leveling at the same time specific criticism at the owners of the New York Mills Corporation. This development did not go unnoticed by A. D. Juilliard officials as is evidenced by a letter from Braman to White on March 10, 1911, in which he complained: "Referring to the enclosed transcriptions of articles which purport to have appeared in the Polish papers there; these are purely libelous and ought to be stopped, and I hope you will take some steps in that direction without delay."[42]

If Braman and his associates felt injured by the venom of Leśnicki's publication, they must have been doubly disconcerted in September, 1911, when Jan Gomólski began publishing *Słowo Polskie*

[The Polish Word]. Progressive in its political orientation, with an active interest in workers' concerns, the paper's first issue pledged to fight discord and disunity, "an extremely formidable and dangerous enemy who goes by the name of ignorance, dissension, inefficiency, conceit, vanity and slovenliness." These vices, Gomólski told his readers, must be eliminated. "Progress will be our motto and our battle cry," he proclaimed.[43] In October, less than a month after his first issue, Gomólski threw his support behind Tuman and his associates by openly praising their efforts and castigating those who were slow to embrace the union cause. The splendid efforts of those forming the union, he impressed upon his readers,

> "must continually struggle with those who still fail to understand their own interests, with those who are delaying joining the ranks of the union, and with those who are all but too eager to listen to the various instigators and agitators. Every battle is difficult and trying, and, as we have observed, this battle has created plenty of extra work for the unionists in N. Y. Mills. However, dear Citizens, you should neither lose heart nor develop misgivings. The cause which you are standing behind and fighting for is just, beautiful and noble. Consequently — fight bravely and boldly! Complete the task you have started but do not be reckless. Be sensible and do not allow any bad individuals to join the ranks, those only wishing your downfall, or those who will only damage the cause with senseless clamor and who are never around when there is work to be done. Do not allow those to take office who only know how to give advice and demand help from others. Let the common simple workers join the ranks of the union. Let the simple workers lead the union — and by way of a simple, honest path you will fight for your own, and simply, as well as unerringly, you will most certainly achieve your objectives."[44]

With the support of the Polish press, the union organizers pressed forward with increasing success. By the end of 1911, nearly 400 employees signed on as members of Local 753. Soon after its formation, the union sent its executive committee to negotiate with management over the issue of wage deductions for faults in the cloth. The union was prepared to argue that it was unfair to penalize workers for instances where flaws occurred due to defective machinery. When the committee members went to the company offices on Main Street they were led to a back door that opened onto an elevated loading dock.

There was no stairway from the dock to the ground. "They opened that door and told the committee to jump, to get out," recalled Józef Piszcz. Then, each of the members of the executive committee was summarily fired. Immediately, Local 753 took action to insist that those terminated be returned to work. Soon, Charles A. Miles arrived to lend the support of the national union. Miles went to speak with the General Superintendent of the New York Mills Corporation, but was informed that the company would not carry on any discussions with the union.[45]

Given the refusal of company officials to negotiate with Miles, the labor organizer called upon the national president of the U.T.W.A., John Golden, to use the weight of his office to present the workers' grievances. In response, Golden wrote to W. Pierrepont White as follows:

"Dear Mr. White,

I have been instructed by the executive council of my International organization to bring the following facts before you relative to some recent happenings in the New York Mills of which you are head, and which we are loath to believe you know anything of.

A number of the employes [sic] of said mill decided to form a union that joint action might be taken on any matters that might arise between them and their employers, believing that they had the same rights as any other body of people to band themselves together for their own mutual protection; the employers for instance. Immediately after they had begun to do this, a number of the active ones in the organization were discharged, without cause so far as they knew outside of the fact that they were officers of the new union. First the local president, Michael Luma [Michał Tuman], was discharged, and ordered to immediately quit the companies house in which he lived, when he asked for the reason for his discharge, he was told to get to H__l out of the place; next came the discharge of the Treasurer of the Union, this man had worked for the firm fourteen years, when he asked Supt. Fish for the reason for his discharge, he was informed that he, Supt. Fish, knew nothing about the matter, and advised him to see the Boss, he done so and was informed by the Boss, in these words! you are through that's all, and if Supt. Fish wants to know why let him come and ask me, since then the secretary and trustee of the new union have also been discharged, which looks to us like one of the clearest cases of discrimination we ever saw. or experienced, leaving no doubt in our minds but what the sole cause of this unwarrantable discrimination, wherein old and faithful employes are being sacrificed simply because they have exerted their right to belong to an organization. The mens names in addition to the president of the local union who have been discharged, Thomas Osyka [Tomasz Osika], Treasurer, Louis Krupa [Ludwik Krupa], Secretary, and Thomas May, Trustee. In addition many complaints are registered as to excessive fining which has become more pronounced than ever of late, in some cases reaching as high as $3.00. It seems to me that no man with the spirit of fair play within him will tolerate such conduct, which is bound to react against those practicing such unfair tactics, and as matters are in a very unsettled condition in the New York Mills on account of the harsh treatment being accorded the help, as outlined above, I am instructed to request that you make an investigation of the matters mentioned in this communication, and if found to exist we feel there will no doubt as to your attitude in having this kind of treatment stopped at once. I might add that our only motive in bringing this matter to your attention is in the interest of harmony, and for the reason that we have been unable to obtain redress by the officials at the mills."[46]

White forwarded Golden's letter to Braman in New York City, and the stockholder quickly wrote to tell White to "pay no attention to the letter. I note that this man constitutes himself judge and jury. As I stated some time ago, there is no half-way course in dealing with the people he represents; it is either a complete surrender or a strike if you begin a discussion. They are going to be extremely cautious as to what they do in times like the present when so many mills throughout the country are shut down, and with dark prospects ahead. We should continue the course we have laid out relentlessly, but with good judgment."[47]

Nevertheless, over the next several weeks those terminated by the New York Mills Corporation were gradually hired by the Walcott & Campbell Spinning Company. This apparently resulted from a communications gap between the two companies, rather than from any attempt by either to settle the employees' grievances. Indeed, Chester Braman complained about this circumvention of the company's efforts to discharge the union members in another letter to White. From the perspective of the Polish workers, however, it appeared as if their own protests were having an effect. Many credited the rehiring of the union members to a "mass Demonstration" by the workers. This was, according to *Slowo Polskie*, "the first victory of the workers." Information on this early "mass demonstration" is sketchy, although it appears from company correspondence that it had nothing to do with the temporary rehiring of the union officers.[48]

Although it began rather inauspiciously, Local 753 continued to grow. The following spring, national interest in the labor movement reached what was at that time probably an all-time peak. The infamous Triangle Shirtwaist Factory fire in 1911 that killed 145 Jewish, Italian and Polish immigrant women garment workers in New York City focused national attention on the need for industrial safety regulation. In New York State, Assemblyman Edward D. Jackson of Buffalo introduced a bill at the urging of the New York State Federation of Labor to address another form of exploitation of women and children by reducing the number of hours they could work to a maximum of fifty-four per week. Faced with this potential regulation of a large segment of the labor force, the textile mills of the Mohawk and Hudson Valley regions, together with several canning factories in western New York, pooled their resources to hire a variety of lawyers, retired judges and legislators to oppose the proposed restrictions.[49] Among the most able of those arguing against the Jackson Bill before a committee empowered by the New York State Legislature was Attorney Thomas D. Watkins of Utica who claimed to represent a group of textile mills with a total capitalization of $35,000,000. On behalf of these interests, Watkins argued that such a measure would so reduce the output of the mills as to cripple them in comparison with foreign manufacturers. Watkins was followed by a "representative of New York Mills" who "provided substance to the charges, indicating that the concerns he spoke for would have to move knitting operations to Georgia, where workers were allowed to labor sixty-six hours a week."[50] In fact, the New York Mills Corporation stood in the forefront of the drive to defeat the fifty-four hour limitation. Company officials exerted pressure on state legislators, actively campaigned among fellow-manufacturers to present a united front, provided funds for the support of lobbyists, and sent their own management personnel to testify before investigating committees in Albany.[51]

Indeed, the management of the A. D. Juilliard Company consistently opposed any attempts to place restrictions or limitations on the authority of employers. As early as December, 1909, Chester A. Braman wrote to W. Pierrepont White to warn him of the possibility of an attempt being made to limit the hours workers could be made to labor each week. "As you are the Legislative Committee," he pointedly noted, "we trust you will keep track of this matter so that we will not be in danger of having a disagreeable surprise. It is a great pity that we haven't an effective Manufacturers Association in this state whereby our strength throughout the state could be quickly marshalled [*sic*] and used as a unit."[52] Two months later Braman cautioned White about a bill introduced in the New York State Assembly that would provide stricter employer liability laws. "This is an outrageous law from our point of view and ought to be blocked," he informed White. "There ought to be some way of promptly stopping this fool legislation, and we could do it if we were properly organized, beyond a question."[53] Once again, in April 1910, Braman revealed his great concern to White, emphasizing that

> "it is of the utmost importance to the textile industry of the State that this bill should not become law. If it does it will be almost ruinous to the New York Mills and no trouble or expense should be allowed to stand in the way of keeping it from getting out of committee. Please do not take anything for granted, but keep in close touch with the situation until the danger is past.[54]

Concurrent with this interest in the Jackson Bill was a rise in labor organization within the state. In particular, the Labor Forward Movement, led by middle-class professionals and clergy who had an interest in reform movements, provided a very emotional appeal that addressed the concerns raised by immigrant labor, the impersonal nature of large corporations, and the waning sense of community stability in older industrial towns. The Labor Forward Movement hoped to reassure owners and the general public of organized labor's support for the capitalist system, while at the same time attempting to enroll any and all workers, skilled or unskilled, native or immigrant, into the trade union movement. Laced with a heavy dose of Protestant evangelicalism, the movement created much excitement in New York and succeeded in making some headway in recruiting Polish and Italian workers. Indeed, Charles A. Miles, who attempted to use the enthusiasm generated by the Labor Forward Movement to assist in enrolling workers in the United Textile Workers of America, maintained in a speech in Auburn, New York, that "Aside from the spiritual work carried on by the churches I do not know of anything that ought to draw from us more enthusiasm and effort for the good of mankind" than unionism.[55]

As the interest in business regulation and the organization of labor increased, several major strikes made news around the country. Chief among these was the strike of some 25,000 textile workers in Lawrence, Massachusetts, which began in January, 1912. The strike originated as a protest to a reduction in wages that accompanied the implementation of a Massachusetts state law reducing the number of hours that women and minors could work, legislation very similar to the Jackson Bill in New York. This strike continued on to a successful conclusion for the workers in late March, making national headlines not only because of its magnitude, but because of the involvement of the socialist-oriented Industrial Workers of the World [I.W.W.] and the violent confrontations which occurred during the work stoppage. The strike was well known in New York Mills because it received extensive coverage in Utica's several English language newspapers, as well as in the Polish language *Slowo Polskie*. It was of particular interest to the Polish workers in New York Mills, many of whom had friends or relatives involved in the events unfolding in Massachusetts. Further, both New York Mills and Lawrence were textile manufacturing centers, both were interested in state legislation placing limits on the number of hours that women and children could work, and both worked in environments where the bulk of the employees consisted on immigrant labor.[56]

The strike in Lawrence was also looked upon with great apprehension by officials of the New York Mills Corporation. "As a matter of fact," Braman wrote to White, "the trouble at Lawrence is not a strike, it is a revolution." The only solution, Braman emphasized, was for employers to refuse to treat with unions at any level, and to band together into their own organizations, to "stand together and work shoulder to shoulder with those of like mind."[57]

While the strike in Lawrence progressed, conditions in New York Mills deteriorated further. On January 11, 1912, a delegation of workers met with George Fish and presented him with a resolution passed by Local 753 requesting a fifteen percent increase in pay, elimination of the fine system, and the development of a "price ticket" system to inform weavers of their exact rates of pay. The latter resulted from continuing misunderstandings wherein the weavers expected a certain pay for work completed, only to find later that they frequently received less than anticipated. The resolution, signed by some 800 employees, was dismissed out of hand, the representatives being informed that the company would neither listen to their requests nor negotiate with them.[58]

Soon thereafter, several Utica newspapers reported that known union activists were being subjected to management retaliation. Substantial fines were assessed for even the smallest of transgressions. Three women who were absent to attend a funeral were each fined $2.00, the foreman at Number 1 fined weavers $.50 per thread for each thick thread found in a cloth, while in Number 2 fines for similar thread "offenses" reached $1.50 to $2.50 per person per week. Shortages in payroll envelopes became commonplace as employees were not compensated for the total number of hours that they worked. When a female weaver at Number 1, a union member, asked to have her loom fixed she was grabbed by the neck, escorted out the door and fired on the spot. Over a period of seven weeks, Michał Tuman's weekly pay envelope was short $1.00, $.50, $1.15, $1.35, $1.75, $1.75 and $2.00. Then he was fired. Gradually, foremen became even more abusive in their treatment of employees, as when a female weaver inquired about a shortage of $2.00 in her pay envelope and was kicked and punched for her inquiry.[59]

Meeting with rebuff at the local level, the union requested the assistance of national organizer Charles A. Miles, who served W. Pierrepont White with a formal letter of complaint from the U.T.W.A. on March 3. That letter, over the signature of U.T.W.A. Secretary-Treasurer Albert Hibbert, read as follows:

"I am writing you for the purpose of bringing to your attention certain matters that concern the best interests of the Employees and the Mills under your charge.

I have been informed that the Employees have presented to you certain matters and up to this time no consideration has been given to them by the Officials; a representative of our Organization has made efforts to secure an interview with some one in authority but with no success. The Operative [sic] have been very patient in the matter and have acted upon our advice that they keep at work until the General Office can make an attempt to secure a conference with the officials of the Firm for the purpose of reaching an amicable understanding to the end that the things complained off [sic] can be investigated, and if found to exist, remedied. Our Organization believes that if there are differences of opinion between the Employer and the Employee, that the most sensible way to bring about harmony is to get together and by arguement [sic] and reasoning reach a point where we can both agree.

I suppose you are in possession of the complaints that have been made together with their request, and I am writing you to ask that you agree to meet a Representative from the General Office to discuss the matters complained of, believing that such conference will result in good to both sides.

I am sending a copy of this letter to the principles [sic] officers of the Firm and express the hope that they may meet with your favorable consideration."[60]

Michał Tuman,
first president of Local 753

Jan Czyżycki,
recording secretary of Local 753

Tomasz Osika,
treasurer of Local 753

Michał Wolak,
vice president of Local 753
(as he appeared in later years)

Company officials in New York City remained adamant in their refusal to negotiate. On March 1 Braman wrote to John P. Campbell of the Walcott & Campbell Company to reassure him that "from the information I receive, only a small number belong to the union, which is in a tottering condition." He further reiterated to Campbell what was by this time the traditional A. D. Juilliard refrain, "If you talk to even the employees there is danger of being quoted outside, and let the union leaders once get the idea that you have any fear and you will have a strike on your hands with startling suddenness. There are but two things to do under the circumstances, as I see them, i.e. dismiss any of the agitators that you find in the plants, or officers of a union, and get in other nationalities as fast as the circumstances will permit, and remain perfectly quiet."[61]

Three days later, on March 4, after receiving the letter from U.T.W.A. official Hibbert, Braman wrote to White noting that the union "did the same thing last year. Pay no attention to them whatever. For any manufacturer to have anything to say to these people would be unwise in the highest degree; you would open a discussion that would not close without a compromise or a fight. As I have so often said, there is nothing that is so deadly to these people as silence on the part of the manufacturer." Then, after some discussion of an upcoming employers meeting, Braman reaffirmed his belief that "Practically a union does not exist there except in name only. Frantic efforts have been made and are being made to hold the few hundreds that formerly belonged, together, but our information is to the effect that dues are not being paid, that the officers are not in the employ of the mills, and the man who seems to be the most active is the editor of the 'Spiritual Hammer' who seems to be a new-comer, and public opinion is adverse to a strike. In this condition of affairs there is very little danger of trouble, and to raise wages under the circumstances would be a confession of weakness and might bring about disturbance."[62] Clearly, Braman continued to believe that the union was a hollow shell, not to be viewed as a serious threat to determined, firm employers. He was soon to learn the price of such contempt.

Some time during the week of March 17-23, Miles went to visit White to voice the workers' concerns. Miles explained the disputes between labor and management then taking place in Lawrence, Lowell, Fall River and New Bedford, Massachusetts, but indicated that neither the national union nor the Juilliard employees wished to see any trouble in New York Mills. At the same time, however, he tried to impress upon White that the employees were very serious in their grievances and wanted some indication that their concerns would be addressed. "I told him that unless the employees of the mills had their demands complied with at once that our union would not be responsible for what might follow." After some discussion, White agreed to meet with Miles a second time after each had an opportunity to reflect on the first meeting. Braman's continuing insistence that there be no contact between employers and employees no doubt had its effect because when Miles returned for the second meeting White refused to meet with him again in the capacity of company president. True to his instructions from Braman in New York, White intended to avoid any appearance of negotiating with union representatives. Miles warned White that failure to negotiate might lead to a work stoppage, but the president remained adamant in his decision to avoid negotiations.[63]

In an effort to establish some channel for communication, the workers sought assistance from the one institution that was indispensable to their lives — the Church. They approached Rev. Aleksander Fijałkowski, who replaced Father Płaza as the pastor at St. Mary's the previous year, to act as a mediator on their behalf. Born in Dobrzyn, in the Płocki region of Poland, on March 24, 1885, Fijałkowski, like many others, emigrated in 1903 at age eighteen to avoid the military draft of the occupying powers. Because of the partitions then in effect, Poles found themselves drafted to serve the interests of foreign states, sometimes even being forced to take up arms against fellow Poles. After arriving in New York he taught briefly in Schenectady before enrolling in Saints Cyril and Methodius Seminary in Detroit, Michigan. He later moved to St. Bernard's Seminary in Rochester where he completed his studies for the priesthood in 1910, being ordained for the Diocese of Syracuse on June 11 of that same year. He served as an assistant at the Sacred Heart Parish in Syracuse for some eighteen months before being assigned to St. Mary's. In many ways he was typical of the "Polish" priests in America at that time, serving as both a religious and temporal leader of the community. Among his parishioners at that time he was known for his "fire and brimstone" sermons and his attention to every detail of parish life.[64]

Dutifully responding to his flock, Fijałkowski went to the company offices several times to relay the employees grievances, along with their requests for better treatment and an increase in salary. The company representatives rejected his good offices and intentions, informing him that "The employes do not make big wages, but they work steady and have no cause for complaint."[65]

Throughout March, the Utica newspapers continued to headline labor walkouts around the country, particularly the massive Lawrence textile strike. On March 1 the *Utica Observer* reported that mill owners in Lawrence had offered a five percent increase in wages. Within the next few days came the news that dozens of mills throughout New England were following suit with various proposals for wage increases and other reforms. Although the strike continued, it was obvious to all that the work stoppage was having the desired effect of forcing the mill owners to negotiate.[66] If a strike was effective in Lawrence, why not in New York Mills?

As the end of March drew near, W. Pierrepont White apparently became convinced of the seriousness of the situation and the reality that his employees might indeed go out on strike, judgments which Braman obviously did not share. In any case, soon after the rejection of Miles' initiatives on behalf of the U.T.W.A., representatives of the Company went to St. Mary's on the evening of Saturday, March 23, to speak with Father Fijałkowski. Ironically, the officers who rebuffed his earlier attempts to present the workers' grievances now called upon him to use his influence with the people to prevent the anticipated strike. The next morning, in his sermon, Fijałkowski informed his parishioners of the visit by the company officials. In an attempt to act as peacemaker, he urged them to show patience, to try once again to reach a negotiated settlement of their grievances.[67]

At 4:00 p.m. that same afternoon Local 753 hosted a mass meeting of workers in Kozak's Hall. The executive committee reviewed the situation, including the latest company overture via Father Fijałkowski, and asked for a motion on what course of action to take. The long-suffering workers were in no mood to cast themselves once again upon the mercy of the absentee landlords and their insensitive foremen. In an emotion-charged atmosphere, the workers' shouts echoing through the hall were all the vote that was needed: *Strajk! Strajk!* Strike! Strike![68]

Chapter 4

Strajk!

Once the decision to strike was made, the executive committee decided to wait a few days before actually beginning the work stoppage to allow time to prepare a statement of grievances and plan for the needs of the workers once the walkout took place. After work on Monday and Tuesday evenings the committee met to discuss the various issues, draft their statement of demands, and plan the coordination of strike activities. These meetings did not go unnoticed by company officials, who held a series of secret meetings to plan a strategy for dealing with the strike threat. On Wednesday morning the company acted. Before the lunch break superintendents and department heads spread the word among the workers that the company had decided to consider a five percent increase in wages. Though not stated publicly, in making this offer the company was certainly attempting to forestall a strike, or at least to win over enough of the employees so that any attempted work stoppage would not have sufficient support to succeed. Against the eventuality of a walkout, A. D. Juilliard also sent a representative to North Adams, Massachusetts, to hire workers who could be brought in to take the place of strikers should that become necessary. Whether the possible salary increase was authorized by Juilliard officials in New York is doubtful given Braman's firm opposition to any kind of concession. More likely it was done on the authority of White who appears to have held a more realistic view of the workers' resolve to strike.[1]

Neither the union executive committee nor the workers themselves were impressed with this eleventh-hour initiative. On Wednesday evening the executive committee held another meeting to discuss the company's actions and review its own progress during the previous two days. Support for the strike remained high. The committee agreed to include in its demands a fifteen percent increase in pay, recognition of the union as a collective bargaining agent, establishment of a piece work pricing schedule, improvement of company owned houses, better treatment of the workers by management, the discharge of bleachery superintendent Fred Braman, the son of corporate stockholder Chester A. Braman, and assurances from the company that all workers would be allowed to return to their jobs once the strike was settled. Reports also indicated that contact was made with officials of the Utica Trades Assembly, which agreed to support the strike, and the United Textile Workers of America which promised that if the work stoppage lasted longer than two weeks it would provide $4 per week to each striker as long as the strike lasted. With goals now clarified and the support of fellow unionists assured, the executive committee agreed to begin the strike the next day.[2]

On the following morning, Thursday, March 28, the employees arrived at work at their normal time of 6:30 a.m. An hour later, by prearranged agreement, they halted work and walked out. The strike had begun. All four of the A. D. Juilliard mills closed immediately, while at the Walcott & Campbell Spinning Company, an independent factory located nearby on Sauquoit Street, about 150 of the 400 workers left, causing that plant to close at noon. In all, 1,119 workers went out on strike, to be joined later by an additional 877 for a total of 1,996. Commenting on the strikers, the *Utica Daily Press* reported that "about 1,400 are Polish speaking, from 40 to 50 Italian, from 80 to 115 Syrian, and from 35 to 40 French. The remainder are English speaking."[3] Meanwhile, *Słowo Polskie* announced with obvious emotion that the striking workers had taken a stand "against the capitalists to battle for bread for themselves and for their children. They are fighting against exploitation and oppression, and therefore deserve our recognition and sympathy. In addition, we wish them the perseverance necessary to achieve one of the largest victories ever."[4]

After leaving the factories, the workers hurried about the village nailing placards headlined *"Strajk"* to trees, telephone poles, buildings, and anywhere else that might command attention. Other groups of strikers journeyed to surrounding communities to announce the strike, seek the support of other union locals, and warn people not to come to the Mills in search of employment while the strike was underway. As the placards announcing the strike appeared in the village, many residents, apparently unable to understand that "strajk" was simply the Polish phonetic spelling of the English word "strike," feared that some violent uprising might occur. Fortunately, they soon learned the truth and panic was avoided.[5]

At 3:00 p.m. a mass meeting of workers convened at Kozak's Hall [sometimes called Kozak's Grove] attracting a large crowd. Given the tenuous relationship between the various ethnic groups employed in the mills, and the attempts by management to play one group off against another, the strike organizers made sure that all of the workers were invited; not only the Poles, but the French, Italian, Syrian, and English as well. The list of demands was read and adopted, after which speeches were made in various languages by representatives of the different ethnic

EXTRA!
Strajk w New York Mills, N. Y.

— Dzisiaj w Czwartek o godz. 7-ej rano, wyszli robotnicy zatrudnieni w fabrykach płóciennych na gremjalny strajk, żądając podwyższenia płący i dogodniejszych warunków zatrudnienia w różnych sekcjach zajęć. We Środę przedstawiciele tut. fabryk płóciennych na odbytym posiedzeniu uchwalili pewną podwyżkę robotnikóm, której jednak robotnicy nie przyjęli, uważając ją za bardzo niską i niepewną. Strajkujący robotnicy w liczbie około 3 tysiące, stanęli z kapitałem do walki o chleb dla siebie i dzieci swoich, do walki z wyzyskiem i uciskiem, dlatego należy się im uznanie i sympatja oraz życzymy im wytrwania a wreszcie pomyślnych rezultatów i jak największego zwycięstwa.

This announcement of the strike appeared in the Utica newspaper *Słowo Polskie*, March 28, 1912.

groups. Union officers carefully cautioned the strikers to use only peaceful means to obtain their goals, to keep off the streets when possible, and to stay away from the saloons. A committee was then appointed to present the list of grievances to company officials as representatives of the United Textile Workers of America. That evening, the *Utica Observer* reported that "The feeling is general among the strikers that if their grievances are exposed and brought forcibly to the attention of the officers of the mills that good results will be obtained."[6] Their hopes proved little more than wishful thinking.

While the employees met at Kozak's Hall, company representatives busily tried to win public support by providing their version of events to the many reporters from Utica's various newspapers who quickly arrived once news of the walkout reached the nearby city. To the press, company officials expressed both surprise and indignation. They claimed that the employees had given them no indication that a strike was planned, nor had they submitted any grievances nor requested any increase in pay. The employees, company officials insisted to the press, made an average wage of $10 per week, considered good by standards in the textile industry. "We pay a good scale of wages here," a company spokesman asserted. "We cannot afford to pay more without increasing the prices of our products. But we did announce to our employees yesterday that a readjustment of the wage scale throughout the mills was in progress and that the new scale would mean better prices in every case where the conditions of the business warranted. We pay about $20,000 each week in wages to our employees, an average of $10 a week to each employee. This is a high average for mills of the character of ours."[7]

In truth, the employees tried repeatedly to meet with company management since the previous year, and the A. D. Juilliard officials, both locally and in New York City, were well aware for some time that a strike would occur if they continued to ignore worker grievances. Not only did the workers attempted to speak with local Juilliard officials, but Father Fijałkowski attempted to open a dialogue with the company, Charles A. Miles spoke with officials in both New York Mills and New York City, and U.T.W.A. officers met and corresponded with these same company officials.

As far as wages were concerned, the company's statements to the press were also very misleading. The average worker in New York Mills did not make $10 per week, nor was the pay scale at A. D. Juilliard comparable to other textile factories in the state. The annual report of the New York State Department of Labor for 1911 indicated that in September of that year the average wage of male textile workers in the various Utica mills was $1.39 per day, while those in nearby New York Mills received only $1.16, a differential of 16.5%. The same source also indicated that the average weekly salary for female operators in New York Mills, for a sixty hour work week, was $6.96, and for female weavers $8.00 per week, neither of which approached the $10 per week figure cited by the company.[8] Although these figures clearly indicated that the workers in New York Mills had a legitimate complaint regarding low wages, comparable figures for March 1912 indicated that in reality their position was growing worse rather than better. The New York State Department of Labor figures for March 1912 show that the average wage of male operatives in New York Mills was $1.17 per day, and that of female operatives $1.11 per day. The average statewide for the same period was $2.21 for males and $1.28 for females. Thus, the disparity for male operators increased from 16.5% to 47.1% during the six months between September 1911 and March 1912. Also, when one compared similar job functions, the disparity was just as great as the averages. While male operatives in New York Mills made $1.17 per day, those in comparable positions in Cohoes, for example, earned $1.75 per day.[9]

Company officials were obviously not only feigning innocence in regard to any previous knowledge of employee grievances or an impending strike, but were also providing inaccurate and misleading salary information in an attempt to shape public opinion against the strikers. The company's policy continued to be one of obfuscation. Of course, the newsmen did not know this, thus they dutifully reported the company's version to their readers.

Following the company's statement, one of the reporters mentioned a rumor that the employees planned to send a delegation to the company offices to present their demands for a ten to fifteen percent pay increase.

"Will your company give such an interview?" the reporter asked.

"We positively will not," replied the spokesman. "Our plant has not made any money in the past six years and we simply cannot afford to do it. We propose to complete our readjustment of the wage scale and allow our employees to return to work under the increased advantages of that scale. We will not go beyond this."[10] It is difficult to understand how the New York Mills Corporation could not be making a profit when wages were reduced during the previous year, thus cutting costs, and at a time when production was increasing. The press, however, did not question A. D. Juilliard's assertions.

Fearful lest the strike turn violent, like so many others around the country, the company also took action to protect its property. "This is a time for the display of good common sense in every step that is taken," Braman wrote to White. "No one should appear alarmed, but sit tight and see that the mills are protected at all hazards." Before the afternoon was over management officials informed Oneida County

Sheriff Daniel Becker of the strike and emphasized that the company held the sheriff responsible for the protection of its property and the maintenance of order in the village. Becker, moved by the urgency of the company appeal, immediately set out for the village with Deputy Sheriff Corbett. Upon arrival, Becker met with company officials who expressed further fears that the strikers might resort to violence or sabotage. At the company's urging, he swore in seven special deputies from among the mills' superintendents and foremen to act as guards. Becker placed this force under the command of Deputy Sheriff Corbett while he visited the different locations to see for himself the extent of the emergency. Despite the company's histrionics, the *Utica Observer* reported that "He found everything as peaceful as a lamb in a clover patch."[11]

Following the meeting at Kozak's Hall, the union's executive committee held its own press conference to plead its case to the public. "The strike was not ordered till every other means of settlement was exhausted," the committee's prepared statement began, explaining that contrary to company statements, repeated requests had been submitted to the company without any result other than cuts in wages, an increase in harassment and abuse, and dismissals. Also contrary to what the company claimed, the average weekly wage was not $10.00, but anywhere from $2.00 to $9.00, with experienced weavers making between $6.00 and $9.00 per week while the less experienced made as little as $2.00 to $5.50. Salaries for workers in other positions ranged from less than $2.00 per week to as much as $8.00. The average was about $7.00 per week. As evidence, they produced the pay envelope of a woman employee who received $1.46 for a full week of work, including one evening of overtime! The strikers then noted that textile workers in New England were successful in gaining wage increases through collective action. "Are we to be blamed for asking for decent living conditions?" they asked.[12]

The union officers also voiced complaints about the company's treatment of its workers. The condition of the company houses was atrocious, they asserted, while some of the bosses treated the workers "inhumanely." To emphasize this they cited cases of workers who were fined, threatened or physically assaulted. They told of how Michał Tuman was shorted in his pay for seven weeks before being fired. They told how Tuman, Walenty Mądry and other union activists were blacklisted to prevent them from finding other employment. They told of the girl who was punched and kicked because she questioned the accuracy of her pay. Further, the strikers claimed that some employees only recently arrived in the country, and unfamiliar with the conduct of business in America, were robbed of a portion of their wages by unscrupulous bosses who demanded payments for jobs and favors. "More pay and better treatment" was their slogan, the workers explained.[13]

As the first day of the strike drew to a close company officials made another attempt to divide the workers, offering to pay a very high $3.00 per night to any of the strikers who agreed to help keep the fires burning in the large boilers supplying the steam used for heat and power in the several plants. When no one came forward, management explained that "serious damage might be caused if the fires were not kept going," and there were also insurance requirements to be considered. Not a single striker broke ranks to accept the rather lucrative offer.[14]

By Friday morning word of the strike spread throughout the surrounding communities. Before the sun rose very far, Tomasz Mótyka, vice president of Local 753, conferred with Rudolf Ząbek, the president, before meeting with his strike committee. Born in Poland in 1851, Mótyka was sixty-one years old at the time of the strike, thus affording him the status of an elder statesman within the Polish community. An educated man, he frequently tutored children during the winter months and took part in a myriad of other civic activities. Now he led his committee of five workers including, in addition to himself, Michał Smoła, Jan Solnica, Antoni Sokal and Piotr Karpiński, to visit the company offices on Main Street to present the strikers' list of grievances and demands to Superintendent Fish. In general, the strikers believed that Fish was a fair man who always treated them politely. They still hoped that if he could be made to understand their grievances some accommodation might be reached.[15]

The men were greeted and ushered into a meeting room where the two sides discussed the workers' grievances and the company's position on the various points for nearly two hours. Fish expressed some sympathy regarding the complaints about abusive treatment, stating at one point: "If any boss mistreats you, come directly to me and I will act fairly towards you in the matter." Yet, while Fish professed concern for the workers' well-being, the strike committee realized immediately that he was also trying to promote a sense of individual initiative and loyalty as an alternative to recognizing the union as a collective bargaining agent. Although Fish offered some general hope of accommodation on the posting of piecework rates, improvement of company-owned housing and the general treatment of workers, he remained firm on Juilliard's refusal to recognize the union, to increase wages, or to discharge Superintendent Braman. Further, since Fish offered no specific proposals other than the five percent raise he previously agreed to take under consideration, the meeting finally ended without reaching an accord.[16]

Following the conclusion of the meeting with Fish, the strike committee went to Kozak's Hall where it called an open meeting for 4:00 p.m. As the hour approached, the hall filled to capacity, with people standing for lack of sufficient seating. The committee reported Superintendent Fish's promise to meet individually with those harboring grievances, but noted that he categorically refused to recognize or treat with representatives of the union, and similarly rejected the demand for a fifteen percent increase in pay. Following the committee's report, union organizer Charles A. Miles took the podium to express the hope that it was not too late to reach an amicable settlement. He congratulated the workers both on their excellent state of organization and on the fact that their strike was being conducted in a peaceful and orderly manner. He then reminded those gathered in the overcrowded room of the benefits of collective action, and reaffirmed the justice of the workers' demands. Although most of the meeting was conducted in Polish, interpreters and representatives of various groups were provided with opportunities to speak in English, French, Italian and Syrian. The *Utica Daily Press* reported that "The meeting lasted for several hours, but was entirely orderly. It was evident from the stillness maintained and the attention shown that all were deeply interested, and there was occasional laughter and applause, but there was nothing like boisterousness at any time and no noisy demonstration."[17] While the strikers remained calm and orderly, their mood was nevertheless one of steadfast defiance. "We'll fight for our demands if it takes all year," one striker emphasized to reporters.[18]

At the conclusion of the meeting the strikers voted on a formal statement of their grievances drafted by the strike committee. Enthusiastically adopted, the statement was distributed among the strikers and to the press. It read:

"The reason we mill workers went out on strike is because in the whole year of 1911 all were badly mistreated. Supers and bosses abused us unmercifully so that we mill workers were compelled to quit. At Mill No. 1 the superintendent for one thick thread in goods fined or took 50 cents for each thread. From girls who made $6 a week on piece work on winders they kept $1 each time. Boss kept $1.50 to $3.50 a week from weavers on counter pieces of work. Once three girls stayed out of work on account of death in their family. The boss fined them $2 apiece.

Mike Tuman had his pay short $1 one week, the next week 50 cents, the third week $1.15; fourth week $1.35; fifth week, $1.75; week before last, $1.75, last week, $2, and then because he joined the union the boss discharged him at the end.

A certain girl weaver was short $2 on her pay and when she asked the loom fixer about it he kicked and punched her on the head. One boy weaver made 11 rolls of goods for which he should receive $11. All they gave him was $6. In spinning room No. 1, one girl asked the foreman to fix her machine and because she belonged to the union Mr. Patrick took her by the neck and fired her out.

In No. 2 Mill, Boss Carl for one thick thread in the goods keeps back on the weavers $1.50 to $3.50 a week. Card room workers work from two to three nights for nothing. In spinning room No. 2 if these workers belong to the union they fire them out from work. In Mill 1 if a man in the loom room gets sick and stays out, the boss makes the man next to him run his and the other man's machines, and if the man refuses to do so they tell him to quit.

Supt. Bramman discharges old workers in the mill, or cuts their wages, and has one man to do two men's work, and treats the people like slaves. Has them work overtime three hours, for which he pays them six cents. If anyone don't want to work overtime for such a big salary, he discharges them and abuses the people worse than animals. Supt. Foster treats his help bad, too. This is the way the working people are treated in New York Mills.

Doings at Walcott & Campbell's Spinning Company are no better than at the New York Mills, Nick Gelin worked on a machine and made $8 a week on piece work. Then Supt. Breheny cut his pay to $6.50 a week. Nick did not want to work for that pay. The super told him to get out. Some workers work 75 hours a week and get only $5. Foreman Daniels told a certain man to work for $2 and when he wouldn't he told him to get out.

It is not truth that the mill workers get $10 a week. If any workers working on piece work for $2 or $3 a week for a month, then the fifth week they may get $10 a week for a treat. Company houses occupied by workers rent from $1.50 to $3 a week. Our patience got to an end and so we all went out on strike to better our conditions. We will not make any trouble. We will hold our peace and finish the strike as we started it."[19]

Reacting to this statement, company officials once again insisted that there was never any indication of employee dissatisfaction before the strike began and that wage scales compared favorably with other textile firms. They reiterated their willingness to welcome the employees back to work under the new, increased wage scale, but could not agree to a fifteen percent increase as it would force the company out of business.[20] In general, however, the press no longer accepted these statements at face value. Most of the area newspapers printed lengthy articles describing both sides of the dispute, while some actually pointed out to their readers that the statements of the company representatives were not always accurate. On March 28, for example, the *Utica Observer* carried a story outlining the workers' assertion that they did not make $10 per week as claimed by the company, noting that "one of the women employees of the Mills showed an envelope that contained $1.46 for a full week's work, including overtime for one night."[21] Two days later the *Utica Daily Press* informed its readers that, contrary to company statements, it learned that the employees indicated to the company as early as January that they had grievances that needed to be addressed. The article went on to describe the presentation of grievances to the company on January 11, followed by the company's refusal to negotiate communicated to the workers on February 13.[22] On the same day, the *Utica Observer* presented even stronger evidence, quoting Charles Miles' statement that several days before the strike he met personally with W. Pierrepont White, president of the A. D. Juilliard Company, and specifically warned him that a strike was imminent. White, Miles emphasized, refused to negotiate. "This statement of Mr. Miles," the newspaper concluded, "is a flat contradiction of the statement issued by an officer of the mills on the day of the strike. The officer said no demand had been made by the employees for more wages and that the Mills Company had no knowledge a strike was coming."[23]

It was clear that the employers could not count on the local press to be their exclusive instrument in rallying public support. Juilliard's case was further damaged late Friday afternoon when nearly fifty men from North Adams, Massachusetts, imported to strengthen the company's position just before the strike began, decided to return home. John and Louis Smith, members of that group, confided to reporters that there was a great deal of dissatisfaction among its members because Juilliard promised them a minimum weekly wage of $10 to come to New York Mills, but their wages for the first week had only been $8.[24] The disclosure that these men planned to return to North Adams because the company did not honor its earlier agreement, together with the other revelations of company falsehoods, must certainly have damaged Juilliard's credibility among the general public.

Evidence that company officials in New York were not happy with either the newspapers' reporting or the fact that their officers in New York Mills were communicating with the press can be seen in Braman's letter to White on March 30 in which he strongly reiterated the Juilliard policy of silence.

> "I am very much disappointed and surprised to notice from the newspaper clippings received, that some of the officers of the New York Mills have evidently been talking to the reporters. The management at the mill are firm in their denial of having seen or talked to any newspaper men from the beginning, but the fact remains that the articles contained items which could not have been guessed at or obtained in any way except from someone in authority at the New York Mills; and I cannot impress you, Mr. Fish and Mr. Coughlin too strongly with the importance of absolute silence under all conditions. See no one from the newspapers, strikers or anyone else, and make no comments on articles that have been printed or are about to be printed, under any conditions. I have been through such conditions as we are now passing through there, and know that any statements, whether written or verbal, made to strike committees or newspapers, whether these representatives be life long friends or enemies, are invariably misconstrued, and will be used against the interests of the New York Mills.
>
> There is nothing at this time of so great importance to you who are in authority there, as absolute silence.[25]

Following the meeting at Kozak's Hall, while company officials and strikers lobbied for the collective ear of the press, Charles Miles met with Patrick J. Downey, a representative of the New York State Department of Mediation and Arbitration who arrived in New York Mills that morning in the hope of facilitating an agreeable settlement to the dispute. Downey approached Miles to learn what might be done, from the union's standpoint, to settle the dispute.[26] "You can do nothing with me in that regard," Miles asserted. "It rests with the mill owners whether or not they want to end the strike or have a fight that may last for months."[27] Miles went on to explain that the union was fully prepared to negotiate, but that the company flatly refused to engage in any discussions whatsoever. Downey then left to discuss matters with the company officials. Meeting with Superintendent Fish in the company's offices, Downey, in the words of the official report of the Bureau of Mediation and Arbitration, "recommended that a conference be held with a committee representing those on strike." Fish, responded that "a conference at that time was impracticable as the company had not as yet determined whether they would re-open the mills or shut them down indefinitely." Clearly, Fish was reiterating the company's hard-line refusal to negotiate, while at the same time attempting to frighten the workers back to their jobs by threatening to close the mills permanently. Downey left for Albany later in the evening without obtaining any agreement from the company to meet with the strikers or in any other way engage in a dialogue that could lead to a settlement. Nevertheless, Miles was pleased with Downey's intervention, hoping that his involvement might eventually persuade A. D. Juilliard to negotiate.[28]

By this time, however, Juilliard's policy for dealing with the strike was firmly established. As defined by Braman, the company's

> "course for the present should be: First - To provide sufficient watchmen inside and outside our Mills to guard them properly. Second - To handle all incoming and outgoing freight, providing guards, if necessary, to do the work. Third - Insist upon the Sheriff maintaining order at all times throughout the Village. Fourth - In case of riot or serious trouble immediately demand that the State protect our property to the extent of furnishing militia if necessary. Fifth, and most important - Hide any concern we may feel; keep everything absolutely to ourselves, and work in unison without undue excitement."[29]

The same day Downey was in New York Mills, William C. Rogers, the state's chief labor mediator, visited with A. D. Juilliard representatives in New York City, including Augustus D. Juilliard himself. Rogers urged those present "to instruct the officers of their company at New York Mills to meet a committee of their employees in an effort to adjust the dispute." The attitude of Juilliard and his associates, however, appeared to be every bit as reluctant to negotiate as the appearances given to Downey in New York Mills. In fact, after his meeting with Juilliard, Rogers reported to the Commissioner of Labor that "The policy of the owners seemed to be one of delay in the expectation that the strikers would voluntarily return to work."[30] This assessment was no doubt correct for no sooner had Rogers left the Juilliard offices than Braman was busy writing to White to tell him that members of the State Board should be treated "pleasantly and courteously" because "a man in this position is always a politician," but also to reassure him that "this board I believe has no legal authority and merely acts in a sort of advisory capacity."[31] It was clear that Juilliard

officials harbored no intention whatever of negotiating or cooperating
with the state mediators.

On Saturday morning, March 30, citizens awoke to read in their
morning papers that all remained peaceful in the village despite the
strike. "Up to the present," the *Utica Saturday Globe* assured its readers, "the strike has been conducted in a more orderly manner and it is
the purpose of the leaders to direct it along this line."[32] The *Utica
Observer* went even further in its effort to quell public fears of violence
by stating that "Sheriff Becker said to-day that he considered the strikers
very orderly people and that no trouble is expected in the Mills."[33] In
general, the reaction of local citizens throughout the strike was a typical
middle-class response exhibiting its greatest concern for the preservation
of order and the protection of private property.

Saturday was pay day at the mills, with both company officials and
local residents fearing that some disorder might break out as the strikers
arrived to claim their pay for the week before the walkout began. As a
precaution, Deputy Sheriff Corbett and several deputies were on hand at
the mill offices, but, as the *Utica Observer* later reported to its relieved
readers, "There was no disorder of any kind. The employees were well
behaved, jovial and sure of winning their fight. Most of them hurried
to their homes with their pay envelopes."[34]

"After your money is gone, what then?" reporters asked.

"Stick together and fight to win," the strikers replied, adding
quickly "No trouble. No, no. Just stick together and win."[35]

With the press on hand in force, the strikers shrewdly took advantage of the opportunity to cast further doubt on the veracity of the
company's statements by showing their pay envelopes to the reporters.
They pointed out that virtually every one of the envelopes was short
payment for one-half hour, and that about three-quarters contained other
shortages as well. "One day laborer, a married man with four small
children," the *Utica Observer* informed its readers, "had $5.28 coming to
him for three days work. The company took $4.80 out for rent, leaving
him 48 cents for his family·[36] The *Utica Daily Press* noted that "Of all
the envelopes given to the committee but one was right."[37] Agnieszka
Taraska, for example, had completed ten jobs at $1.30 each, but re-
ceived only $9.75 instead of the $13.00 due her. Amounts varied, but
in the company's defense reporters noted that sometimes weekly pay
could vary considerably because weavers and other piece work employees would not be paid for a job until it was completed. Thus, a
pay envelope one week might contain $4 and the next week $14. "But
in all the envelopes — and there were scores of them — that were
shown," the newspaper concluded, "there was not one except in the
cases of loom fixers, above $10. The majority varied between $6 and
$9, and in many cases were for overtime as well as for a full week's

work."[38] Thus, the local press once again lent support to the case of the strikers by making public evidence that drew company statements into serious question.

Early that afternoon members of the executive committee of Local 753 met with Charles Miles at the Utica Labor Temple where they voted to reaffirm their commitment to continue the strike indefinitely. Clearly, this placed a severe financial strain on the families of the strikers, necessitating that steps be taken to provide assistance. Miles reiterated the promise of the national union to provide financial assistance to the strikers, and all present agreed to appeal to other unions for assistance. Representatives of the Utica Trades Assembly immediately pledged their support.[39]

At 4:00 p.m. the strikers once again convened at Kozak's Hall to learn what transpired during the day. With little progress to report, Miles informed them of his discussion with the state mediator the previous day and took the opportunity to explain to those assembled the probable impact of the new fifty-four hour law recently passed by the state legislature. He also urged them to continue their strike "in the same manner as it has thus far been carried on, that is, peaceably and honorably."[40] Following Miles, Louis Muziński of Boston, a national representative of the United Textile Workers of America, spoke to the workers about the textile strike in Lawrence, Massachusetts. Next, union president Rudolf Ząbek spoke to the assembled crowd in Polish. For the benefit of non-Poles, speeches followed in French, Italian and Syrian, whereupon the meeting ended peacefully with the strikers remaining enthusiastic and determined to continue their walkout.[41]

By the end of the second day of the strike, its effects were already beginning to be felt in the surrounding area. On Friday the *Utica Observer* noted that the closing of the Walcott & Campbell Spinning Company created a serious shortage of yarn among the area's textile mills. "The mills that depend upon the yarn manufactured by the company will be compelled to close unless the strike is ended within the next few days," the newspaper opined.[42] Should this occur, several thousand textile workers throughout central New York would be out of work. Then too, there was a very real possibility of the strike spreading. On Saturday evening Local 386 of the United Textile Workers of America, a Utica-based local composed mostly of Poles under the leadership of Michał Kostor, met at Kościuszko Hall on Lincoln Avenue in Utica to review the New York Mills strike and determine their own course of action. Organizer Miles addressed those assembled, after which the Utica union voted to present the owners of the Utica Steam and Mohawk Valley Cotton Mills with demands for a fifteen percent increase in pay and a maximum limit of twelve looms that could be assigned to a single operator. A committee was formed to deliver the workers' demands to Henry F. Mansfield, general superintendent of the two mills.[43] Thus, inspired by their compatriots in New York Mills, workers in the Utica textile mills took up the fight for better treatment.

On Sunday morning, March 31, the first Sunday after the beginning of the strike, the Polish people of New York Mills took time out from their worldly cares to attend Mass at St. Mary's Church. Many were anxious to hear what, if anything, their priest would say about the struggle for "more pay and better treatment." His word would be important to his flock; indeed, to many his support or condemnation of the strike might influence their future actions. Father Fijałkowski was deeply involved in all aspects of his parishioners' lives, and himself harbored a highly developed sense of Polish ethnicity. On the other hand, he was in a difficult position regarding the strike. As a clergyman, he must oppose any form of violence, a stance that could easily be misinterpreted as siding with the company. Further, as not only the spiritual but the temporal leader of the parish, Fijałkowski had to be concerned with the financial implications of the walkout. With parishioners' donations as the primary source of parish revenue, a long strike would precipitate a fiscal crisis. Thus, he was certainly under both moral and financial pressure to take at least a compromising stance regarding the strike.[44] No doubt he labored long over his sermon for this, the last Sunday before the holy week observances preceding Easter. Yet in the end Fijałkowski stood squarely and unequivocally behind a theme that characterized many of his sermons since his arrival in the village: *"jedność,"* unity. Regardless of the immediate consequences, Fijałkowski advised his parishioners to remain united. *Jedność, jedność, jedność,* he emphasized repeatedly in his remarks. And, lest the families of the strikers be placed in even greater financial crisis, he advised the congregation to "Save what money you have very carefully. Do not give any of it to the church until the strike is settled and you return to work. Keep it for your families. Remain united in your fight for better wages and better conditions and see to it that no disorder occurs in the proceedings of your strike."[45] The most respected leader in the Polish community had spoken. The strike would continue.

A drizzling all-day rain kept villagers inside for most of the day, but at 4:00 p.m. that afternoon the strikers assembled for their scheduled meeting at Kozak's Hall. There they listened to further speeches in Polish, Syrian, French and English, and heard their leaders tell them that the company remained adamant in its refusal to deal with them as a union. Indeed, it was obvious that union recognition was the most divisive of the issues separating employers and employees. "This strike will not be settled except [when] the United Textile Workers of America

Father Aleksander Fijałkowski

are recognized in that settlement," Charles Miles reiterated to the reporters covering the meeting at Kozak's Hall. "Our union gave the company plenty of time to settle their differences with the employees. If they had done this before the strike was called, recognition of the union would not have been made an issue. But it will be a paramount issue from now until the strike is ended. No offer of increased pay will be received or accepted unless it comes from the company through our union."[46]

Members of the strike committee also took advantage of the presence of reporters to press their concerns regarding better living conditions and the lack of company attention to the houses it rented to workers. The *Utica Daily Press* reported the next day that many of the company houses were damp, unhealthy, and had not been repaired in some time. It also noted that there was no sewer system, and thus "no water closets in the houses. Outdoor vaults are used, and these have not been emptied all winter, and in many cases the stench is readily perceptible to the person passing by on the street quite a distance away."[47] There was a single water pump to serve the company houses on Campbell Avenue, and it was currently broken. On Cottage Street sixteen families were served by one pump. "Every home had one of those cisterns to catch rain water for clothes and dish water," Bertha Kozak reminisced. "But for cooking they had to go out on the street. I remember that the pump was right in the center of Cottage Street and everybody would come with a pail and they stood in line one after the other." On Garden Street where eight houses contained sixteen families totaling some sixty people, there was but a single water source. In addition, the water in these outdoor wells was unfit for human consumption, having been contaminated by ground seepage from both the nearby mills and what the newspaper termed "the leakings of privies."[48]

The following day news of the strike in New York Mills was temporarily eclipsed by the dramatic announcement that the Utica Steam and Mohawk Valley Cotton Mills voluntarily agreed to a ten percent across-the-board increase in wages for all of their 2,500 employees. In addition, the Oneita Knitting Company announced a revised salary schedule providing varied increases for the several hundred workers that it employed. Together with other announced increases, it was estimated by Utica area employers that some 10,000 workers would be affected, with most receiving increases in the range of five to ten percent. Although Miles was quick to point out that wages were not the only grievance of local textile workers, it was obvious that the New York Mills strike served as a catalyst in convincing area mill owners to make a serious attempt to avoid a confrontation that would lead to its spread.[49]

At a meeting held at Kościuszko Hall on Lincoln Avenue that evening, the Utica unions developed plans for the submission of additional grievances to the various employers, but there was apparently little support for any immediate action and even organizer Miles counseled against a strike until the owners could respond. The new wage offer succeeded in mollifying enough workers so that the immediate threat of the New York Mills strike spreading to the surrounding area was avoided. The *Utica Observer* concluded that the offer of a flat increase was to be "heartily commended and the general belief is that the employees will be satisfied with the increase. The company has always shown a disposition to be fair with them in the matter of wages."[50] Despite this development, A. D. Juilliard made no such move toward settlement. Instead, it immediately took a more aggressive posture toward the strike.

During the day Patrick J. Downey, the state labor mediator, returned to New York Mills for a meeting with White. To date, the Bureau of Mediation and Arbitration made as little headway as the strikers in seeking a negotiation session with the employers. Thus, Downey was back in town to once again suggest to White that he should agree to a conference with the strikers. He further indicated to White that, since the strikers were amenable to a conference, there was a possibility of resolving the stalemate. White remained evasive, but agreed to "take the matter under consideration" and provide Downey with an answer in a few days.[51] Given his instructions from the A. D. Juilliard offices in New York City, it is obvious that White had no intention of negotiating and was only playing for time. The attitude of the company officers remained one of stonewalling any attempted settlement. Indeed, those in New York City continued to believe that most of the strikers were actually content and would go back to work if not for the pressure of others. The union, Braman asserted to White about a week later, "was not popular with the workers and nothing would have come of it had it not been for the trouble at Lawrence, Mass." The trouble lay with outside forces, Braman maintained, "assassins of industrial peace and their foreign renegade assistants."[52]

The next morning — Tuesday, April 2 — the company brought in approximately fifty men and women from surrounding communities to work in the bleachery and packing rooms. The new workers were protected by some twenty-five armed mill bosses, newly sworn as special deputy sheriffs with the authority to act to protect both property and workers in the mills. Spokesmen for the company explained that no new goods were being produced, but that goods already on hand in the bleachery, which would otherwise spoil, were being completed. Although the company denied any attempt to reopen the mills, and newspapers theorized that by cleaning out their older stock the company was probably determined to close the mills for an indefinite period, the strikers feared that the importation of non-union workers might be the

first step in an attempt to resume mill operations. At a special meeting
called to discuss their various options, a series of Polish, French,
Syrian, Italian and English committees were formed to visit the homes
of their respective workers and make sure that each family received the
assistance it needed. Further, a determination was made to begin
picketing in order to persuade non-union workers not to enter the mills.
Picketing began at 4:00 a.m. the following morning.[53]

By 5:00 a.m. groups of picketers not only blocked each entrance to
the mills, but also situated themselves along roads leading into town
and in positions where the street cars could be watched. Soon, several
non-union Italian workers arrived by street car from Utica. They were
immediately surrounded by the pickets and ordered out of town. Fearing
violence, they obeyed.[54] A few minutes later, two more Italian workers
from Utica attempted to enter the village along Campbell Avenue.

"Where are you going?" demanded the pickets.

"None of your business," replied one of the Uticans.

Then, as the pickets began to surround their quarry, one of the
Italians produced a knife with a blade that appeared to observers to be
"as long as a crutch."

"Scat," he shouted, brandishing the knife menacingly in the air.

As the pickets recoiled, the two Italians beat a hasty retreat back
toward Utica.[55]

This was not the first time that Italians from Utica were used as
strike-breakers. Only the previous month the *Utica Observer* carried a
report of their being imported into nearby Rome to replace striking
freight handlers at the New York Central Railroad yards. The first
Italians apparently settled in Utica about 1815, with a small influx in
the 1870s, followed by large-scale immigration in the 1890s, reaching a
population of some 6,000 by 1900. Most of these early arrivals
worked in Utica's low-paying brickyards and construction industry, and
later in that city's textile factories. In general, their lot was not much
different from that of the Poles and they soon began to organize themselves for both religious and secular support. In July of 1895 the
church of St. Maria di Monte Carmelo [St. Mary of Mount Carmel]
was founded and Father Antonio Castelli began holding services for
Italian parishioners in an old school building on Catharine Street
belonging to St. John's Church. The new Italian church dedicated to
St. Mary of Mount Carmel opened on June 29, 1902, followed shortly
by the establishment of a school in 1904 and the secular *Societa Ital-
iana di Progresso ed Aiuto* [Italian Society for Progress and Assistance]
and *Figli d'Italia* [Sons of Italy] organizations. In 1905 the *Circolo
Elettorale* was founded in an effort to form an Italian voting bloc. In
general, the leaders of Utica's Italian community appear to have been
solidly in favor of group organization, and labor organization in

particular. *La Luce* [The Light], one of Utica's Italian language news-papers, carried extensive and sympathetic coverage of the textile work-ers' strike in Lawrence, Massachusetts, continually encouraging its readers to organize and avoid divisive infighting.[56] The use of Italians as strike-breakers apparently resulted from the continuing large-scale influx of new immigrants into the community. As these people arrived, with little knowledge of either America or its ways, in most cases in immediate need of jobs and as yet unacculturated into the infrastructure of Utica's resident Italian community, they could easily be induced to move to nearby towns and villages by offers of employ-ment.

In addition to the Italians, however, the company also tried other methods to mobilize a work force. The local German newspaper, the *Utica Deutsche Zeitung* [Utica German Newspaper], reported one humorous event which took place when a group of picketers noticed a large crate being moved from Number 3 to Number 1. Curious, they approached to examine the crate and were very much surprised to find inside a stoker whom the company was trying to smuggle from one mill to the other to tend the boilers.[57]

Later, around 11:00 a.m., one of the non-union workers came out of Number 1 and approached some of the picketers whom he knew. The strikers picked the man up onto their shoulders and deposited him into a pile of mud. Though witnesses noted that the temperament of both sides was good-natured, the muddied worker fled as quickly as he could.[58] The pickets meted out similar treatment to anyone suspected of strike breaking activities. The *Utica Observer* later reported that:

> "Scores of Polish women, clad in callico and gingham dresses and with heavy shawls over their heads, aided the men in picketing the streets and watching for non-union help. They walked arm in arm through the mud and slush, or stood in groups on street corners, where they held up every stranger who attempted to go near the mills. Early this morning two Polish women caught an Italian workman by each arm and asked him in the Polish lan-guage if he was a strike-breaker. He replied in Italian. The two women promptly slapped him soundly across the ears. The frightened Italian broke loose from them and ran away. It was learned afterwards that the man is an employee of the Utica & Mohawk Valley Railroad Com-pany, but that didn't save him from getting his ears boxed. The Polish women are working on the system of boxing first and asking questions afterward."[59]

At noon, the strikers surrounded the company-owned boarding houses in an attempt to prevent meals being taken to the non-union workers in the mills. Seeing this, the deputy sheriffs, now some one hundred in number, intervened to carry food to the company workers, while also warning the strikers not to interfere. The pickets did not attempt to stop the deputy sheriffs, who were clearly armed, but their displeasure was evident and not a few grumbled verbal threats to starve the workers out of the mills. Throughout the rest of the day, anyone approaching the mills was stopped and required to identify themselves as deputies before being allowed to pass. Although an evening newspaper reported that the deputies "were without fear of trouble, as they know the strikers personally,"[60] it was obvious that tensions were beginning to escalate.

As the pickets became more vocal, Frederick B. Adams, a Utica attorney called in by Sheriff Becker to advise him on how to deal with the strikers, arrived outside the office at Number 1 where, according to a reporter from the *Utica Observer*, "a swarthy Polander caught him by the coattails and pulled him towards the setting sun."[61] Faced with some fifty pickets demanding to know who he was, Adams did not hesitate to tell them.

"See here, boys," he commanded, "line right up and listen to me a few minutes. I'm going to talk to you. This sort of thing has got to stop. You have no right to hold me up, stop me on the street or ask me anything about my business. I'm the attorney for the sheriff and I am here on business for the sheriff. But it doesn't make any difference who I am, you have no right to interfere with me."

"How do we know that you are not a scab?" demanded a picket. "Some men come here all dressed up, go in the mills like gentlemen, pull off good clothes and go to work in overalls. It's got to stop."

Adams remained adamant. "You have no right to stop any man who wants to go into the mills of this company. You've got to stop it or we'll make you stop it if we have to bring 1,000 men here to do it."[62] Neither the pickets nor Adams would change their view.

That evening the *Utica Observer* reported that "The strike situation at New York Mills took a serious turn today. The pickets of the strikers have the village in a state of siege. Every street car is watched. Every stranger is held up and questioned. Ugly feeling cropped out in several places this morning, and in one instance a non-union man drew a knife on the strikers."[63] Fearing the worse, the community braced for the resumption of picketing the next morning. Yet, the most important developments of the day occurred after the evening edition of the *Utica Observer* was distributed.

Around 6:00 p.m. Deputy Sheriff Jack O'Neill and several colleagues attempted to escort a non-union worker through the pickets surrounding Number 3. When the pickets objected, the mill bosses, *now deputized as law enforcement officers*, began wielding their clubs about, slashing at the pickets with a vengeance born of disgust and frustration. Michał Jankowski, Aleksander Gilkowski and Franciszek Stampha were beaten and cut, while Marya Raczkowska received a severe cut on the head from one of the officers clubs. One woman threw a handful of red pepper into the eyes of Deputy Sheriff Robert Morehead, causing a very painful temporary blindness. Deputies O'Neill and Corbett were similarly spattered with pepper. Although the woman escaped, the following morning deputies arrested Katarzyna Rogała and charged her with the deed. Scattered minor incidents occurred throughout the night, mostly when chunks of ice were thrown at deputies by some boys out for an evening of adventure.[64]

As soon as the melee at Number 3 ended, Sheriff Becker telephoned a call for assistance to the surrounding communities, hoping to have some 300-400 deputies sworn in by the next day.[65] Unfortunately, as the *Utica Observer* explained to its readers, "Some of these men are questionable characters. A few are men who have served terms in the Utica jail. One is a Utica saloon keeper who has been arrested and arraigned in City Court on a criminal charge. A number are bosses from the Mills, men who use their brief authority brutally in some cases, without judgment in others, and who are openly prejudiced against the strikers."[66] The deputizing of the mill bosses would not be the only time that Becker exercised extremely poor judgment during the strike.

Caught by surprise over the sudden escalation of the confrontations, followed by Sheriff Becker's call for reinforcements, and anxious to disavow any plans to incite violence, union organizer Miles issued the following self-serving statement to the press:

"It is generally conceded that I have made every effort to maintain peace and order, and conduct the strike along peaceful, intelligent lines. I regret that the officials of the mill are failing to cooperate in the maintenance of peace. It will be readily understood that the swearing in of mill bosses as deputy sheriffs and clothing them with the power and dignity of the law is absolutely unjust and unfair. An officer of the law is expected to represent justice and protection for all and must essentially be non-partizan, but all of these men are bound to the company's interest from which they receive their salary now and in the future. Under these circumstances it must be obvious to all that the striking employees would receive slight consideration and absolutely no protection from their former bosses who have now been clothed with the authority of the law, and must act upon the minds of the strikers as the red flag does upon the bull. Organized labor is sometimes blamed for violence resulting from just such actions as these, and I protest against the use of such methods of disturbing the peace in New York Mills."[67]

The strike began its second week on Thursday, April 4. Around 6:00 a.m. that morning the A. D. Juilliard Company loaded a number of strike-breakers onto automobiles and drove them into the village. As they approached the picket lines, the drivers raced their vehicles at high speed toward the mill gates, splattering mud and scattering men and women on all sides. Fortunately, none of the strikers were seriously injured. Their outrage at this wanton act of disregard for the lives of the pickets was only heightened when the non-union workers soon reappeared as deputies armed with clubs, threatening to attack the strikers if they did not clear the streets.[68]

At about the same time, some 600 strikers gathered in front of the company offices on Main Street. Without provocation, a group of some thirty deputies demanded that the strikers leave, and Deputy David Alexander began to assault a woman picket. As other strikers came to her rescue, a general meleé began. Salt was thrown in Alexander's face. Fists and clubs were employed without mercy, once again victimizing the strikers. One woman and four men were arrested and taken by police car to the Utica jail.[69]

About an hour later, around 7:00 a.m., pickets stopped bosses John Meehan and Harry Patrick, accompanied by several non-union workers, when they attempted to enter Number 1. As the *Utica Observer* reported, "A crowd of deputies hurried to the place and commenced rough tactics with the strikers." In the fracas which followed, deputies swung wildly about with their clubs, battering both men and women, while the strikers responded with stones and chunks of ice. One of the deputies struck Bridget Gadziała over the head with his club, knocking her to the ground. When her husband Michał attempted to protect her, the deputies beat him severely. Katarzyna Balda and Józef Smoła were each assaulted with clubs, the former suffering a large gash on her head. Another striker, according to one account wielding a rubber hose, slashed Meehan across the mouth causing a very painful injury. When order was finally restored, six men and one woman were arrested and sent off to jail in Utica.[70] A list of the injured strikers, published in the *Utica Observer* the following day, contained the additional names of Josephine Dziziel, Helen Doronogo, Marya Rouczka, Maryanna Kupiec, Louisa Leś, Marya Kawa, Louisa Kaczówka, Katarzyna Bieva,

88   *United We Stand*

Kazimierz Przybyła, Bridget Borak, Michał Kaczówka, Stanisław Kaczówka, Jan Furgoł, Jan Masak, Jan Kurgan, and Jan Starsiak.[71]

Further disorder occurred at noon when Leokadya Rosiński was arrested for disorderly conduct by two "amateur deputies." When they attempted to escort her away from the scene they were attacked by about a dozen other Polish women who "swooped down upon them, tore Katie loose from them, slapped the officers soundly across the ears, and carried Katie away in triumph." In commenting upon the incident the *Utica Observer* said "It was noticeable that the deputies who knew their work and did it right had no trouble with the strikers in patrolling the streets. The pickets respected their authority though they complained when it was exercised."[72] The *Utica Daily Press* sided more with the deputies, noting that "the ugly attitude which became manifest in the strikers the day before reached a point where it was vented in deeds of violence and scenes of riot and disorder. Fighting, stoning, the throwing of vitriol, salt and pepper, and cursing marked the scenes evident to the attempt of the bosses to enter the mills."[73]

Some of the strikers involved in the altercations of April 4.
Note the bandages on the head of the striker to the left of center.

Faced with these disorders, Sheriff Becker began to seriously doubt the ability of his deputies to control the situation. Indeed, the actions of some of these deputies had in large measure caused the tensions to escalate to their present state. Fearing an increase in violence if the outbreaks continued, he determined to seize control of the situation by declaring a state of martial law throughout the village. Soon his deputies were rushing about town posting proclamations at conspicuous points around the village which read:

> "Know ye, that riot and disorders having occurred in the village of New York Mills, Oneida County, N. Y., I, as the sheriff of said county, command all groups and loiterers to disperse and I forbid all manner of disturbance and gathering on the public streets of said village."[74]

To back up his proclamation, Becker immediately made a formal request for support from the New York State National Guard. Soon the muffled tramp of marching soldiers echoed through the once peaceful village.

Chapter 5

Martial Law

By noon, officers of the local National Guard companies were notified and men were being summoned from their homes and places of employment. The 28th [Company A, First Infantry] and 44th Separate Companies [Company B, First Infantry] from Utica assembled about 1:30 p.m., while the 31st Separate Company [Company M, First Infantry] from Mohawk, some dozen miles east along the Mohawk Valley, came into the city around 3:15 p.m. As they arrived at their rendezvous point, the three companies, numbering some 250 soldiers, boarded trolley cars for New York Mills. The troops were almost entirely made up of Anglo-Saxon Americans, their officers being prominent in local business and politics. The commanding officer was Major Henry J. Cookinham, Jr., the scion of a prominent Oneida County family. Cookinham was a long-time member and officer in the Oneida Historical Society, and had only recently published a respected history of Oneida County. Given the socioeconomic class of the officers and their men, there was every reason for the strikers to fear that their sympathies would lie with the company owners.[1]

Arriving in the village, Company B, under the command of Captain Thomas M. Sherman, the son of James S. Sherman, who was then serving as vice president in the administration of William Howard Taft, quickly detrained and marched to Mills No. 3 and 4 where the soldiers "threw out patrols, clearing the sidewalks at the point of the bayonet and surrounding the mill with double guards." Company A performed similar service, the 1st Platoon being detached to No. 2, and the 2nd Platoon to No. 1. Company M, arriving slightly later than the other two, quickly reinforced the troops occupying the area around No. 1. Saloons were closed, alcoholic beverages were prohibited, and patrols were dispatched to disperse any groups of strikers that might be found. Once secured, the troops settled down to the routine of occupation, walking guard duty through the cold rain and ice which typified the inclement weather of that unusual spring. Dividing into platoons which served four hours on duty and four hours off, the soldiers slept on the hard floors in the mills, with their mess tents pitched on the mill property or in the surrounding yards.[2]

The militia musters in its foul weather gear.

Changing the guard at Nos. 3 and 4.

Both the strikers and the general population of the village were taken completely by surprise at the appearance of the National Guard. The *Utica Observer* reported that "Residents of New York Mills are greatly wrought up over the bringing of the soldiers to the village. There was no need for this, the business men say. The strikers say so, too, and with emphasis."[3] Indeed, there was great consternation on the part of village residents, and the strikers appeared very bitter over what they regarded as another attempt by management to cow them into submission. Though fearful of what the soldiers might do, the strikers remained defiant. "Let the soldiers come," they declared to reporters. "We'll keep all scabs out of the Mills just the same."[4]

Late that afternoon the strikers held an emergency meeting at Kozak's Hall where they heard that the United Textile Workers of America and the Utica Trades Assembly offered to hire attorney Timothy D. Curtin to represent the strikers arrested during the morning's altercations. Further, the Utica Mule Spinners Union and the the Utica Trades Assembly each voted $25 per week to assist the strikers in New York Mills. Should the strike last longer than two weeks, the Utica Trades Assembly voted unanimously to donate its ten percent raise each week to the strikers, a sum likely to reach about $2,000 per week. Within the next few days, additional support was forthcoming from the Utica-based Knitters and Cutters Union Local 606, Boiler Makers Union Local 223, Machinists Union Local 425, Iron Molders' Union Local 112, Teamsters' Union Local 445, and several other area labor organizations.[5] The strike committee's planning proved exemplary, resulting in a continuous outpouring of much needed support during the walkout.

That evening six of those arrested during the day were arraigned before Justice of the Peace W. C. Aldridge in Whitesboro. The five men were charged with drunkenness and rioting, while the lone woman was accused of throwing pepper into the eyes of a deputy. The accused all pleaded not guilty, and the cases were adjourned until April 14. Each prisoner was released on $200 bond, with Józef Smoła signing the bonds. "I know them," Smoła explained. "They are good people. They work hard and have families. I sign all their bonds while my money lasts." After two adjournments, those arrested were eventually released following "a strong lecture by the judge ... as to conduct while the strike is in progress."[6]

Good Friday marked the beginning of the Easter weekend. All week long the religious celebrations of Holy Week at St. Mary's Church diverted some of the strikers' attention from the picket lines and served as a calming influence in an otherwise tense situation. In keeping with this spirit, the St. Stanislaus Society, which planned to march on Good Friday in its usual paramilitary attire to usher in the Easter weekend, decided against such a public display. With the arrival of the National Guard, the Society's members feared that the sight of 125 Poles marching down Main Street in their dress uniforms, armed with swords and guns, might convince the authorities that they meant to open hostilities. To avoid any misunderstandings, the Society wisely decided not to march, relying instead upon a children's procession, accompanied by adults in their finest dresses and suits, to celebrate the holy days.[7]

Perhaps because of the solemn religious holy days, the *Utica Observer* was able to tell its readers Friday afternoon that "New York Mills is as quiet as a Quaker sermon today." Indeed, after the initial surprise and disgust of the strikers subsided, they actually formed a rather friendly relationship with the guardsmen, whom they came to regard as an improvement over the company "thugs" sworn in as deputies. "The strikers and the soldiers are on such good terms," the *Utica Observer* reported the same day, "that the Polish people are beginning to tell the militia about Kosciouski [Kościuszko], Count Pulaski, Joe Smoly [Smoła] and John Kozaka [Kozak]."[8] One of the first actions the guardsmen took was to order the deputies and private detectives hired by the company off the streets and into the mills, away from the strikers. This, and other such actions, soon convinced the strikers that the National Guard was not there to further abuse them, and they actually came to appreciate its presence as a means of protecting themselves from the excesses of the deputies hired by A. D. Juilliard.[9] "The general opinion prevailed yesterday," the *Utica Daily Press* reported, "that the guardsmen were conducting themselves in excellent fashion and not a few of the strikers expressed satisfaction over the employment of the militia, saying that they were sure that the guardsmen would be fair and just in their dealings with both strikers and employers." A reporter for the *Utica Daily Press* quoted one of the strikers as stating that "Every bit of disorder has been engendered by deputies and we are glad that the militia has come to take place over these men. The deputies have started trouble wherever it was possible for them to do so."[10] The *Utica Observer* added that "The strikers like the soldiers. In every part of the village the people say the militia is far preferable to the special deputies employed by the sheriff."[11]

The conduct of the guardsmen also elicited a vast change in attitude by organizer Miles. Upon their arrival he pronounced the calling out of the guardsmen to be "a dastardly outrage and an attempt to intimidate the strikers." By the next day, however, he was telling reporters that the soldiers were "A vast improvement upon the deputies."[12] That Friday evening he issued a statement intended to further arouse public sympathy for the strikers, while at the same time ingratiating the strikers with the guardsmen. "So far as the militia are concerned," he began,

"I regret that men who have joined the force for the protection and maintenance of national defense should be humiliated by being drafted to New York Mills with the obvious expectation that they could intimidate the strikers who, up to this time have created no breach of the peace. On the other hand I am glad that the militia are here under responsible commanders, otherwise I fear that the band of so-called private detectives, composed largely of strong-arm men, many of whom have unenviable records, would have beaten the heads off our peaceful strikers without the least provocation. Whoever is responsible for bringing deputies into New York Mills is guilty of a crime against the community which is nothing short of an outrageous attempt to intimidate men and women who are struggling to raise from the borders of starvation the standard of American living and citizenship."[13]

Relations between strikers and guardsmen were, in fact, so amicable that on Saturday representatives of the Society of St. Stanislaus went to Major Cookinham to explain the purpose of their organization and its religious affiliation, and to inquire whether he had any objections to their marching in full uniform and weaponry in the Easter Sunday procession. Given the peaceful atmosphere prevailing in the village, Cookinham interposed no objections.[14] Thus, the following morning, to the great consternation of Juilliard officials and their deputies, the Society of St. Stanislaus led the Easter procession down Main Street to the Church of St. Mary, Our Lady of Częstochowa, where the Polish parishioners spent the morning celebrating Easter Sunday. The *Utica Daily Press* reported that "The men in line made no more hostile demonstrations than to wave their hands and shout 'Hello' to the militiamen on patrol."[15]

The Easter weekend passed quietly. On Monday morning the *Utica Observer* informed its readers that "There were no disorders of any kind at the Mills yesterday or last night. The strikers assert very solemnly that there won't be any, either, unless somebody else starts it. Attempts have been made to show that the strikers are desperate in order to justify the big expense that is being forced upon the county by a sheriff who lacks confidence in himself and his deputies. But any man who wants to sit down by the fireside with the strikers and talk about the conditions will conclude that the strikers are a very human lot of people and that bayonets are not necessary to keep them in order."[16]

The end of the Easter weekend also meant a return to strike activities. Monday afternoon saw an open meeting of strikers held at Kozak's Hall. More than 1,200 operatives attended this huge rally to hear a succession of speakers using Polish, Italian, English or Syrian encourage them to remain united and firm in their stance. Polish organizer Joseph Tylkoff of the U.T.W.A., who arrived in New York Mills the previous Saturday, spoke on his experiences during the recent textile

The St. Stanislaus Society marching down Main Street ca. 1912.
A procession like this during the 1912 strike caused great fear and
consternation among company officials.

A meeting of strikers at Smoła's hall.

strike in Lowell, Massachusetts, urging the workers to remain united in their efforts to seek redress. Charles A. Miles began by recounting the efforts made to obtain a negotiated settlement prior to the beginning of the strike, noting that because of the company's refusal to negotiate "The responsibility of this strike is entirely on the shoulders of the mill officials." Miles continued on to paint an encouraging picture of the strikers' accomplishments to date, expressing in the process his confidence that the strike would eventually be decided in their favor. The mills were closed, thus placing a financial burden on the company. The national organization agreed to provide financial support, and the relief committee reported that contributions from other unions, groups and individuals were arriving each day. Subscription lists for support were even then being circulated in Utica. "I want every man and woman here to realize," Miles continued, "that we are up against a situation which is as it is and not as we would like to have it. We are in the situation primarily to win. If we are going to win we must continue to unitedly take all necessary steps. We must make the best possible use of all financial benefits." He reminded the workers that they were not the only people on strike, that "Thousands all over the country are making the same fight for better conditions." Then, in a conclusion met by loud cheers and applause, he stated forcefully: "We have got to win. You know as well as I that the firm can not start until we say so."[17]

U.T.W.A. Organizers Charles A. Miles (left) and Joseph Tylkoff (right). Miles was very effective in obtaining U.T.W.A. support.

Ludwik Leśnicki of Utica, the socialist-oriented editor of the weekly newspaper *Młotek Duchowny*, next took the podium to deliver a compelling oration in Polish extolling the virtues of a legal strike in the pursuit of just goals as the only means that workers had to deal with the mistreatment of employers. "We are living a life of strife," he told his spell-bound audience. "Progress means fight. We shall not stop fighting until every man in our rank is satisfied."[18]

The relief committee then reported that several hundred dollars in contributions had already arrived, with no demands for support thus far being made by individual strikers. In addition, the Polish businesses in Utica and New York Mills pledged to provide needy strikers with bread for the duration of the strike.[19] Further support came from the trustees of St. Mary's Church who announced that their building fund for a new church currently stood at more than $2,000, and that, should it be necessary, the entire sum would be used for relief of the needy. Although the parish was Polish, and the vast majority of the strikers likewise Polish, it was determined that "no discrimination be made in the distribution of relief even if the relief should be from the church fund."[20]

Following the speeches, the strikers adopted resolutions designed to prepare them for the continuation of a long strike. First, they agreed that those strikers who lived in the three hundred company-owned houses would refuse to pay their rent when it came due at the end of the week. In case of evictions, arrangements were undertaken to provide living accommodations for families in private residences or nearby community buildings. Finally, an appeal was issued by Tomasz Mótyka, vice president of Local 753, as follows:

> "For years and years we have been subject to all kinds of abuses at the hands of the mill companies. We have been fighting for our rights and the last phase of the fight has come — a strike. We are organized, but our union is too young to support a large family of 2,000 strikers. We are proud bearers of American laborship, and we believe that every liberty loving American will support us in this fight. We believe that the strike, in its legal form, is nothing but a request for our right, better treatment and more pay, which will make us able to support our families and make us able to perform our duties as citizens. This strike, when eventually a victory, shall be a benefit to both workingmen and business men. With this understanding we left our places in the mills and struck, and we believe that we are to be supported during our fight. All

donations are to be sent to the strikers' committee, New York Mills."[21]

The strike committee was adamant that it would not seek any meeting with the employers unless the company first requested a meeting. "We sent our delegation to the company, with a statement of our grievances, at the commencement of the strike, and our demands were rejected, as well as recognition of our union refused," one leader stated emphatically. "The next action towards a settlement is therefore clearly up to the company. None will be taken by the strikers."[22]

That evening, at a regular meeting of the Utica Trades Assembly, organizer Miles made "a stirring appeal" for the appointment of a committee to organize support for the strikers in New York Mills. Such a committee was quickly approved with Charles E. Weaver serving as chair, E. J. Collmer as secretary, and John Shea as treasurer.[23] The committee immediately developed an organized plan for soliciting and collecting donations of food, clothing and money, and issued the following resolution to the press:

> "Whereas, The textile workers of New York Mills, after long years of suffering and struggle upon the merest subsistence, owing to the low rate of wage paid in the cotton mills, have made every effort to bring about a readjustment of their conditions by conference with their employers; and

> Whereas, Their employers have refused all consideration of their just demands, refusing to recognize their committees or raise their meager wages, the average of which over a period of 12 months, including several months of overtime, amounts to the miserable sum of $6.95 per week; and

> Whereas the homes of the workers are but poor, desolate and unsanitary shacks, bare of the ordinary conveniences for cleanliness; and

> Whereas, the employees have been subject to fines, abuse and sometimes curses; therefore, be it

> Resolved, That we, the committee representing the Utica Trades Assembly, resolve to do our best to support our fellow workers in their struggle to raise to the American standard of living, and inasmuch as many of the poor

toilers are women and children whose small wages compel them to live from hand to mouth.

We appeal to all our fellow citizens in the name of common humanity to cooperate with us in supplying food and clothing to alleviate the sufferings of these struggling toilers."[24]

The company, for its part, maintained a tight security on both its property and its public statements. "I never knew such a hullabaloo over a strike of a few ignorant foreigners," Braman wrote to White from his New York City offices, "all this excitement is exactly what they like and will prolong the difficulty."[25] Time and again reporters would ask for comments or statements, only to be told by company officials that their policy was not to issue any statements or comment on anything relating to the strike.

Given the reluctance of the company to make any further statements, the strikers attempted to garner additional public support through a campaign to depict their terrible living conditions. On Wednesday, April 10, the relief committee announced that a house-to-house survey of Polish strikers found more than 100 families in need of assistance ranging from food to clothing and shoes, while a similar search by the Syrian committee identified 37 families in need of assistance. The committee further stated that the company-owned houses were in a deplorable condition because A. D. Juilliard neglected repairs for so long. Indeed, that very day, to emphasize the plight of the strikers, H. J. Grant, a member of the relief committee from the Utica Trades Assembly, sent a letter to the State Board of Health requesting an investigation into the matter before an epidemic broke out. Describing conditions in the company houses, Grant maintained that "The floors are loose and often contain holes through which the stench from below enters the rooms above. The outhouses are without exception in unspeakable condition and filled to overflowing. In most cases the contents are oozing out on the floors. Some of these outhouses are scarcely 10 feet from the houses and around them the children play and eat their meals. Especially is this true of places on Mill Street." The relief committee also decided to establish a distribution point for food and clothing, donated by the Utica Trades Assembly and local merchants, at Kozak's Hall, a central location in the village.[26]

About that time a very sympathetic article appeared in the *Utica Saturday Globe* outlining the plight of the strikers in very compelling human terms. Titled "Where Lard is a Luxury," the article noted that conditions were terrible among the strikers with no relief in sight.

"There is a Polish family consisting of husband, wife and four small children to whom the writer's attention was called. The head of the family earns $8 a week and pays $3 every other week for rent. The breakfast of this family consists of bread and coffee, the latter without either milk or sugar. Dinner consists of boiled potatoes and cabbage without any meat. For supper there is served sometimes, perhaps, potatoes with a little bologna, sometimes bread, with lard, and coffee. No butter enters this home and lard is considered a luxury that is used only once a day.

This is not an exceptional case. There are scores of families in New York Mills who live in the same way to whom such things as meat, unless infrequently and of the cheapest kind, butter, milk and sugar are unknown except by name and memory. Today there is absolute want in many homes. There are little children crying for food and a few days ago, when the weather was severe, these little children were crying both for food and fire. There are kind hearts, however, among the strikers and those who have are ready to share with those who have not. Few, very few, have much to give and if the cessation of work lasts long practically all of the strikers will be reduced to the same level."[27]

On Thursday, April 11, as the strike entered its third week, many of the strikers began to drift out of town in search of other employment. The *Utica Observer* estimated in its April 11 edition that "Nearly all of the French people employed in the Mills have gone away, as have about 150 English and 200 Poles. These men are skilled mill workers and they found employment without difficulty in other cities at wages in advance of what they received in New York Mills."[28] With the strike now two weeks old, the $4 per week benefit promised by the U.T.W.A. could be paid to each striker in accordance with the union bylaws. Checks were distributed to each of the union members through the relief station at Kozak's Hall. Vouchers for groceries that could be obtained from sympathetic stores identified by the strikers were provided to strikers who were not members of Local 753, some 1,000 in number.[29]

The strikers were not the only ones in need. During the previous few days the Utica newspapers carried several stories regarding the poor living conditions of the national guardsmen. Walking guard in the cold rain and snow of a dreary April, sleeping on hard floors in unheated mills, the picture which emerged in the newspapers was one of cold, sickly, unhappy men contracting serious illnesses from their long exposure to the elements. Unable to fathom these stories, members of the 31st Separate Company from Mohawk stated that they "wished to emphatically deny the stories that some of the members are sick, as such a report only causes worry at home." The soldiers further stated that while "some members had colds," they were "not handicapped in their work on that account. They are enjoying their experience and claim that the feeling between the strikers and the militia is so friendly that a few evenings ago the strikers treated the soldiers to egg sandwiches and hot coffee."[30]

By this time it was obvious that the company was losing the propaganda war for public sentiment. Also, other events were then transpiring that placed additional pressure on the company to renounce its hard-line stance in favor of negotiation. While the strikers lobbied for public support, the State Board of Mediation and Arbitration continued its own efforts to bring about a settlement. Patrick Downey met on several occasions between April 3 and April 10 with W. Pierrepont White of the New York Mills Corporation and John P. Campbell representing the Walcott & Campbell Company. In each of these instances, in keeping with the A. D. Juilliard company policy, the responses of White and Campbell were so ambiguous as to amount to a refusal to meet with their striking employees. In his report to the State Department of Labor, Downey noted that "Mr. White's answer to the proposition for a conference being so indefinite and his attitude being so evasive, nothing could be accomplished." Because of this obvious impasse, William C. Rogers, Deputy Commissioner of Labor and chief negotiator for the Bureau of Mediation and Arbitration, visited Augustus D. Juilliard in New York City on April 10 to further urge him and his associates "to instruct the officers of their company at New York Mills to meet with a committee of their employees in an effort to adjust the dispute." But Rogers also met with nothing save obfuscation and delay.[31]

Seeing that no progress was being made to resolve the dispute, and fearing the consequences that a prolonged strike might have on other industries in New York State, the Commissioner of Labor personally notified W. Pierrepont White that "if the attitude of the New York Mills Company and Walcott and Campbell was as reported to him, namely that they had persistently refused to meet a committee of the employees, he would order a public investigation." The threat of a public investigation of the conditions and employee grievances at New York Mills was potentially a serious blow to the company. The information furnished to the newspapers by Local 753 was enough to influence general public opinion over to the side of the strikers. Should the State Department of Labor conduct a full-scale public investigation it would no doubt verify the instances mentioned in the union's list of grievances, as well as uncovering the low wages, poor working conditions, shorting of employee pay envelopes, and other abuses which occurred, some of which were also violations of the New York State labor laws. Clearly, the company did not want to become the subject of a State Department of Labor investigation. Thus, White quickly informed the Commissioner of Labor that he felt confident that "by the latter part of the week a settlement could be effected." White also requested "an extension of time" to facilitate the settlement. Given the positive nature of White's communication, the Commissioner agreed to the extension.[32]

Neither the A. D. Juilliard officials in New York nor White had any intention of giving up the struggle that easily. During a series of strategy meetings company officials decided to use the time extension granted to them to pursue a more aggressive stance in the hopes of both influencing public opinion in their favor and placing pressure upon the strikers to return to work without the necessity of a negotiated settlement. To do this, however, the company first had to forestall any intervention by the State Board of Mediation and Arbitration. "I think it would be a serious mistake to have the State Board of Mediation take up our case," Braman informed White, "as it would mean delay, a great deal of notoriety, and is bound to end unsatisfactorily to the mill." Should White be approached by representatives of the Board again, Braman instructed, he should say only "that we expect our matter to be settled very shortly, and ask him to defer 'butting in' for a time." If the Board proved unwilling to be put off, White was to let Braman know "immediately and we will bring political influence to bear upon him through Tammany Hall. I repeat, it would be a very serious and costly mistake to allow these politicians to institute an inquiry, and we shall combat it to the last."[33]

The brief reprieve granted the company was also used to increase recruiting of strike-breakers and influence public opinion against the strikers. In an attempt to force Father Fijałkowski to use his influence on behalf of the company's interests, Braman told White to "send for the Polish Priest at New York Mills, and tell him that the present doings of his flock there must undergo a marked change at once or we shall take immediate steps to get them out of our houses, at the same time assuring him that if we once get the Polish people out of New York Mills we will see to it that a large number are never again employed there. Inasmuch as he is depending on the building there of a Polish church, and has spent a large sum for a lot, this may have some effect on him."[34]

In the same letter Braman indicated for the first time that company officials were willing to alter their obviously unsuccessful policy of declining comment to the press. Sensing the need for a press offensive to supplement his behind-the-scenes efforts to pressure the strikers,

Braman told White that "the time is approaching when it will probably be necessary to publish our side in some form in the papers, and I have today dictated the enclosed, which may be subject to revision, as I intend to take it home tonight and consider the wording very carefully."[35]

The original draft of Braman's statement began with the assertion that "The strike at the New York Mills was instigated, as usual, by outside agitators who make their living, and many of them fortunes, by playing on the ignorance of the work-people." It went on in very harsh, pointed language to describe how the "loud-mouthed liars and scoundrels met with scant encouragement," but by "playing on the credulity of their countrymen" they were finally able to create a small union which, nevertheless, did not enjoy the support of the majority of workers. Braman's diatribe continued on to castigate both the Utica newspapers and business community for their actions during the strike. As to the press, "Not one of the papers of this city has had a word to say in favor of law and order, but have published column after column of flap-doodle, all of which no sane person will believe is not against the interests of the city of Utica." With regard to the business community, "It has always been supposed that one of the main objects of a Chamber of Commerce was to encourage the industries of a community. Has anyone ever heard of any action or protest against the outrageous proceedings at New York Mills during the last week from that body or from any member of it? This body of business men seemingly view the matter as they would an entertainment, with smug indifference; but the time is coming when the members of your Chamber of Commerce, your pulpits, and your people at large, will have to stand up and be counted in matters of this kind."[36] The sarcastic, accusatory tenor of these words was reflected throughout the draft statement, an obvious manifestation of the tremendous anger welling within the New York executive.

To a reasonable mind, Braman's draft statement was at the least unpolitic, and at the most inflammatory. In the course of the statement he also contradicted some of the earlier assertions of the company officials in New York Mills. For example, at one point he indicated that the employees had been attempting to present grievances for nearly two years, an obvious contradiction of the company's earlier claim to have had no prior knowledge of the unrest which led to the strike. In addition, at a time when the company was seeking support for its position, Braman's blatant attacks on the press and the business community could only serve to strengthen the strikers' cause. White was quick to recognize the potential danger of the draft statement, informing Braman that "In regard to the article which you drafted, really it is a most creditable thing for vituperation. However, there are many points in it to be taken and cared for properly, but in its present shape would not be received any better than banker Schiff's tirade against the newspapers at the dinner." White went on to explain the local political milieu and the power of those who operated the newspapers. He cautioned against publication of the statement in its draft form. "Each locality has its own way of doing business," he concluded, "and it is usually considered advisable to see that the local customs are observed."[37]   Because of White's counsel for caution, the final version of the statement subsequently released by Superintendent Fish was considerably more moderate in tone. As released, this lengthy denial of union allegations and argument in support of the company read as follows:

> "The statements which have been printed during the past two weeks regarding conditions at the New York Mills are so misleading, and in most cases so grossly inaccurate, that we are impelled in fairness to ourselves, and to the public, and more especially to the large class of intelligent textile workers in this and other localities, to submit the following facts:
>
> The strike was instigated by outsiders who had no connection with the mills, and who advised our former employees to leave their work, although an increase had been granted them.
>
> The majority of the operatives, about 2,000 in number, are of Polish extraction, very many of whom can neither speak nor understand the English language. As a class they are law-abiding, industrious and frugal, and were well thought of by their employers. They were apparently satisfied with their wages and treatment, and their frugality is evidenced by the fact that the post-office records at New York Mills show that they remitted an average of $1,000 per week to the old country, as well as acquiring property here.
>
> The company has made no effort to operate the mills, nor has it given notice to its former employees to vacate its houses, the only work that has been done has been to keep up the fires under the boilers, in order to protect the insurance on its property and to save its perishable property, yet all are familiar with the violence and disorder which has taken place, the expense of which must be borne by the community at large, the mills and the employees who can illy afford the loss. This is due to a great extent to tolerating the presence and methods of the men who have no interests at stake except their own salaries which they receive by inciting strikes and riots.

The charges that our mills are unsanitary are absolutely without foundation. This can be proved by consulting the records of the State Factory Department.

During the past four years we have spent an average of over $100,000 per year in additions and improvements to this property. Every house has been papered and painted during this period, and contracts had been placed for a large number of modern, five room houses, before the present trouble begun. The yards surrounding the tenements are thoroughly cleaned every spring and fall, and this spring cleaning is progressing as rapidly as the weather will permit.

It must be recognized by all who are familiar with conditions at New York Mills, that the maintenance of cleanliness and order in the company's tenements is a most vexatious problem for the company.

The rents of the company's houses run from 75 cents to $2 per week. The employees receive the same wages paid for similar classes of work in other mills, and in view of the low rent it cost[s] our employees much less to live than it costs the employees of any of the mills in the surrounding country.

Charges that the state labor law relating to employment of women and minors is openly violated in the operation of our plants, can equally be disproved by referring to the factory inspection department at Albany.

The charges of ill-treatment and abuse of employees by superintendents and overseers have not the slightest foundation; we will welcome any reliable evidence of such misconduct at any time, and will pay $250 reward for legal proof showing that such acts have occurred in our plants and have been committed or sanctioned by our superintendents or overseers.

The company has always taken a deep interest in the matter of education in the village. It presented the school board at No. 1 Mill with land for a school house, and the minutes of the school district show their appreciation of this fact.

The company also contributed liberally to the fund for the building of a new Polish Catholic Church in New York Mills.

With reference to the wage schedule, this company always has paid, and always intends to pay as high wages as are paid by any other manufacturer in the same line of business, and had voluntarily granted an increase in wages to its employees before the strike. It would appear that the object of these outside agitators is clearly to make an effort to take the control of the business out of the hands of its owners. In fact, for the past week it has been common talk in the vicinity of the mills that the mills are the property of the employees, that they can do as they please with them for they were built with their labor, losing sight of the fact that the mills have been in existence 75 years, and the very large majority of its employees have lived in this country no more than five years. This unthinkable proposition is, of course, doomed to complete failure, and in the meantime the company, its former employees and the community are paying the bills."[38]

Following the issuance of the statement, the company continued its new policy of overt action by taking a reporter from the *Utica Observer* on a tour of one of the mills. There, the paper obligingly informed its readers, "He found a well-lighted, thoroughly sanitary plant, spotlessly clean in every part. The machinery, much of it new and recently installed, was of the best type obtainable. Some of it was imported from England. All of it was apparently in excellent condition."[39] This favorable picture of the textile mills was circulated in the newspaper's April 12 edition, thereby providing serious contradiction of the conditions reported by the strikers. It apparently never occurred to the reporter that the plant might actually be considerably different in operation. By the time the reporter visited the plant the company had two full weeks to clean the premises, air out the rooms, and otherwise make the setting presentable. Without the machinery in operation the constant banging of the equipment was absent, as was the haze of lint which always enveloped the weavers.

The reaction of the workers to Fish's statement was a series of individual denials. However, a formal reply was postponed until the strike committee could develop a detailed, reasoned response. Once the union leaders consulted one another, Miles issued the following response on behalf of the union:

"The first statement of Mr. Fish that the strike was caused by outsiders is not true. The demands on the part of the workers were made entirely on their own initiative and the strike was declared by local men without the consent of the international officers.

Mr. Fish next states that his employees were apparently satisfied with their wages and treatment, yet these same employees entirely on their own responsibility presented demands for an increase in wages and an adjustment of other conditions, signed by 800 of their members without consulting anyone outside of their own membership.

Mr. Fish further states that the charges of violation of the state labor laws in regard to the employment of women and minors in the plant can easily be disproved by referring to the Factory Inspection Department at Albany. The fact of the matter is that on the last occasion when a factory inspector called at the New York Mills to investigate complaints of women working overtime, the lights were turned out and the women ordered home.

Mr. Fish further denies the charges of ill treatment and abuse of employees and offers $250 reward for legal proof showing such acts having occurred in 'our plant.' The following affidavits are herewith presented with a view of securing the reward and not with any desire to give unpleasant notoriety to the abuses perpetrated upon the employees. I regret that the statement of Mr. Fish compels me in justice to our cause, to make public these unpleasant facts."[40]

Accompanying the statement to the press were three sworn affidavits which supported the workers' claims. In the first, Marya Lopata accused the company of shorting her wages, stating also that she was the victim of "rough treatment at the hands of a boss" that caused her to miss a day's work. When she did not report because of her injuries she was dismissed. A second document by seventeen-year-old Katarzyna Kosmider claimed that she worked two weeks without pay, after which her salary was not the full amount to which she was entitled. She further claimed that one of the mill bosses struck her on the back and across the face with a belt, and then discharged her when she complained. The third affidavit, attested to by Anna Kulpa, claimed that she was not paid for three weeks of work, following which her wages fluctuated widely without any explanation.[41]

Following the presentation of the statement and the affidavits, Miles asserted to the assembled reporters his conviction that some of the abuses attested to by many of the aggrieved employees "never came to the knowledge of Superintendent Fish." Whether this was a reflection of the continuing belief among many of the striking employees that Fish was fair and would be just if their grievances could be made known, or whether it was merely an attempt to leave room for future conciliation by insulating Fish from direct involvement in the abuses, cannot be determined. Nevertheless, Miles quickly added that, "The very fact that such conditions can exist without the knowledge of Superintendent Fish and other responsible officials of the mill is an all sufficient reason for the establishment of an organization among the workers with properly constituted representatives to make these abuses known to the officials of the mill."⁴²

On April 13 the *Utica Saturday Globe*, obviously tiring of the long stalemate, complained that "Although the village is as orderly as any ward in Utica, a force of deputies at $3 a day and three companies of militia are still on duty at an estimated cost to the taxpayers of $600 a day. How long this expense is to continue no one knows. Apparently no one cares, except for the taxpayer, and of course no one considers him. What is a taxpayer for anyway if it be not to foot bills, however contracted?"⁴³ Then, following a brief summary of Superintendent Fish's statement, the *Globe* opined that "The statement, while vigorously defending the policy of the company, holds out no prospect for peace. On the contrary, it shows that the company takes the position that it is in the right throughout and, inferentially, that peace can be reestablished only by the strikers returning to work under the same conditions as before. This the strikers assert they will not do — and so the fight goes on, each side set in its views, the deputies and militia on duty and the taxpayer wondering when it will all end."⁴⁴

The *Globe* was not the only paper concerned with the cost of keeping the National Guard in New York Mills. As early as April 5 the *Utica Observer* pointed out to its readers that "The county will foot the bills for the militia and the special deputies at New York Mills. It will be a sum that will make the taxpayers do a war dance."⁴⁵ The cost of the operation, especially in view of the calm which prevailed in the Mills and the continual observations of both residents and visitors that the National Guard was unnecessary, was increasing daily as an issue of controversy. What people lost sight of, however, was that without the guard the excesses of the company's deputies and detectives would no doubt have continued unabated, perhaps leading to a much more serious outbreak of violence.

On April 15 the front pages of the Utica newspapers were crammed with information on a disaster of immense international proportions that drastically reduced coverage of the local strike. On its maiden voyage from Liverpool to New York, the enormous White Star passenger liner *Titanic*, the supposedly unsinkable and most lavish commercial ship ever built, struck an iceberg and sank in the frigid North Atlantic. First reports of the disaster indicated that the passengers and crew had all been rescued, but these soon gave way to the stark reality that more than 1,500 people, over half of those aboard, perished in an icy grave. Among the *Titanic's* passenger list were many of the most prominent in American and British society: the John Jacob Astors, the Benjamin Gugenheims, the Isadore Strausses, Major Archie Butt, President Taft's military aide, and the George Wideners, benefactors of Harvard University. Among the other victims were Arthur Ryerson, a prominent Philadelphia businessman who owned a camp on Otsego Lake and was a non-resident member of the prestigious Fort Schuyler Club in Utica. Captain E. J. Smith who commanded the giant ship and went to the bottom of the ocean with it was a cousin of Mrs. Owen Owens of Seymour Avenue in Utica. Among the victims, too, were hundreds of less prominent steerage passengers, immigrants hoping for a new life in America. Numbered among them were English, Welsh, French, German, Polish and Italian laborers, the very classes of people, and in a few cases the former countrymen and neighbors of those who now toiled in the factories of the New York Mills Company. The tragedy was all inclusive in scope, engaging the attention of editors and readers in all of the Utica newspapers, whether English, Polish, Italian or German editions. For days the tragedy at sea was the focus of popular attention, yet it did not completely overshadow the continuing saga of the strike in New York Mills.[46]

Though largely unnoticed at the time because of the *Titanic* disaster, Monday, April 15, was also the day that A. D. Juilliard chose to take the next step in pressuring the strikers back to work by resuming production at its mills. All during the previous week and well into the weekend company officials were busy contacting recruiting agents in Utica, Rome, and throughout Central New York to obtain a force of strike-breakers sufficient to once again begin operations. At 6:30 a.m. that Monday morning the whistle located in the tower of Number 1 blew as it normally would to call employees to work before the strike. Several hundred Italian strike-breakers soon arrived in trolley cars, alighting under guard at the corner of Main and Mill Streets. As they entered the mills amid taunting cries of "scab" from the assembled picketers, several English and a few Syrian strikers joined the strike-breakers and returned to work. The force was sufficient to begin operations at Number 1 and the bleachery, while providing about a seventy-five percent work force at Numbers 3 and 4. The large Number 2 mill remained closed. Given the number of new workers, it was immediately obvious that this was no case of merely completing and shipping goods on hand. Rather, the company was making a serious attempt to produce new goods and return the situation to "business as usual" in an effort to discourage the strikers and force them back to work. The National Guard companies turned out in full force to keep the strikers away from the strike-breakers, but no incidents of violence were reported.[47]

Taken completely by surprise, the strikers were furious over the restarting of the mills, many fearing that evictions from company houses would follow to make room for the new workers. Indeed, the whistle which blew at Number 1 also served as a call to further action by the strikers. Hundreds took to the streets. The newspapers reported that "At no time since the soldiers have been at the mills have so many strikers appeared on the streets. Men and women out singly, in pairs, fours, sixes and sometimes as many as 25 and 30 appear in a body on the streets. They are exceedingly wrought up over the opening of the mills and everywhere one can hear mutterings about 'The Scabs,' as the strikers call those who are taking their places."[48]

Within hours the strike committee blanketed the village with large red, diamond-shaped placards designed to boost the spirits of the strikers. Printed in English and Polish, the black lettering read:

> We Are
> Winning.
> We Will Win
> If We
> Stand Together,
> If the
> Mills Are Kept Tied Up Tight.
> Therefore Stick.
> Stand Together or They'll Hang One After
> the Other.
> Don't Scab.
> Attend All Meetings.
> Pack the Halls Full and Keep the Mills
> Closed.
> Put This on Your Coat. Pin it
> on Tight So That Every-
> body can see that
> I Am Not a Scab.[49]

That afternoon the strikers met at Kozak's Hall to discuss the new turn of events and the actions which might be taken to continue the strike. Uncharacteristically, it was closed to reporters and the general public. At the meeting, attended by an overflow crowd of some 1,400 strikers, a motion to continue the strike passed unanimously. "We'll stay out all summer," strikers leaving the meeting told reporters. "Let them bring all the Italians here they want to."[50] Organizer Miles likewise tried to project an image of optimism, telling the press that the new workers were largely "unskilled and next to worthless," thus the company's attempts to start the mills were doomed to failure.[51]

Regardless of the public image of confidence displayed by the strikers and their leaders, the restarting of the mills was cause for serious concern.

During the day additional strike-breakers arrived by trolley and entered the mills. The new company employees ate lunch in the factories so as not to encounter the pickets, but a few of the English and Syrians who lived in the village were escorted by members of the National Guard to and from their houses at lunch time. In total, an estimated 500 workers were on the job by the end of the first day of resumed operations. Some of the strike-breakers, however, did not last very long. That same afternoon between fifty and seventy-five Italians walked off the job in what they termed a dispute over the wages the company promised them. "Eight dollars a week no good," one announced as he left Number 1. "When you take 60 cents a week carfare out of that — bah!"[52] Company officials claimed that the workers who left were simply incompetent and that their statements about wage disputes were made to gain sympathy with the Polish pickets. Regardless of which version is correct, by the end of the day company officials were justifiably happy with the day's events. Large numbers of strike-breakers were brought it, Numbers 1, 3, 4 and the bleachery were successfully restarted and, to their surprise and delight, some of the English and Syrian strikers reconsidered and came back to work. No violence occurred, and there was no sign of any impending clash. The mill officials were certain that within a few days the remaining strikers would see the futility of their struggle and return to work without the necessity of compromise.[53]

On April 17 the National Guard companies from Utica and Mohawk, having spent two weeks of dreary, monotonous work in New York Mills, were relieved by companies from Binghamton and Oneonta. The units from Utica and Mohawk rendered good service in New York Mills, treating the people of the village fairly and gaining the respect of residents and strikers alike. The press reported that "The Utica and Mohawk boys were given a hearty farewell and good wishes were showered upon them by the friends they made during their two weeks' service in the village. The soldiers were courteous and thoughtful in their treatment of all people in the New York Mills and their conduct won them the good will not only of the mill owners and bosses, but of the strikers and other residents of the village."[54] There were few who disagreed.

That afternoon some $1,200 in groceries were distributed to strikers by the U.T.W.A. Organizer Miles spent most of the day conferring separately with the Polish and English strike committees, and courting additional support from the Utica and Syracuse Trades Assemblies, both of which voted further aid, as did the Central Federation of Labor in Albany. The company's initiative in issuing an official statement to the press and restarting the mills clearly placed the strikers on the defensive, requiring that Miles expend much energy and time courting the newspapers and seeking further support to repair the damage.[55]

Meanwhile, the company continued its initiative. As Miles scurried about between Utica, New York Mills and Syracuse, and the leaders of Local 753 sought to reassure their members and promote continued unity, company officials announced that the quantity of goods produced in the reopened plants was nearing capacity and, to counter Miles' earlier claims of problems with "unskilled" labor, that the workers were learning quickly. At the same time, Superintendent Fish left the village for New England where, although he did not explicitly say so, it was assumed that he would be recruiting new employees to fill the remaining vacancies in the mills. "This act seems," the *Utica Daily Press* concluded, "to be the first determined step on the part of the mill officials to end the strike."[56] Indeed, through its recent public statements and its reopening of the mills the company was making a *very* determined effort to effect public opinion, erode the confidence of the strikers, and force a settlement without having to deal with the U.T.W.A. Its new aggressive activities, however, did not go unnoticed.

On the same day that the mills reopened, William C. Rogers of the State Board of Mediation and Arbitration paid another visit to Augustus D. Juilliard in New York City. Once again, Juilliard would not commit himself to any specific action to achieve a negotiated settlement. With all of the company's efforts apparently directed toward resuming operations, and no noticeable indication that it was prepared to meet the strikers in negotiation, Patrick J. Downey once again met with White, Fish and Campbell, requesting that they agree to "receive a committee of their employees." They refused. When Rogers and Downey communicated the respective refusals of company officials in both New York Mills and New York City to the Department of Labor, the Commissioner's patience wore out. "Immediately," in the words of the Bureau's official report, he "notified the mill owners that unless they made a public announcement through the press, of the time, date and place at which they would meet a committee of their employees with an understanding that they would do their part in adjusting the strike, he would order an investigation forthwith."[57]

Faced with imminent government intervention which could lead to an embarrassing public investigation and possible forced arbitration, White complied. In order to put the best possible light on what was about to transpire, White did not once mention the Commissioner's ultimatum, rather he maintained the company's standard line that it was, and had always been willing to meet to address grievances with any committee the Polish people might choose to send. White indicated in his statement that the company representatives would be available in the mill office on Main Street at 2:00 p.m. on the following Saturday and Monday. While distributing the statement to the press, however, White added the verbal proviso that the company representatives would meet with the strikers "as former employees and not as union delegates." Also, proof of the hastiness of the company's effort can be seen in the comment of the editor of *Słowo Polskie* that the announcement reached that paper's offices only moments before it went to press.[58] White's formal statement, as issued to the press, read as follows:

New York Mills, April 17, 1912

To the Public:

It has been brought to our attention that the Polish people at New York Mills are being daily informed that the superintendent and officers of the New York Mills Company would not meet or talk with any committee of the Polish people as employees of the company.

We have also been informed that it has been stated to the Polish people that committees and individuals who were in our employ had been to the main office and were sent away without a chance to see any officials.

Statements of this character are untrue. The day before the Polish people stopped work an announcement was made to them that their pay would be raised. Since the mills shut down the superintendent and officers have been at all times, and are now ready and willing to meet a committee of our former employees and talk over for adjustment all matters of difference between them and the people working in the mills. We are now ready to meet a committee at any time that a day may be set and in order that there may be no possible misunderstanding, we will be at the main office, No. 2 Mill, at 2 p.m. next Saturday, and also 2 p.m. next Monday to meet a committee of our former employees.

This statement is made that those who have been erroneously informed may know the position of the company.

New York Mills Company,
By W. Pierrepont White,
President[59]

White's statement was clearly geared to gather public support and place the strikers in a position where they could either take advantage of the opportunity to meet the employers on the latter's terms, or continue the strike and run the risk of losing substantial public support by appearing to be the party unwilling to compromise. In fact, the *Utica Observer* clearly stated its hope "that the Poles will take advantage of the opportunity offered them for a conference with the mill officers. Since the commencement of the strike there has been a feeling that the mill company would not give a courteous hearing to the strikers. But the officers generously issued the invitation and it now remains for the Poles and their leaders to take advantage of it and end the present trouble amicably."[60] Clearly, the company's maneuver was working. The press was reacting favorably, and there was every reason to believe that the public would follow its lead.

To be sure that the point of its efforts was understood by the strikers, and to exert as much pressure as possible upon them, the company also circulated rumors to the effect that should the opportunity for discussions on Saturday and Monday pass without response, there would be no additional moves on their part to meet with the "former employees."[61] On Friday, April 19, the eve of the Saturday time set by the company for the first meeting, representatives of the A. D. Juilliard Company jubilantly announced to assembled reporters that "More wheels were turning today and we will turn every one before long."[62] The barrage of such statements was almost endless between the Wednesday announcement by White and the Saturday meeting time. The company expended every effort to portray itself as the agreeable, accommodating party, while at the same time giving the impression that all was well in the mills and that full production would soon be reached with or without the strikers.

That afternoon, following White's statement, the strikers held another meeting at Kozak's Hall where they reaffirmed their determination to stick together, but also decided to send a six-member strike committee to speak with company officials at the appointed hour on Saturday. Although White's unofficial comments to the press indicated that he would not treat with representatives of the union, his official statement said only that the company officials would be willing to meet with "a committee of our former employees," neglecting to rule out union officers. Given this loophole, the strike committee simply ignored White's unofficial statement about not receiving union representatives and declare themselves ready to meet with company officials. Though seemingly a minor semantic point, the omission of the prohibition against union representatives in the official statement provided a means by which both sides could sit down while still maintaining their official public postures. The company claimed to have met with "their former employees," while Local 753 claimed that its representatives met with company officials. This opportunity to negotiate a settlement would not be lost.[63]

Miles was now placed in a position of having to reiterate union claims, while at the same time being tactful enough not to sabotage the impending talks. Seeking a delicate and graceful way to portray the decision to meet the company officials as a *union* decision, while at the same time not blatantly offending White, he issued the following statement after the meeting at Kozak's Hall.

> "Mr. Pierpont White has issued the first official statement we have received intimating that the company was desirous of meeting a committee of the strikers. The last committee that interviewed Mr. Fish was distinctly informed that the company would not consider their demands, and that no further talk was necessary.
>
> That my position in this matter may not be misunderstood, I desire to say that I have never advised the strikers not to send a committee if the company should desire to meet one; in fact the constitution of our international organization provides that a local committee shall, wherever possible, adjust all grievances with their employers.
>
> Out of consideration of the taxpayers of the county, I have advised the strikers to maintain peace and order and it has been maintained. In the interest of all parties concerned I have advised the sending of a committee, and I sincerely trust that an honorable adjustment may result. On the other hand, I shall positively instruct the members of our organization to absolutely refuse a settlement that does not meet the requirements of a square, honest adjustment of wages and conditions."[64]

Miles' statement reiterated his and the U.T.W.A.'s willingness to negotiate, restated their previous attempt, and cautioned that failure to arrive at a just settlement offer would result in a continuation of the strike. Noticeably absent, however, was any reference to the "committee of strikers" being a *union* committee. It was obvious to all concerned that the issue of union recognition was the major impediment to a settlement, thus Miles attempted to make his point while referring to those who were to meet with White simply as "a committee of strikers." It was a tactful response.

The following day the first meeting between the contending sides since the beginning of the strike took place. Significantly, the employers did not take exception to the fact that the "committee of strikers" was led by Tomasz Mótyka, vice president of Local 753. "The committee was received courteously," the *Utica Observer* reported, "and given an impartial hearing by the company."[65] During the meeting the company offered a variable increase in salary from five to twelve percent, depending upon the type of work done. The strike committee countered with their initial demand for a flat fifteen percent increase, the establishment of a published pricing system for piece work, and the elimination of the fine system. The committee also restated its desire for attention to the condition of company housing, and company officials signaled their willingness to take steps in that direction. The question of union recognition was not pressed, although the strikers did ask for recognition of a "shop committee" to present future grievances. The company officials, though maintaining that to their knowledge no mistreatment of workers previously occurred, indicated that mistreatment would not be permitted and legitimate grievance would be heard and acted upon. Similarly, the initial demand for the dismissal of Superintendent Braman at the bleachery was not pressed, but the committee did demand the reinstatement of all strikers once the work stoppage was settled. The company agreed to do so "as soon as the opportunity offered." After about one and one-half hours the meeting adjourned to allow the committee to report back to the strikers.[66]

At 9:00 a.m. on Monday, April 22, the Polish and Syrian strikers met at Kozak's Hall in what was described as the largest and "most enthusiastic" meeting since the beginning of the strike. There they heard the report of their committee and voted on the proposed settlement to the strike. Although newspapers that morning and the previous evening predicted a quick end to the strike, the strikers voted to reject the company offer as too "vague." The company's refusal to agree to a specific proposal for settling future grievances, its refusal to agree to a shop committee, unclear wording about the reinstatement of strikers, and the ambiguous use of percentages to define raises were all cited by various union officials as reasons for the rejection of the offer.[67]

At 2:00 p.m. that afternoon the strike committee again met with company officials to formally reject the initial offer and present their objections and counterproposals. During a two and one-half hour session the strike committee indicated that it wanted some firm assurance that the strikers would all be reinstated immediately upon resolution of the strike. On this issue the company was only willing to state that most of the strikers would be rehired immediately, and the remainder "when the opportunity is presented." Although little detail of the rest of the meeting is available, progress on the other issues appears to have been made for early that evening, during another meeting in Kozak's Hall, the majority opinion was that the company's offer was now reasonably favorable. While not yet ready to recommend acceptance,

Tomasz Mótyka, vice president of Local 753 and chairman of the 1912
strike committee. The sign to the left reads "Równość, Wolność,
Braterstwo" [Equality, Freedom, Brotherhood].

Miles did tell the strikers that "The proposition made by the company at this afternoon's conference seems to be favorable to both parties concerned."[68] After some debate, the strikers voted to accept in principle the new proposal for settlement.

On Wednesday morning, April 24, the *Utica Daily Press* announced to its readers the erroneous information that the strike was settled *with the company's original offer*. "The strike resulted in a defeat for the employees, for they will return to work this morning under conditions very similar to those they left." The newspaper, apparently citing mill officials, went on to a brief discussion of the terms of the settlement, indicating periodically that the employees failed to achieve their full demands. Following its coverage of the settlement stipulations the paper noted that Miles' version of the settlement "differs materially from that presented by the mill officials." It then printed lengthy sections of Miles' statement, including his assertion that "I regard the settlement as a desire on the part of the firm to comply with our demands for that square, honorable adjustment which was the basis of our demands. I trust that the relations of the company and the employees may be more amicable in the future than in the past to the great advantage of all concerned."[69]

In a similar vein the *Utica Observer* stated that the "operatives have been badly advised from the start," and that the "terms of the settlement are precisely those offered by the company before the strike occurred."[70] In general, the Utica newspapers all followed this lead. During the strike they had, on the whole, been rather objective, on many occasions even appearing to show sympathy for the strikers. Yet, as part of its last-minute offensive the A. D. Juilliard Company was successful in exerting pressure upon the Utica newspapers to adopt the company's point of view. Once the settlement was announced, the English-language newspapers each adopted the company's version of the settlement and proclaimed defeat for the strikers. Some, like the *Utica Observer*, went so far as to castigate Miles as an outside instigator who ill-served the workers by acting against their best interests. The *Utica Daily Press* claimed that the strike leaders purposely kept the company proposals secret from the workers, who were simply told that the company refused to negotiate. "This school of instruction continued," it concluded, "until the New York Mills Company published in the various local papers a notice calling a meeting of the former employees and the officials at two definite dates."[71] It was obvious that the publicity efforts, posturing and outright pressure employed by the company in the final days of the strike had a convincing effect on the press, which was forceful in its assertions of company victory and condemnation of the union's efforts.

Obviously, the company was as interested in portraying the settlement as a victory as Miles was in casting it as a victory for organized labor. The newspapers, by accepting the company's version and clinging to the notion that any demand not fully realized was a defeat for the union, supported the idea that labor had lost. Indeed, the company continued to maintain in public that it won, and to issue statements to the effect that the strike was for naught as the workers eventually accepted the same offer given to them the day before the strike began. But there is evidence that suggests the company's position did not result from mere bravado, but from an honest belief that it had won. On April 26 Chester Braman wrote to W. Pierrepont White to caution against too much exultation: "We have, apparently, won, and for conscience sake let us let well enough alone. What we want now is to run our mills in peace, and not try to obtain any glory through the newspapers."[72]

Of all the English-language Utica newspapers, only the *Utica Sunday Tribune* took a neutral position, informing its readers that the settlement "appeared satisfactory to both the company and its employees [and] was regarded as a matter for general congratulation." The paper went on to note that "Probably no other strike of equal magnitude in the number of the strikers and the extent of interests involved was ever conducted with as little manifestation of ill feeling as this one."[73]

Miles, by speaking in general of honorable and fair settlements was able to assert that labor, as he told the Utica Trades Assembly, won a victory.[74] Further, the official report submitted to the annual convention of the United Textile Workers of America maintained that "The strike ended in a victory for the union and a compliance by the firm of the demands made upon them. " The report stated that to Miles was due "all the credit for the settlement of the affair."[75] Miles, to his credit, provided another scenario in his own official report to the convention, stating that "though all the Police Department, militia, and private detectives were brought in, the splendid solidarity of our Polish brothers and sisters remained unbroken." Noting that the official report on the strike settlement credited him with the victory, Miles flatly asserted: "I tell you it was due to the unexampled loyalty and unselfishness of our Polish brothers and sisters."[76]

Amidst these conflicting viewpoints, where did the truth lie? Surely, anyone who has been involved in serious negotiation over complex issues knows that a final agreement wherein one side attains *everything* that it demands is extremely rare. Negotiation is a process whose purpose is to settle disagreements through the give-and-take of compromise, and it is from this perspective that the final settlement of the strike must be viewed. To maintain that one side or the other lost because it did not achieve every one of its goals in its entirety is simply not valid.

The basic demands of Local 753 at the beginning of the strike included (1) a fifteen percent increase in wages, (2) recognition of the union as the collective bargaining agent for the workers, (3) establishment of a posted piecework pricing schedule, (4) improvement of company owned houses, (5) better treatment of the workers by management, (6) the firing of bleachery superintendent Braman, and (7) assurances by the company that all striking workers would be allowed to return to their jobs once the strike was concluded. In light of these demands, how did the two sides fare in the settlement?

On the issue of wages, the company, despite its assertions to the press that it offered a five to twelve percent increase before the strike, only announced that it would *consider* making a five percent increase. The workers demanded a fifteen percent increase. According to the final settlement, weavers would receive a 14.5% increase and those in the spinning department and other areas would receive increases varying from 5% to 12.5%.[77] While not the flat fifteen percent increase demanded by the strikers, the raises were considerably above the original amount mentioned by the employers. Further, the agreement was a firm one, unlike the vague promise to "consider" an increase made earlier by the company. This was a negotiated settlement in which neither side obtained exactly what it wanted, but clearly the workers received considerably more through their strike than they would otherwise have obtained.

On the question of the union the company remained adamant against any formal recognition. Clearly the company came out ahead on this proposition, however the union could claim at least some progress. The strike did force the company to deal with the union's strike committee, whether it admitted to doing that or not. In the interests of effecting a settlement, the company maintained a public posture of non-recognition, while at the same time negotiating with the union strike committee led by Tomasz Mótyka, under the guise of it being "a committee of workers." In fact, the June 1912 issue of *The Textile Worker*, a publication of the U.T.W.A., claimed that although the company would not formally recognize the union, it gave "a promise to treat with committees of the operatives."[78] Official recognition or not, the company, which steadfastly refused to treat with the workers in any fashion save as individuals, negotiated with their committee to end the strike.

Under the settlement the company agreed to establish and post a piece-rate schedule, thus providing employees with information on pay scales so they could better calculate what was due them. This was an important concession to the union because many of the workers' grievances involved pay shortages and misunderstandings impossible to address without a firm pricing schedule. Without such a schedule, workers would continue to be at the mercy of the employer's whim. This was certainly a victory for the workers.

The fourth demand, that of improvement of the company housing, was also included in the settlement. The company agreed to improve existing company housing, to install modern facilities, and to construct additional units of more modern design. This was a significant concession not only because of its impact on the workers' standard of living, but because of the potential expense to the company that such improvements would require. Once again, it was clearly a union victory.[79]

On the question of better treatment from management the company made a formal statement prohibiting ill-treatment of the workers. It also agreed to hire, at its own expense, an interpreter agreeable to the workers who could assist in presenting grievances to the company officials. In practice, this individual could become a union representative to management. Another union victory.[80]

With regard to the firing of Superintendent Braman, the company refused and the strikers dropped the demand. A victory for the company.

Finally, with regard to the rehiring of the strikers, the company would not agree to immediate reinstatement of everyone because to do so would lead to difficulties with the "scab" force that it employed. Nevertheless, it did agree to take the majority back immediately and the remainder as soon as possible. In practice, virtually all who wished to return were rehired within about two weeks. In general, the issue was decided in favor of the employees.

Thus, of the seven fundamental issues, two, union recognition and the termination of Braman, could be classified as company victories. Five were decided to the greater advantage of the workers: an increased wage scale, establishment of a piece work schedule, improvement of company houses, better treatment from management, and the rehiring of the strikers. Given this record, it is difficult to conclude that the company was the victor. Rather, the settlement must be seen as a good compromise. An agreement in which each side obtained some concessions, and in which each could be pleased.[81]

The strike lasted 27 days idling, at its peak, some 2,028 workers for a loss which the State Department of Labor estimated at 42,400 working days, 67.7% of the time lost in all textile disputes in the state during that year. The U.T.W.A. contributed some $2,600 to the support of the strikers, who also received generous support from other local unions, from organized labor as far distant as Syracuse and Albany, and from the general public. It was estimated that the work stoppage cost the workers some $60,000 in wages, "while the mill companies have lost a like amount in the curtailment of business." The cost to the taxpayers of Oneida County was estimated in excess of $20,000 in payments for deputies, guardsmen, and other attending costs.[82] But

122   *United We Stand*

aside from these immediate "costs," the strike had other serious and
lasting impacts for the company, the workers and the community. The
strike set into motion processes of community identity and community
action that would never be reversed.

One immediate consequence of the strike in New York Mills was
an increase in wages for textile workers in Utica who benefited from the
stand of their colleagues in Local 753 when the Utica employers decided
to offer wage increases rather than risk the spread of the strike. The
many sympathetic newspaper articles published during the strike, coupled with the lack of any serious violence led to the general public
perception that the strikers were neither wild-eyed foreign radicals nor
ignorant slave labor. The generally fair treatment of the strike by the
press thus began a long process of upgrading the status of the Polish
community in the eyes of the general public which, though it might
still regard the Poles as inferior in status, at least began to realize that
they were people with normal human feelings, hopes and aspirations.

A similar increase in self-perception occurred within the Polish
community itself. Although some Poles complained that the strike did
not succeed as much as they hoped, the majority felt a new sense of
jedność, of unity and community solidarity. Once again they banded
together with specific goals in mind, and once again they achieved some
positive results. The company was forced to deal with them, and their
lives would be materially better because of their action. Though often
bitter memories of the struggle would remain in their minds, as they
would in the collective remembrance of the community in general, they
demonstrated once again that collective action worked. In the words of
Charles A. Miles, "the strike ended in victory for the union," and that
victory was due to "the splendid solidarity of our Polish brothers and
sisters." They were now a cohesive community with its own collective
self-identity, an identity and cohesiveness that would survive as a permanent legacy to generations then unborn.

Chapter 6

Bóg i Ojczyzna

The successful strike of March and April 1912 caused worker pride to soar and led to a renewed feeling of confidence within the Polish community in New York Mills. Nevertheless, following the strike membership in Local 753 declined briefly as those who were not satisfied with the settlement abandoned the union and some of those who felt that the situation was satisfactorily resolved also tended to remove themselves from union activism in the belief that all of their goals were accomplished. Most, however, remained loyal, keeping their dues current, and soon membership once again rose. In November, 1912, William Bork, a U.T.W.A. representative in Utica, reported that the "Textile workers union is growing in membership. Conditions of organized labor [are] improving."[1] As a consequence of the strike, wages were indeed improving. *The Annual Report of the Bureau of Labor Statistics* for the period ending September 30, 1912 listed a single union in New York Mills which numbered 1,050 members. At the same time, the summary statistics presented a picture of the changes in wages over the period from October 1, 1911 through September 30, 1912. Although the summary data did not make distinctions by specific task, thus fluctuations in wages between the more and less skilled positions are lost, nevertheless the general picture which emerges is one of wage increases following the conclusion of the 1912 strike. The average daily wage for male workers in March, before the strike, was $1.17, while in September it was $1.50, an increase of 28.2%. For female workers the March figure was $1.11, while that of September was $1.39, an increase of 25.2%. This meant that the average weekly wages for men rose from $7.02 before the strike to $9.00 in September, while weekly female wages increased from $6.66 per week in March to $8.34 in September.[2]

The Twelfth Annual Convention of the United Textile Workers of America convened in Boston, October 21-25, 1912. Jan Sroka and Michał Smoła attended as the first representatives of Local 753 to take part in a national U.T.W.A. convention. There they listened to reports on strikes conducted during the previous year, including their own in New York Mills. In his organizer's report, Charles Miles lauded the "unexampled loyalty and unselfishness" of the workers of New York Mills for the "splendid victory" which they achieved.[3] No doubt Sroka and Smoła were filled with a justifiable pride.

One of the ideas the successful strike confirmed in the minds of the Poles in New York Mills was that collective action did, in fact, work. Consequently, community activists continued to think in terms of organized means of addressing group problems and providing for the well-being of the community. Kazimierz Dziedzic, a civic-minded activist who arrived in New York Mills in 1906, led a movement to improve community living conditions. Going door-to-door evenings and on weekends, he, along with others, organized private home-owners to have water piped into the village and later succeeded in leading petition drives that resulted in the paving of sidewalks and installation of sewers. Another problem was the continuing arrival of immigrants from Europe who generally had little knowledge of the United States or the local community, and even less financial resources. To address this, on June 15, 1912, Jan Sroka, Józef Smoła, Jerzy Kozakiewicz, Michał Tuman, Stanisław Puła, and several other concerned individuals founded the *Klub Krakówski* [Kraków Club]. Named in honor of the city from which Sroka, the organization's first chairman, emigrated, the new society was formed to provide financial aid and advice to newcomers, including information on how to become a citizen. Organized as a political action group, its founders "were people who understood that laws, privileges and one's own well-being have to be fought for. In order to achieve these goals, one has at first to measure one's own strength, to create an organization purely political in character to endeavor to attain one's goals by means of a concerted effort." To achieve these the group hired people to serve as witnesses to render assistance at citizenship hearings, and otherwise encouraged people to learn English and become active citizens.[4] Eventually this would evolve into the New York Mills Polish Democratic Club, a very strong political action group. Clearly, the lessons of collective action and group solidarity learned during the 1912 strike were quickly put into practice in other arenas.

Life in New York Mills continued to bloom. Civic, cultural and religious activities in the village all increasing in both breadth and depth as the Polish residents continued to develop into a close-knit, cohesive community. The Polish Falcons presented plays in Smoła's Hall, the Polish band gave concerts, and various singing groups performed to the delight of enthusiastic audiences. The Society of St. Stanislaus continued to contribute to both religious and civic activities. On Sunday, March 16, 1913, it presented as a gift a "new, beautiful canopy" that was blessed at St. Mary's Church. "Honor to the Society of St. Stanislaus for such a gift," proclaimed *Słowo Polskie*, which kept its readers informed of every new development in the community.[5]

In addition, new businesses began to appear. The *Sklep Krakówski* [Kraków Store], a business partnership with shares selling at $5.00 each, incorporated with a board of directors including Józef Smoleński, Józef Smoła, Jerzy Kozakiewicz, Michał Tuman, Andrzej Lorek, Jan Sroka, Adolf Leszczyński and J. Wentka. Dr. Leon P. Jankiewicz, a prominent Utica physician, opened an office in the village, while other entrepreneurs, the beginnings of a prosperous middle class, included such diverse activities as Stefan Zamoryłło's hardware and paint store, Jan Wolak's bakery, Józef Nowicki's grocery and butcher shop, and Antoni Zamiarski's funeral services. "It is worth applauding the citizens of New York Mills," Gomólski commented in *Słowo Polskie* as the small village continued to evolve, becoming in the process not only a focus for concerted labor organization, but a cohesive and self-sustaining community.[6]

On May 3, 1913, one of the largest gatherings since the height of the strike took place in celebration of the anniversary of the Polish Constitution of the Third of May. Poles from Utica and the surrounding communities were invited to attend and participate, and the newspaper accounts of the festivities indicate that they turned out in great numbers. At 2:30 p.m. a procession began on St. Stanislaus Street, marching slowly south along Main Street. Leading the long parade was a wagon filled with children, followed by Tomasz Mótyka, president of Local 753, who walked along on foot. By 3:45 p.m. the procession began arriving at *Park Narodowy* [National Park], the picnic area owned by the Kozak brothers. At 4:00 p.m. Mótyka opened the proceedings by inviting Ludwik Lesnicki to the podium as the first speaker of the day. Once the editor and publisher of *Młotek Duchowny*, the strongly anti-Catholic social and economic weekly with socialist overtones published briefly in Utica between 1910 and 1912, Leśnicki reviewed the events leading up to the writing of the Constitution of the Third of May, noting that the Polish people and the Polish working class owed debts of gratitude to those who created the Constitution. The best way to honor their memory, he insisted, would be for everyone present to educate themselves, to become informed, to organize and to give what they could to community service, "not forgetting that the world belongs to the brave." Leśnicki then turned to the fate of the Polish worker in a foreign land, calling for unity and an awareness that "the people have to think for themselves, act on their own, and not wait for leaders who might be even now carrying on some 'business' with the enemies of the people." Finally, turning his attention to the absence of Father

Fijałkowski from the ceremonies, he took the opportunity to criticize the absent cleric: "I don't see your pastor here. He did not come because for him the worker's hand stinks. Therefore don't push yourselves toward him in the future, and wait until he himself comes to you, and here with you will talk to you about your destiny and advise you."[7] Although Leśnicki had a reputation as an anti-cleric, the fact that he openly criticized the pastor of St. Mary's, the single most important institution in the lives of the Polish people in the village, is a good indication of the strength and stature enjoyed by the union at that time. Later *Słowo Polskie* commented: "Father Fijałkowski does not find it suitable [in good taste] to go along with the people."[8]

After a brief speech in English, Jan Sroka took the podium to observe that "We came together here, oppressed in the Old Country, destitute, and we began in a foreign land to organize and concentrate and to learn and inform. And we are doing well not to wait for the orders of the gentry and 'protectors,' but rather we in our way, like the working class, gather together to honor the past and talk of the future." Continuing, he reviewed some of the important points of the Polish Constitution, concluding by telling his audience that "You have already been told today that you have to think for yourselves, work on your own, talk for yourselves, because you know what bothers you and where as well as what is the remedy. You will always find us ready to serve you because this is our 'obligation'; because we are here so that we can be of service to you. And we are ready to pay any price to be of assistance to you. Neither prison, nor fines will keep us from this work that is so much needed."[9]

The Polish orchestra played a variety of national, patriotic and worker songs, after which the crowd reassembled in the hall at National Park to hear speakers comment on the state of affairs in Poland. "In conclusion," *Słowo Polskie* stated with obvious pride, "it should be noted that the anniversary took place without the least confusion, everything ran smoothly and seriously, as was appropriate to the importance of the occasion. This was because the people know how to observe the anniversary which they organize by themselves without the help of 'lords or semi-lords'." The following week Local 753 published a message of thanks to the Polish unionists in Utica for taking part in the May 3 celebrations, "With best wishes for an early tearing off of the noose of economic servitude."[10]

The anniversary of the Constitution of the Third of May was the most celebrated of Polish secular holidays, with the prominence accorded labor leaders at the celebrations attesting further to the status of organized labor in the community after the 1912 strike. Yet the Poles, who always maintained close ties to the Old World, were also becoming increasingly concerned over deteriorating economic conditions in their eastern European homeland and the growing political tensions threatening to place their relatives in Europe in even greater danger. As concerns increased, there was a public meeting in Smoła's Hall at the end of May, 1913, to discuss means by which aid could be given to the Committee of National Defense, a branch of which already existed in New York Mills. *Słowo Polskie* commented that "All, for whom the good of Poland touches the heart, should find themselves at the hall."[11]

On June 22 another meeting convened in Smoła's Hall with a huge crowd estimated at some 500 people in attendance. Father Fijałkowski presided, opening with an explanation of the goals of the meeting. Sroka then took the podium to speak on the topic "Why we are exiles." Several other village leaders spoke, their orations being interspersed with recitations and children singing nationalistic songs. Once again Tomasz Mótyka "spoke with verve, taking a stand and not sparing any bitter words for the loafers who are always ready to damage the national cause. Smoła's Hall was booming with loud applause during Mótyka's talk," *Słowo Polskie* explained, "because the speaker was telling the honest truth and it was felt that he believed in what he was saying." When he finished, Eugenia Mótyka recited *"O Polska Nasza"* [Oh, Our Poland] before Sroka spoke once again. *Słowo Polskie* reported that his "talk showed that he knows the needs of the immigration and he knows where to look for the causes of our calamities and adversities. Sroka's talk was interrupted by the applause of the listeners; it was filled with profound thoughts and wonderful suggestions for the people of this small Polish colony which has gone forward boldly on behalf of the whole area with its hard work and thorough understanding of its obligations."[12]

With the speeches and diversions completed, the gathering settled down to the serious business of electing officers and organizing a fundraising drive for the relief of their compatriots in Poland. Once again union activists were prominent among the leadership of this collective action movement. Jan Sroka won approval as president, Stanisław Federowski as vice president, Jan Czyżycki as recording secretary, Jan Solnica as financial secretary and Michał Samoń as treasurer. Those elected as trustees to be responsible for the organization's finances were Jan Puła and Tomasz Mótyka. It was then voted unanimously to send collectors to individual homes to solicit donations. Elected for this purpose were Petronela Miłanowicz and Karolina Pietruszka. In its next edition, *Słowo Polskie* reported to its readership that "In Utica there is yet no committee, in Little Falls nothing is heard of one — New York Mills, a smaller community, did what was needed."[13]

Still, the community continued to grow in both numbers and organization. On August 2, 1914, Father Fijałkowski organized the *Towarzystwa Różańcowe Męskich*, the Male Rosary Society, to promote rosary observances and participation in church activities. Under the traditional Polish motto *"Bóg i Ojczyzna* ["God and Fatherland"], the new organization sought to contribute to both the religious and secular life of the village. Its first activities included the purchase of a banner for the church for $225 in 1915 and the acquisition of linens for the altar at a cost of $30 in 1916. Once again, it was union activists who took the lead in this new endeavor, with Tomasz Osika being elected president of the new society, assisted by secretary Andrzej Kobielski and treasurer Ludwik Krupa.[14]

One of the most significant achievements during this period was the construction of St. Mary's school in 1915 under the leadership of Father Fijałkowski. Soon, an order of teaching nuns, the Sisters of St. Felix, generally known as the Felicians, arrived to assume responsibility for the education of the Polish community's youth. Lessons were conducted in both Polish and English, with the result that many of the village's children enjoyed the advantages of bilingualism.[15]

Despite the increasing demands on the people's limited time that all of the new activities required, concern for the well-being of the union remained uppermost in the minds of many. By 1913 the need for a permanent union meeting place was obvious to all.[16] "The union committee understands," *Słowo Polskie* explained to its readers, "that wanting to eradicate all evil it must have a haven as a rallying point where the workers in their free time will be able to gather and recommend ways to improve their adverse circumstances."[17] A building committee was formed consisting of Jan Solnica, Antoni Sokal and Jan Furgał. They attempted to purchase a building for a union office, but once again the Poles ran into difficulty, being thwarted in their attempts by a man who refused to sell property to the Poles. Finally, after further fruitless searching, Jan Solnica arranged to purchase two vacant lots on St. Stanislaus Street, near St. Mary's Church, from the parish in mid-1913, transferring them to a workers' committee in November 1913 of that year. Dated July 17, 1914, the mortgage of the new *Dom Robotniczy* [Workers' Home], later known as Union Hall, was held by Tomasz Szlosek, Antoni Knutelski, Jan Solnica, Piotr Kozak and Wojciech Nowak. The mortgage indicated a balance due of $3,500 to the assignees for the two lots, each of which was forty feet wide along St. Stanislaus Street and 120 feet deep. The amount was due in three years from that date, with 6% annual interest. Szlosek paid $1,000, Knutelski $800, Solnica and Kozak $600 each and Nowak $500.[18]

To oversee the financial affairs of the new building the members of Local 753 created the *Stowarzyszenie Polskiej Hali Robotniczej Inkorporowane*, the Polish Workingmen's Hall Association Incorporated. The mortgage was signed by Jan Solnica as president and Piotr Górecki as secretary, while the first Board of Directors of the new corporation included Tomasz Mótyka, Jan Solnica, Jan Sliski, Andrzej Lorek, Piotr Górecki and Wojciech Nowak. The Constitution Committee established to provide the official working documents necessary for incorporation was chaired by Ludwik Leśnicki, with the legal assistance of attorney John Buckley. The document the Committee designed was simple, but effective. Open to "Any Polander of general honesty and in full sympathy with the true labor movement," it called for meetings to be held at least once each month on a permanent date with officers selected by the Board of Directors for terms of one year. The six Directors were elected by the general membership for terms of six years, with their terms staggered so that two new members were elected every two years. All officers charged with the handling of "money, funds or property" of the Association were required to post a $1,000 bond "for the faithful performance of the duties of said office." The business of the Association was carried on by the Board of Directors, with changes in the by-laws requiring a two-thirds majority vote of the membership.[19]

The construction of Union Hall proved to be of tremendous significance to the village's Polish community. As soon as it was completed it became a center for social and cultural activities. St. Mary's Parish used the hall for functions that were too large for the small church, Józef Powroźnik led rehearsals and concerts by the newly-formed St. Cecilia's Choir, and men's organizations put on plays, held smokers, and scheduled their meetings there. Union Hall hosted dances, weddings, showers and minstrel shows. The Felician Sisters directed parish plays and children's recitals, while the annual New Year's Eve dance was a social highlight of the year.[20]

Chief among the diversions in the new hall were elaborate theatrical productions and concerts by the Polish band. Early Polish bands marched in parades and played outdoors at picnics and other social functions. They included brass, drums, clarinets, and other popular American instruments of the day. The predominant music at weddings and dances was more traditional in nature, consisting mainly of strings, three or four pieces in number, the lead instrument invariably being a violin, accompanied by a second violin and a string bass played with a bow. Most of the musicians and their instruments came from Poland and they could play without sheet music. There were no drummers, accordions or brass as in later years, and clarinets were only gradually introduced beginning in the early 1920s. "They used to play all the

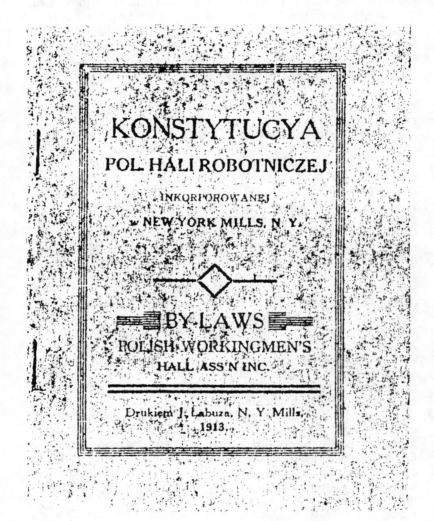

The cover of the constitution of the Polish Workingmen's Hall, 1913.

time, I'm telling you, and that big bass, oh, my gosh, the way he could play that thing. And the violin, too. Why, they were old musicians from Poland. If you would sing to them, boy, they would play, and without any [written] notes. Well, they were all smart, and they could play without notes."[21]

Sometimes a clarinet would be added to the two violins and a bass. As the halls got bigger, clarinets became more standard and trumpets occasionally appeared to increase the volume so it could be heard in the back of the hall. "So when the wedding was at Union Hall in New York Mills, they most naturally had to have five musicians and sometimes six, depending on how big the wedding was. [More musicians] gave out more music, and you could hear it through the whole hall, because the place was really spacious. And if you had a smaller band maybe you couldn't hear it through to the other end of the hall." Dances included traditional Polish regional favorites such as the *mazurka* and *oberek*, as well as waltzes and figure dances.[22]

Regardless of the occasion, the community never failed to pay its respects to its heritage through song or prayer. At social gatherings the Polish band would play a variety of traditional Old World melodies, but the favorite selection was always its sentimental rendition of *Góralu Czy Ci Nie Żal*, the hauntingly emotional "Mountaineer's Song" that served as an unofficial hymn for the village's Polish community. Even the most stout hearted of immigrants, those whose emotions were otherwise hardened by the harsh realities of life and work in the textile industry, could be seen wiping tears from their eyes as the deep voice of Jan Wróblewski led them through the meaningful verses of this touching mountaineer's lament:

> Góralu, czy ci nie żal
> Odchodzić od stron ojczystych,
> Swierkowych lasów i hal,
> I tych potoków przejrzystych?
>
> Góralu, czy ci nie żal?
> Góralu, wracaj do hal!
>
> Góral na góry spoziera,
> I łzy rękawem ociera.
> Ach, góry porzucić trzeba
> Dla chleba, panie, dla chleba.
>
> Góralu, czy ci nie żal?

Góralu, wracaj do hal!

A Góral jak dziecko płacze,
"Może ich już nie zobaczę?"
I poszedł w dal mroczną z kosą,
W guńce starganej i boso.

Góralu, żal mi cię żal,
Góralu, wracaj do hal!

Mountaineer do you not grieve
To leave your fair native land?
Its pine forests and meadows,
Its crystal clear brooks?

Mountaineer do you not grieve?
Mountaineer, return to your meadows!

The Mountaineer turned to the hills,
And wiped the tears with his sleeve.
Farewell, my hills and my valleys,
I must leave thee in search of bread.

Mountaineer do you not grieve?
Mountaineer, return to your meadows!

The Mountaineer wept like a child,
"Perhaps I'll never see you again?"
He walked away into the shadows,
Barefoot, in tattered clothes, carrying his scythe.

Mountaineer, I grieve for you,
Mountaineer, return, pray do![23]

Despite these successes and the renewed enthusiasm which they engendered in the community, all was not entirely well. The gains were many, but the battle continued. The New York State Department of Labor *Bulletin* for the period October 1, 1912 through September 30, 1913 indicated that male and female weavers in the textile mills in Utica received an increase in wages of $1.00 per week on April 17, 1913. Their average weekly rate before the change was $9.50 per week, rising to $10.50 per week after the increase. The textile workers in

Union Hall as it appeared in 1988.

One of the many theatrical productions staged in Union Hall.
The identities of the people are unknown.

New York Mills received no such raises, with skilled weavers making an average of between $9.00 and $10.00 per week at a time when the United States Department of Labor reported the average wage in the cotton textile industry, including *both* skilled and unskilled workers, was $10.10 per week. If the latter was an average for all workers, clearly the skilled weavers were making an average well above $10.00 per week.[24]

By way of further comparison, the *Bulletin* on wages and hours for the year ending September 30, 1913, indicated that of male carders in Utica, 75 received $9.00 per week for 54 hours work, while 25 received $10.00, an average weekly rate of $9.25. In New York Mills at the same time, 30 male carders received $10.00, 40 received $9.00 and 30 received $8.00 for 54 hours work, an average of only $9.00. The differential was not great, but it widened appreciably when one compared male carders in New York Mills to those in Cohoes who received $11.40 per week for 54 hours work. Such conditions caused *Słowo Polskie*, as early as July, 1912, to lament that while some had received a raise, "others experienced a pay cut, and some of the more zealous union members are being dismissed from work to boot."[25]

Aside from lagging behind in wages, there were also continuing problems of inequitable treatment, some of which were exacerbated by Chester A. Braman's continuing attempts to disrupt union activities. Despite the company's assertions of victory following the 1912 strike, there were indications that the collective action of the workers hurt the employers deeply. Braman spent much of the summer and fall of 1912 writing to stockholders to explain why the company could not pay its customary dividends. In a series of letters, he recited a litany of improvements to machinery and the physical plant which he told stockholders actually made their investments more valuable despite the lack of dividends. "While no dividends were earned during the past six months," he asserted, "I consider the property stronger in value and earning power than at any time in the past six years."[26] W. Pierrepont White also stressed the improvements in the physical facilities in his letters to stockholders, but privately in correspondence to Braman he confided that "The labor conditions for 1912 have been such however that the increased savings and the increased earning are not going to put the Company in a position to pay a dividend on the preferred stock on the 1st of February."[27]

Faced with of this reality, White, fearing for his own position, urged Braman to circulate a public statement regarding the improvements made in the mills lest White's credibility within the community be destroyed. Further, it is clear from White's correspondence with Mrs. John B. Ethridge, his cousin, that the economic effect of the 1912 strike was considerably more serious than company officials were willing to make public. "You will note that in 1913 we expect no income from The New York Mills preferred stock," he explained. "They met with a very disastrous strike in March and April of last year, with the result that they have made no money during the twelve months, and therefore will have none to pay during 1913."[28] In a letter to stockholder Augusta M. Wilcox in Orlando, Florida, White explained the economic situation further, noting that "while the Company lost money for the first six months of 1912, on account of the strike, that during the second six months they earned sufficiently so that the end of the year they stood without any loss for the 12 months."[29] Thus, while the economic effects of the strike lasted into the next year, once the work stoppage ended the company once again began showing a profit that allowed it to break even by February, 1913, and to return profits thereafter.

Although the company quickly began showing a profit once the mills were reopened, Braman and the other A. D. Juilliard officials had no intention of allowing another strike to develop. Over the course of the next year Braman relentlessly pursued those known to be union activists, especially the Kozaks upon whom he placed a large share of the blame for the 1912 strike because their hall was used as a union meeting place. In addition to its attempts to entrap the men by sending detectives to purchase liquor on Sundays, the company also placed detectives at work in the mills to infiltrate the union and obtain information from within. In June, 1912, W. Pierrepont White reported to Braman that his private detectives had secured evidence against the Kozaks that would be placed before the Grand Jury at its next meeting, and by the end of that month White reported the conviction of Stanisław Mikus, Bronisław Sliski and Józef Krouse on evidence obtained by these detectives. Not content with this victory, White also attempted to influence the court in its sentencing. "I saw Judge Hazard," he told Braman, "and talked over the situation with him, and told him that a fine did not seem to be of any aid in helping these people to learn to observe the law, and that it seemed to me necessary to try a fine and imprisonment."[30]

Despite the continuing efforts of White and Braman, however, the Kozaks proved an elusive foe. In July Braman lamented that he was "very sorry indeed that they did not imprison Kozak. As long as this man is allowed to get off by paying a fine we will have trouble at the New York Mills. We must reach him somehow and get him out of the town."[31] Nor were the two company executives interested only in the Kozaks. In the months following the conclusion of the 1912 strike the company made a concerted effort to close down all of the union's previous meeting places on the grounds that they were violating the liquor laws. Among the other recipients of this scrutiny were a saloon at 428

Main Street operated by Stanisław Mikus and Wawrzyniec Głód, the Rose Lawn hall owned by Józef Smoła, a tavern at 520 Main Street operated by Jan Zając [using the English name John Roberts], a saloon at 60 Asylum Street run by Bronisław Sliski, and a saloon on Henderson Street operated by Józef Krouse.[32]

At the beginning of 1913 White and Braman were still pursuing the Kozaks and their fellow businessmen. The Kozaks, however, devised a strategem that appeared to have both the company and its detectives quite perplexed. In order to avoid having their liquor license revoked, the Kozak brothers placed the license in the name of Bertha Kozak, while operating the business themselves. Thus, though they might be arrested, they could only be fined. Since the owner of the license was not charged, the license could not be revoked. "The question raised is a novel one," White informed Braman, "and not before decided."[33] Nevertheless, the company persisted in its attempts to run the brothers out of town, while also continuing its efforts against other union activists. By February, 1913, Braman was still insisting that "we must get Motyka. It may be a rather long fight, but we think we will eventually land him. This man has been a trouble breeder wherever he has been."[34] Faced with these continuing assaults upon their members and supporters, the union began to react.

As early as August, 1912, there was a meeting of Local 753 at Kozak's hall to discuss why the company fired Jan Solnica, the union's financial secretary, and Michał Wolak, a union activist. It was decided to pursue the matter further, with the stipulation that if the company did not reinstate the two men a new strike would be considered. In addition, the union decided to press a demand for the firing of Jan Dudrak "who reveals the union's resolutions to all the bosses and singles out particular individuals who conduct more vigorous union activity."[35]

Another serious complaint related to the company's use of a "card system" that required an employee who wished to apply for a different position in any of the factories to obtain a card signed by his previous boss. The workers regarded this as an infringement on their liberties making it very difficult for them to seek better employment. "America is a 'free' country and New York Mills lies in America," *Słowo Polskie* observed. "As it happens there are 'passes' or 'passports' which do not do anybody any good, but rather nail the worker in such a way that even if he lives on [trolley] line 1, he has to work on line 3, because Mr. 'boss' will not hand out a 'pass' and the next one will not give work without the passport. And so the tramway company takes the poor wages of the worker each day because to walk on foot from No. 1 to No. 3 is not very practical."[36]

Given the continuing disparity in wages, and the failure of the New York Mills Corporation to adhere to its 1912 agreement to insure better and more equitable treatment for the workers, in 1913 Local 753 "presented demands for improved conditions."[37] By this time, however, the textile industry was feeling the effects of a recession, while some problems also apparently developed between union and non-union workers as *Słowo Polskie* noted that there were "scabs" among the workers who would not support the union's cause, nor contribute to the construction of Union Hall. In fact, on July 17 it carried strong editorial comments that "To the extent that the building of the hall is moving along briskly, so are the enemies of the working class stirring up a hell of slander and despicable instigations against those who are taking charge of the building project. On one day it is heard that this one or the other is going to take over the hall, on another, the threat of quarrels and dissensions, or even that the hall is going to be a Mason hall. Don't worry about such trivia!"[38]

In any event, on July 11, 1913, an open union meeting was held at Mickiewicz Hall, 730 Whitesboro Street in Utica to try and reinvigorate the union cause. "It is extremely important that all union members attend and straighten out their arrears," secretary Stefania Węgiel wrote in *Słowo Polskie*, "since it is not certain what will be happening in the near future if the company with their '*bosami*' [bosses] do not stop oppressing the worker at each step as they are beginning to do again. Therefore, everybody please come."[39]

Then, a few days later on July 16, some 300 members of Local 753 gathered on the property on St. Stanislaus Street where the hall was to be erected. Called by President Tomasz Mótyka, the purpose of the meeting was to discuss the increase in anti-union agitation by company agents, and to clarify the workers' complaints of ill-treatment that led to a walk-out by twenty-four employees in No. 1. As *Słowo Polskie* reported, "The complaints spilled forth from the lips of female workers carrying children on their arms, [and] there were also many girls complaining about the injustices that they encountered day after day." In one instance, the wife of Mr. Pezdek, who lay sick at home with an illness that would soon cost him his life, stayed home from work to tend to her husband. As *Słowo Polskie* reported, "During the time of Mr. Pezdek's illness the French *nahajka* [from a Russian word meaning knout, the knotted whip used for whipping criminals] from No. 2 turned out to be a lousy descendent of the great Lafayette. When the wife of the fatally ill Pezdek did not come to work on Tuesday, the French *nahajnik* told her that he did not care whether her husband was ill or even dying, she was supposed to come to work if she did not want to lose her job permanently." One of the strongest complaints was apparently against an Irish boss in No. 1 who reportedly used foul language in front of women employees. "If this crimp does not stop using profanity on Polish women, whose shoes he is not worthy to untie," *Słowo Polskie* threatened, then he will soon "get his 'what for' and nothing will help him as he goes before the judge. Let the company translator translate that to him in English."[40]

After everyone had an opportunity to voice their grievances, under the cloudless skies where their hall was soon to be erected, Mótyka said a few brief words before introducing Ludwik Leśnicki, Mr. Wurzowski and Stefan Zamoryłło, each to speak in turn. The reporter for *Słowo Polskie* wrote that "In the eyes of some we saw tears at the time during the speech of the 'revolutionary' who finished his speech more or less in this manner: 'And if the struggle for our fate, a struggle for a piece of daily bread, to which we all are entitled, is a crime, then I am a criminal, and it makes me happy that I can be one. And I will go today or tomorrow, wherever they are fighting for this bread, because I have to go there, because I am needed there, because I ought to be there.'"[41] Following the speeches a committee was formed to pursue the complaints further and report at a meeting to be held the following Saturday.[42]

At the request of Local 753, John Golden, President of the U.T.W.A., directed labor organizer Joseph Minszewski to travel to New York Mills to lend the weight of the U.T.W.A. to the union's efforts to secure agreement on the reinstatement of the fired members and the treatment of workers in the mills. Minszewski later reported that he had "several conferences and meetings, making gradual progress toward a settlement" that prevented the walkout in No. 1 from becoming a general strike. The result, again according to Minszewski's report to the U.T.W.A., was that the fifty-four-hour week recently mandated in New York State for women and children was obtained for all employees, along with the promise of "a ten per cent. increase for piece and day workers."[43] Yet, subsequent events proved that the "settlement" was more elusive than Minszewski made it appear. Within a few weeks Gomólski was reporting to the readers of *Słowo Polskie* that "the union committee returned from the company offices disappointed. ... The company will not give in, and it seems to us that the workers will not give in either! There is only one way to untie the Gordian Knot."[44]

Dissension appears to have continued in the ranks of the workers as *Słowo Polskie* soon noted that the union's pursuit of these matters "does not appeal to the rapscallions for whom the welfare of the worker is a thorn in the finger." Indeed, union leaders told the newspaper that they feared the owners were determined to "chase all the unionists out of New York Mills."[45] On July 24 the Polish newspaper carried a stinging editorial castigating those who did not give the union their wholehearted support:

> "Traitors to the Polish People.
>
> When more than two weeks ago the capitalist flunkies began hurting the Polish workers by firings and cuts in pay, there was no defender of the wronged workers. But when the union committee called an unscheduled meeting, at which there was discussion of the matter of defense before everybody, then the traitors, the foul-smelling scum, the provocateurs with a look of hungry wolves, threw themselves at the committee, threatening and baiting with rancor, snarling in anger about money, money, in order to crush and break the union and help the capitalist flunkies to throw the poor and meek Polish people out of work.
>
> Hands off! you Cains, and especially you damned traitors from the company's stucco building."[46]

Józef Smoła,
union supporter and owner
of a hall where the union
frequently met.

Jan Gomólski,
editor of *Słowo Polskie*, in the
uniform he wore as a volunteer in
the Polish Army in World War I.

Part of the dissension within the Polish community appears to have been inspired by the company's ongoing efforts to disrupt the union. In September, 1913, *Słowo Polskie* reported that company agitators were spreading malicious and slanderous accusations throughout the mills in an attempt to discredit Tomasz Mótyka, Jan Sroka, Jan Puła, the Sliski brothers, and several other union activists. In addition, the unionists were successful in catching a spy, "one of the Polish capitalist flunkies who carried everything heard at the people's gatherings to the company. It is high time to blow these blokes to the four winds because they pollute the air that the decent worker has to breathe."[47]

Aside from the company's machinations, it is also apparent that there were distinct factions developing within the Polish community and the union itself. Central to these cleavages were the role of the church and a growing spirit of independent thinking which some labeled "socialism." It is apparent from the pages of *Słowo Polskie* that not only were union leaders concerned about wavering support, if not outright collaboration with company officials, but that some were in the midst of a feud with Father Fijałkowski who continued to urge restraint and peaceful negotiation. Although the union was able, with the assistance of Minszewski, to secure some promises from company officials, the severe dissension, coupled with the failing national economy, left the union in a weakened condition, unable to press for a more secure agreement.

In 1914 Local 753's official representatives, as recorded with the New York State Department of Labor, were Antoni Knutelski and Franciszek Wadas. During that year the weavers in the New York Mills Corporation filed a grievance over prices and several other issues characterized in official reports as "of minor character." A conference was arranged with company management at which an agreement was reached "in regard to prices" and "promises were made to remedy the other grievances, and the situation was finally adjusted." The published proceedings of the Fourteenth Annual Convention of the U.T.W.A. indicate that these were "not very serious," but were "fraught with dangerous consequences had they not been attended to...."[48]

A clue to the nature of these grievances may be obtained from the pages of *Słowo Polskie* which reported on activities in New York Mills in vivid language, replete with allusions to political conditions in occupied Poland. Employers were characterized as "czars," police were referred to as "Cossacks," and those who were not vigorous supporters of the union were labeled "traitors." The newspapers continuing accounts refer to poor safety conditions that led to recurring accidents such as when a man named Zwierecki injured his toes on a machine in the dye room. In another such incident Józef Domagalski, a worker in the bleachery, was seriously injured when caught in the machinery. As *Słowo Polskie* informed its readers, "He was forced to work all day Friday, that evening, and Saturday until noon without any rest. Thirty hours is a bit too much. Being physically exhausted and half conscious from lack of sleep, he was not careful enough in servicing the machine and he got caught by the hand. In an instant, the machine mangled and broke his hands and ribs. In a hopeless condition he was taken to the hospital."[49]

The treatment of workers in general, and union activists in particular, continued to deteriorate. In August, 1913, for example, the Kiełbasa family was thrown out of their company owned housing without any reason being given for the eviction. "The scabs and spoilers of the union have been rejoicing the past few days because they were able to get a big laugh out of the eviction of Kiełbasa, his wife and children from company housing. Do not rejoice you comics, do not, because he who laughs last laughs best, and you will not be the last to laugh," *Słowo Polskie* warned. "We will be laughing when we get rid of you darling capitalist pawlickers."[50] In another issue Gomólski's acerbic newspaper cautioned that "Every one of you knows that the capitalist slave drivers are just waiting for the moment when they can once again force you under their yoke. It is their goal and they are striving toward it with perseverance. Face them with a solidarity against which the encroachments of the capitalist *fejstrów* [festooners] will crumble."[51]

Supported by both the radical rhetoric of Gomólski's tabloid and the more cautious dissent of the average worker, a committee representing the union went to see the superintendent of the New York Mills Corporation in August, 1913, to seek assurances that grievances would be acted upon and conditions improved. They were told that "the company cannot do any more." The union's officers appealed to the national U.T.W.A. for assistance and within a week Local 753 received a telegram from John Golden assuring them that Organizer Miles would be arriving soon to take up their cause. The intervention of the organizer proved, however, to be unsuccessful. After several days of work, Miles was unable to accomplish any settlement, or to make headway in bringing the two sides together at the negotiating table. The company remained steadfast in its refusal to accede to any of the worker demands, while the union appeared equally unwilling to concede defeat.[52]

The following year, 1914, witnessed an event of great significance to organized labor in the passage of the Clayton Act. Designed to strengthen the Sherman Anti-Trust Act of 1890, it specifically exempted labor unions from being considered monopolies in restraint of trade. Samuel Gompers likened this to a Magna Carta for labor, freeing it from restraints on organization and the use of strikes and boycotts to gain employer concessions.[53]

The beginning of that same year witnessed a continuation of falling prices and rising unemployment, an atmosphere that continued to weaken the union's bargaining position. Records of the New York State Department of Labor indicate that membership in Local 753, which numbered more than 1,000 men and women in the wake of the 1912 strike, decreased to some 900 by September 1913 and to a mere 700 by September 1914. Although most of the union members appear to have remained loyal, as layoffs occurred the number of employees decreased, and with it, naturally, the number of union members.[54] Union officials, however, began to detect something more sinister and calculating in the continuing closure of the mills, as Antoni Knutelski explained in a frank letter to *Słowo Polskie* in July, 1914:

> "Unemployment in the local factories continues to reign, while the factory officials are actually encouraging the people and keep announcing that within a short period of time they will be hiring in the factories all the workers, but they have been promising this for several weeks and the factories are still standing idle.
>
> There exists a significant number of unemployed who are waiting for the time when it might please the factory owners to start work in their mills. Something is deteriorating in the economic situation with heavy American industry. A social structure based on exploitation cannot exist for long, which is something the capitalists know very well, so they are trying with this to throw a scare in the people by closing the factories and provoking crises, so that the people would not be drawn to radical social forces. Currently we are witnessing the economic struggle between the exploiters, that is the capitalists, and those exploited, the working class. Workers, defending themselves from exploitation, are calling strikes for which in turn the greedy capitalists, worried about their profits, are taking revenge by closing factories."[55]

Toward the end of the year, however, the outbreak of war in Europe increased the demand for textiles, causing the New York Mills Corporation to recall workers who had been laid off, thereby increasing union enrollment once again. Freed from possible charges of monopolistic restraint of trade, and buoyed by increasing employment as industry geared up to fill wartime orders from the European powers, the status of organized labor began once again to increase. Despite the upturn in business, and the attendant profits which it generated, the New York Mills Corporation showed no indication that it would restore the wage cuts made during the more difficult economic times of 1913-14. Thus, on April 2, 1916, a union committee visited the offices of the New York Mills Corporation to present demands for an increase in wages, abolition of the card system, double pay for overtime work, and a reduction in the number of looms that the weavers were required to tend. The committee was prepared to argue in the first instance that the average wage of $8.00 to $10.00 per week, while perhaps sufficient for a single person, was not at all adequate to meet expenses once an employee was married and forced to support a family. With regard to the card system, the workers felt that the limitations imposed by it were a restriction on their personal liberty that they would not have accepted in Russia, and certainly would not in the United States where freedom was accorded by law. The card system restricted them to one job, thus preventing them from seeking better jobs or improving themselves. Finally, with regard to overtime, this request affected primarily those in the bleachery who were often required to work well into the evening on weekdays, and sometimes into the early morning on Saturday. This additional work was paid at the regular rate, but the workers felt that the hardship involved for the bleachery workers ought to be paid for at double the standard rate. Regarding the looms, the workers argued that operating sixteen Draper looms or eight hand looms was too exhausting. As evidence they pointed to a woman who, the previous Monday, fainted and had to leave the factory. When these demands were not met, Local 753 notified U.T.W.A. headquarters.[56]

About May of 1916 several weavers quit work because they were each forced to operate sixteen looms. When they left, Andrew Young, who replaced George Fish as superintendent of the New York Mills Corporation when Fish objected to the company's strong-arm tactics, sent each a letter demanding that they vacate their company-owned housing. That night the union held a meeting to discuss the situation. It was reported that when Young heard of the meeting he agreed to take the workers back, to reduce the number of looms they were required to operate, and to allow them to remain in the company housing. Despite this agreement, as the *Utica Herald-Dispatch* later reported, "The men went back to work, but were obliged to work as before."[57]

When a committee attempted to approach Young about this breach of the agreement, he refused to meet with it. As a consequence, Jesse Walker, vice president of the United Textile Workers of America, visited New York Mills briefly in mid-June and spoke with Young, who then agreed to meet with the committee. Following Walker's visit, Joseph Minszewski was once again sent to assist in the negotiations. During his visit, he spoke before the Utica Trades Assembly, seeking their support in revitalizing textile unions in the Utica area, and obtained their pledge of assistance. He also visited Young with a committee from Local 753, but no progress was made. In fact, Young, following A. D. Juilliard's company policy to the letter, refused to negotiate with them at all.[58]

Although its officials refused to negotiate, the New York Mills Corporation was not entirely inactive in preparing for the possibility of another strike. Once again, policies and procedures for eliminating union activity were openly discussed among the various officials, while company officers continued to seek a united front with other area manufacturers and to curry the favor of other potential allies. In one such attempt, Chester Braman, aware of the prominence and influence of Father Fijałkowski among his Polish parishioners, wrote to John P. Campbell at the Walcott & Campbell Spinning Company to suggest that he make a financial donation to St. Mary's as a means of securing Fijałkowski's good graces. The letter read as follows:

> "Do you not think that it would be a good idea to send Father Fijalkowski a check for say $100? This man can be of great service, and I believe that by recognizing him in this way, you will get a liberal return on the investment. We have found him intelligent, and fair in any controversy that has arisen with any of his parishioners.
> We sent him quite a check from the main office."[59]

Although Fijałkowski frequently acted as a go-between in discussions between his parishioners and the company, and he continued to support caution and peaceful negotiation, there is no evidence that the company's attempt to curry favor with the Polish priest was effective in turning him to its side. A letter from Stefan Zamorytło to *Słowo Polskie* about this same time provides a good example of how most of Fijałkowski's parishioners felt about the cleric.

> "As our distinguished readers know, at the present time a battle is going on almost everywhere in the world in which the the worker is taking part on one side and the capitalist on the other. It is as if the worker is waking up from a long sleep and, having rubbed his eyes, he sees what is going on around him and how disgracefully he is being exploited by others. The worker has noticed that the capitalist never works, does not know how to work,

takes all the fruits of the worker's labors and in exchange for strenuous labor pays a starvation wage. The worker has finally figured out that there is no justice and that it cannot go on like this any longer. He is getting up the courage in order to go to his exploiter, present his gripe, and lay claim to a larger piece of the pie.

As a result of the fact that the capitalist does not want to agree to the worker's demands and that the worker cannot accomplish anything by legal means, unions are organized. Having organized, the worker goes to battle with capital in order to attain that which rightly belongs to him. The capitalist, worrying about his own skin, searches for all kinds of opportunities which would enable him to hinder the operations of the workers' organization. Most often, in this matter, he appeals to the clergy for help. The majority of the clergy tends to forget that the clergy has an obligation to defend the common folk. Instead of imitating Christ, the clergy imitates Judas, for when the capitalist pays, they take his side and with all their strength try to keep the worker in the capitalist's servitude as long as possible.

Lucky are the workers in New York Mills, where the pastor is the venerable Father A. Fijałkowski. He is a priest and pastor in the full sense of the word. Father F. not only does not interfere in the organization of workers unions, but he himself works upon improving the material situation of his parishioners. The facts testify to this. Whenever one of the local workers is in any way wronged by the bosses or the superintendents and requests help, the Most Reverend Pastor, in other words the noble-minded Father F., never refuses. On the other hand, he goes with the wronged party to the main office and intercedes in order to redress the injustice.

Though, by acting so, Father F. lays himself open to disapproval from the side of capital, he all the same does not take notice of this and stands firmly in defense of the worker. If all the parishes had such pastors as Father Fijałkowski, the fight over bread would be, without a doubt, much easier. Firstly: no one would bother the worker in his endeavors, secondly: the capitalist, not having the support of the clergy, would more quickly give in to the workers' demands. So hats off to Father A. Fijałkowski, who in every respect deserves it."[60]

When no progress was made in the negotiations locally, Minszewski notified John Golden, national president of the U.T.W.A., who met with the owners of the New York Mills Corporation in New York City in an effort to spur substantive discussions. The only result of this was that Young met with Minszewski and the committee from Local 753 and told them that the company could not increase wages. Further, Young indicated that the company would not abolish the card system, which he defended as something that was actually advantageous to employees.[61]

With no progress in the offering, several union meetings debated the remaining options. Finally, on Friday evening, July 14, a long meeting received and discussed the report of the negotiating committee. This completed, the workers decided, with but one dissenting vote, to go on strike if the company maintained its refusal to negotiate employee demands. A committee was again appointed to see Young in a last attempt at negotiated settlement. Once again, Young refused to discuss the employees' grievances. Thus, on Monday evening, July 17, the committee met and determined to go on strike at 8:00 a.m. the following day.[82]

Chapter 7

"United We Stand"

On Tuesday morning, July 18, 1916, employees of the various factories in New York Mills went to work at 7:00 a.m. as usual. One hour later some 1,000 workers went out on strike from the textile mills owned by the New York Mills Corporation, while another 200 struck the Oneida Bleachery and still 200 more walked out of the Walcott & Campbell Spinning Company on Sauquoit Street. Though mainly Polish, the ranks of the strikers included Italians, Syrians, French and people of other nationalities as well. Their decision to walk out was not easy. Most of the workers were poor, living from payday to payday on barely enough to provide the necessities of life. Many had families to support, while some contributed to families in Europe made destitute by the wartime conditions. Thus, the decision to strike was a painful one, fraught with both predictable and unforeseen consequences. Reluctant though many were, they knew their lot would not improve unless they stood together. Yet, the courage of their convictions did not make their decision any easier and as they left the factories that morning many openly wept.[1]

Predictably, company officials reacted by immediately calling upon Sheriff William K. Harvey to provide protection for their property. Before the day was out the sheriff administered the oath to twenty-five special deputies, while the Walcott & Campbell Company arranged to hire an additional twenty guards from a Utica detective agency to patrol its property.[2]

Throughout the morning the strikers and their families gathered at Union Hall in the sweltering heat and humidity of what was to be an oppressively hot summer. Gradually, a crowd estimated at about one thousand men, women and children, all of them perspiring profusely, completely filled the hall with many forced to stand along the walls or outside for lack of room. At 10:30 a.m., Jan Sroka, president of Local 753, ascended the stage where, flanked by two large American flags and signs reading "Strajk," he called the meeting to order. Speaking in Polish, he outlined the grievances which led to the strike, the attempts to bring these matters to the attention of company officials, and the resulting decision to strike when it became apparent that the complaints would be ignored. After calling upon those assembled to stand fast in their demands, Sroka introduced Rudolf Ząbek, former president of Local 753 during the 1912 strike. Ząbek had since moved to Chicago where he became involved in raising funds for the relief of war victims in Europe. He was visiting New York Mills to speak on behalf of the war relief effort when the strike began. Ząbek called for everyone to obey the laws of their adopted country at which the audience rose as one to pledge themselves to stand by their demands in a peaceful, orderly manner. Ząbek also demanded that the strikers pledge to avoid the use of alcoholic beverages, noting that any union member who appeared in an intoxicated state during the strike would be expelled from the organization. "We are all Americans," he proclaimed loudly, the audience now applauding his every statement. "We want nothing more than what Americans 10 or 20 years ago were striving for."[3] The loud applause rose to a crescendo as men, women and children came to their feet in the stifling hot room, shouting their approval.

Following Ząbek, Joseph Nawer, a Syrian worker, spoke to his people in their native language, covering the same points explained earlier to the Polish workers. When he finished, those assembled elected a committee of twelve, including representatives from each of the ethnic groups present, to manage the negotiations with employers and the details of providing assistance to the families of the strikers. It was also announced that anyone who required financial assistance could apply to the committee for funds from the union local's treasury.[4]

After the meeting the strike leaders met with the press. Antoni Knutelski, secretary of Local 753, assisted by Ząbek, described to reporters the most important of their grievances and demands. First, the two men explained, the workers in the mills were poorly paid. Weavers, among the more skilled of the workers, and therefore among the better paid, made only between $8.00 and $11.00 per week, while spinners made from $8.00 to $10.00 for the same period. Thus, one very important demand was an increase in wages, but the union was willing to leave the actual amount of the increase to negotiations.[5]

Secondly, since the beginning of the year weavers had been forced to manage as many as sixteen Draper looms, where previously they were responsible for only ten. Knutelski and Ząbek asserted that such numbers not only resulted in reduced wages, but were unsafe for the operators. Regarding the safety issue, the Poles explained that under the new rules operatives were required to tend eight double or sixteen single looms. The rapid pace required to manage such a workload often resulted in injuries when fingers became caught while attempting to change shuttles. The workers, their representatives said, were willing to operate six double or ten single looms.[6]

Third, the two Poles told reporters that their people objected strenuously to the "card system," which functioned like a "blacklist," preventing workers from moving about to seek advancement or better employment. Under this system, any worker applying for a new position was obliged to provide a card from the mill where he or she was last employed. By withholding these cards, employers could prevent workers from seeking better jobs. "This limits our personal liberty," Ząbek stressed, noting also that there appeared, as well, to be a pattern of discrimination against union members.[7]

The company's response to the strike was considerably less vocal or detailed. Much as in 1912, the employers indicated their dismay, maintaining that they had no warning of a strike and could think of no legitimate reason why it should occur. An official of the Walcott & Campbell Spinning Company told reporters that until the walkout began he believed the workers were completely satisfied. Those in the spinning mill, he said, received an increase amounting to some fifteen percent only a few months earlier, thus he knew of no reason why they should go on strike.[8] Similarly, James F. Hubbell, attorney for the New York Mills Corporation, adopted the same posture in a more formal statement expressing A.D. Juilliard's position that the strike was both unanticipated and unjustified. In it he said:

> "The company is always ready to listen to any grievance the employees may have or think they have, but the present demand for more money will not be granted. If a committee is sent by the employees, it may be received, but it will not result in anything, as far as more pay is concerned. I do not believe the majority of the employees are dissatisfied. There is a certain element of malcontents who started this thing, and the others simply fell in. I believe most of those who have stopped work are willing to return."[9]

Hubbell's statement completely ignored the attempts representatives of Local 753 and the United Textile Workers of America made beginning as early as April, 1916, to discuss employee grievances with company officials. Whether the attorney, or the New York Mills Company, actually believed that the majority of workers were satisfied, or whether they were simply posturing for public consumption, cannot be determined. Regardless, before long the strikers proved their resolve.

"Today the mills were idle," noted the *Utica Herald-Dispatch* on the second day of the strike. "It was said that not a wheel was turning in any of the big factories and that the only persons at work were a few machinists, who were making repairs. A drowsy calm pervaded the

village and men, women and children loafed wherever they could find a
shady shelter from the intense heat."[10] When a reporter visited the
offices of the New York Mills Corporation to inquire about the complaints raised by the union, Andrew Young, Superintendent of the New
York Mills Corporation, refused to see him.[11] A. D. Juilliard's policy,
as 1912, was clearly to refuse comment on specifics in the hope that
the strikers would soon become disaffected once their money ran out,
and then return of their own accord.

The day was oppressively hot, with some strikers commenting that
they would rather be outside on a day like that than working in any
factory. At 2:45 p.m. an overflow crowd gathered at Union Hall. Jan
Sroka, who presided, delivered a brief speech before turning the podium
over to Rudolf Zabek. The latter spoke for nearly an hour on the general status of labor in the United States. He noted that the condition of
workers had improved greatly in recent years, maintaining also that
when workers are treated well they are more productive. Zabek drew
upon the example of Henry Ford as an enlightened owner who considered all of his workers to be valuable. "He makes it a point to see how
his workmen live and tries to control conditions so that they will live
well," Zabek explained. "He says if living conditions are improved, the
workmen will be more capable. He raised the wages of his workmen
until each receives at least $5 a day, and he is satisfied to pay them this
as he still has a profit. If the company here says it can not afford to
raise wages, it is not true. In many places when wages have been
raised, the workmen have proved themselves more efficient." Next,
Zabek compared labor movements in the United States with those in
Europe. It was Tolstoy, he told his audience, "who said that the spirit
of a strike is not revolutionary, but a passive form of struggle by which
workmen can attain their ends." Zabek applauded the strikers for adopt-
ing this passive form of resistance, assuring them that they "will show
by their conduct that the authorities do not need to send policemen or
deputy sheriffs here, for the workmen will keep order themselves."[12]

A deafening applause followed Zabek's remarks. Then Joseph
Nawer spoke briefly to his Syrian compatriots. Joseph Minszewski
followed Nawer, taking the opportunity to stress the justice of the
strike and to emphasize how the strikers should conduct themselves.
Minszewski also noted that employment opportunities in the textile
industries were good and that if the strike proved long the striking
workers might be taken to other cities to seek employment in areas
where they were then needed. An Italian speaker was called for, but
none could be found. Finally, as a last order of business, the *Utica
Daily Press* reported that "Owing to the heat, it was resolved to have
the next meeting at a cooler hour in the day."[13]

Jan Kwieciński,
representative to the national
U.T.W.A. in 1916

Jerzy Kozakiewicz,
trustee of Local 753.

Józef Piszcz,
community activist and
union supporter.

Józef Nowicki,
one of the village businessmen
who supported the strikers.

"We are ready for a long, long fight, if one is needed," Ząbek told reporters after the meeting. "We are prepared. We did not expect that the company would accept our most important demands. Whether the national organization is back of us or not, we are going to stand by our demands. We will fight it out alone as a local union, if need be, but we will receive some aid from the national organization anyway."[14]

Despite the efforts of both Minszewski and the strike committee of Local 753, the employers steadfastly refused to treat with the workers. At the offices of the New York Mills Corporation the strikers' representatives were informed that Superintendent Young was out of town and may or may not return the next day. At the Walcott & Campbell Company they were told that John P. Campbell, superintendent of that facility, was away on vacation and could not be reached. At the Oneida Bleachery the story was the same, Superintendent Alexander F. Hobbs was unavailable and could not be reached.[15]

At another long meeting on July 20, once again presided over by Jan Sroka at Union Hall, the strikers decided to extend a formal request to mill officials for a meeting with the strike committee. They transmitted the request by telephone, but once again the response from mill officials was that both Young and Campbell were out of town. This made it obvious, the strikers felt, that company officials were simply avoiding them. "We are willing to confer with the employers at any time it is possible to do so," a strike leader informed the press in an attempt to make their position clear. "We are the workmen and they are the owners and we do not expect that they will come to us. We would like to have a conference with them and we are not too proud to ask it. We would like to have a conference and have shown our willingness to confer."[16] This position showed a conciliatory stance, as well as indicating a recognition of the class deference expected during that age.

The strikers also took advantage of the presence of the press to convey their disgust with the so-called "American" workers who continued to cross their picket lines. Long the butt of criticism from Anglo-Saxon Americans that they brought down wage scales and were otherwise detrimental to the welfare of American labor, the Poles were angry that their critics refused to join them in the struggle for better wages and improved working conditions. It was, the Poles reasoned, yet another example of the prevalent racism to which they were constantly subjected. The bitterness of this disappointment was apparent in their remarks to reporters:

> "These people have been frequently ridiculing the Polish people and saying that they are willing to work for nothing and work under any conditions. But now that the Polish people are striking for better wages and for better

treatment from the employers, to be consistent these men who have blamed us heretofore should now be with us instead of being against us. They are always kicking on the Polish people, but now that the Polish people are trying to get better pay and better conditions they at least expected that these men would be favorable to them. We will be very sorry if they continue to work under the circumstances or if they try to get other workmen in. When we ask what pay they get they decline to let us know. We believe they would be out striking with us if they did not receive better pay than we do. They say the Polish people are crazy and do not know what they are doing. If they receive [sic] the same wages as we do they would not think so."[17]

That same afternoon, July 20, the first conference took place between the strike committee and officials at the Oneida Bleachery when Joseph Minszewski and two representatives of Local 753, along with Jan P. Baran who acted as interpreter, spoke with Fred Geissler, a Bleachery official. During the meeting the strike representatives asked that production bonuses then being paid in the Bleachery be paid directly to the workers by the main office, rather than through the supervisors. Geissler agreed. The second complaint voiced by the strikers was, as reported in the press, "that they had been insulted at times and that profane and abusive language had been applied to them."[18] Geissler replied that Bleachery officials would gladly hear any specific evidence of such instances, and that remedial action would be taken to assure fair and proper treatment. Upon the conclusion of the meeting Minszewski reported some progress, but indicated that the crucial questions of abolition of the card system and wage increases were deferred until the return of Alexander F. Hobbs from New York City. No progress was made with either the New York Mills Corporation or the Walcott & Campbell Spinning Company as Andrew Young and John P. Campbell were both said to be away on vacation. The strike leaders determined to await their return to open substantive negotiations.[19]

By the end of the second day of the strike the factories of the New York Mills Corporation were completely shut down, with only a few machinists and watchmen reporting for work. The officers of Local 753 were successful in securing promises of financial assistance for the strikers from the Utica Trades Assembly and several other locals affiliated with the American Federation of Labor.[20] Such support was crucial if the strike lasted more than a few days because Local 753's funds were limited and the walkout was not sanctioned by the national office of the

United Textile Workers of America, thus it was uncertain whether assistance would be available from that source.

Yet, few on either side felt that the work stoppage would last very long. As people lounged about under the trees, playing cards and keeping out of the blistering sun, a lazy calm pervaded the village. "We have a little vacation in hot weather," one striker commented to a reporter. "When we get two or three cents more money we will go back to work."[21]

Despite this attitude, and its posture of public silence, the New York Mills Corporation was taking no chances on a prolonged strike. That very morning, three non-striking Poles employed by the company visited Polish families to tell them that if they did not return to work they would be evicted from company owned housing.[22] While refusing to meet with its employees to discuss a settlement to the strike, the New York Mills Corporation was beginning to use the pressure of fear and intimidation to force the strikers back to work. It was also busy counting the number of employees still reporting for work, while at the same time sending agents to nearby localities to inquire about the availability of additional labor to supplement its nucleus of bosses, machinists and company officials not on strike.

Active in these recruiting efforts was Józef Myśliwiec, a long-time employee hired as a translator and recruiter because of his fluency in both English and Polish. Myśliwiec was successful in attracting many Poles to New York Mills from the textile centers in Massachusetts, thereby earning the favor of company officials. When the union was successful, during the 1912 strike, in obtaining the company's agreement to hire a translator to act as a personnel officer to assist the Polish employees, Myśliwiec was given that role because of the trust company officials placed in him. "If a Polish person wanted a job and the boss wouldn't give them one," Bertha Kozak recalled, "they'd go to see Joe and then Joe would help them out. He'd talk to the boss and ask the boss the reason why. He was for the people. The Polish people didn't resent the position he held because they were happy they had someone who helped them out on their side because, you know, some people who couldn't get a job, they'd go '*do Myśliwieca*' and he'd help them out. He'd talk to the boss."[23]

Gradually, Myśliwiec's role in administering personnel matters grew to encompass the handling of job tickets issued by bosses when they needed help, and to management of the company's houses. By 1916 he had already become a part of management, trusted by company officials to deal with their Polish employees, although not attaining the status within the company that Anglo-Saxon's with positions of equal importance enjoyed. Nevertheless, Myśliwiec was management, not labor, and when the strike came he chose to stay with the company rather than walk out. This, coupled with the active role that he played on behalf of the company during the strike, cast him as a traitor in the eyes of his fellow Poles. More than a half-century after the strike, some of those who lived through it still recalled with bitterness and anger the role that Myśliwiec played.[24]

By Friday morning, July 21, the New York Mills Corporation, with the aid of Myśliwiec and others, assembled some 150 workers, mostly Anglo-Saxon Americans along with a few Italians from Utica, who gathered at Mill No. 3 in an attempt to resume partial operation of the velvet and corduroy production in that facility. To its attempts at spreading fear and intimidation, the company obviously planned to place further pressure on the strikers by preparing to reopen manufacturing operations. In doing so, the company hoped that the sight of the mills in operation would be sufficient to lure many of the strikers back, perhaps causing a split between the Poles and the other groups, or among the Poles themselves. Any such schism within the ranks of the strikers would make it considerably easier for the company to emerge victorious.[25]

The significance of the company's actions can be seen when Jan Sroka opened the daily meeting of the strikers with a call for unity, after which he introduced Joseph Nawer, who spoke to the Syrian strikers for over an hour. Following his oration some fifty of their number signed an application for a union charter for a new Syrian local. All of the Syrians received lapel buttons to show their support for the strike. Benjamin Shiro, business agent and corresponding secretary of Local 35 of the Hod Carriers and Building Laborers of America, then addressed the Italian strikers in another speech which lasted nearly an hour. As a result, several Italian strikers signed papers making an official application for the establishment of an Italian union local. "Victory will be ours in a short time if you stick together," Shiro exhorted his followers. "The only way for workers to get right conditions and money from employers is by organization. In this fight you are not Polish or Italian or Syrian, but all one. You must tell the mill people that you want no card system; the time is past for that sort of thing. You want a committee which, when anyone is discharged, can go to headquarters and ask why that person was discharged and tell them they must take him back or you will shut down the mill. United we stand, divided we fall."[26] Shiro was interrupted several times by applause from the Italians. There would be no fear, he asserted, of the Italians returning to work until the strike was satisfactorily settled.[27]

Given the language barriers, the strike committee decided it would be more effective to enroll strikers into unions comprised of their own nationality than to try and mix all of the nationalities into Local 753.[28]

Although seemingly a rational move to facilitate communication, this had the effect of fragmenting the strikers, leaving them open to divisions that might not have occurred had all of them been enrolled into a single union as was the case during the 1912 strike. In retrospect, this was probably a mistake because the separation of ethnic groups into different unions was not conducive to either unity or understanding.

When the Syrians and Italians finished pledging their unity with the Polish strikers, Ząbek, referring to the morning's attempts by the New York Mills Corporation to bring workers into its facilities, called for the establishment of picket lines to dissuade those who had returned to work, or any others who might be so inclined. Then, reminding the audience of the "difficulty that would be encountered by pickets of one nationality in trying to appeal to workers of another nationality," and of the "possibility of friction if any argument should occur between pickets and workers," he suggested that one method by which such misunderstanding and trouble could be avoided was for the pickets to use printed cards bearing a statement of the strikers grievances.[29] Picketing lent a physical presence that psychologically bolstered the spirits of the strikers, while at the same time presenting an emotional barrier to those who wished to enter the mills. It was a necessary step, though also one that would certainly increase the possibility of confrontation.

On the same day Sheriff Harvey placed signs about the village that contained, in English, Polish and Italian, the following notice:

> "In the name of the People of the State of New York. All persons in the villages of New York Mills and Yorkville, so-called, who are unlawfully assembled are commanded to immediately disperse.
>
> The sheriff's department is not interested in any manner as to the outcome of the strike now pending, but its duty is to see that order is preserved, and it will discharge said duty. All persons violating the law will be arrested.
>
> William K. Harvey,
> Sheriff"[30]

Saturday, July 22, was pay day in New York Mills. Some 1,000 strikers received their wages, but several complained that their pay envelopes were shorted. They went with an interpreter to the mill officers to resolve the situation.[31] Although no overt trouble occurred during the disbursement of pay, the morning was not to pass in complete peace.

That morning the first acts of violence occurred when three people, two of them strikers, were assaulted by a special deputy thought to be

David Alexander, the same man who was conspicuous as a company instigator during the 1912 strike. The incident began when a New York Mills man, on his way to work in neighboring Whitesboro, stopped along a sidewalk in the former village to await a friend. Witnesses reported a deputy approached and who ordered him to move along. When he attempted to explain that he was just waiting for a friend to walk to work, the deputy struck him with his club without warning. Soon after, a striker who paused on the sidewalk to roll a cigarette was shoved by the same guard who insisted that he keep moving. Still later, a woman who "failed to move promptly when ordered to do so" was jabbed about the chin and breast with a nightstick by the same deputy. Outraged by the deputy's conduct, Minszewski indicated to the press that he planned to bring the incidents to the attention of Sheriff Harvey so that the situation could be resolved before it became serious.[32] Indeed, the incidents of that morning appeared at the time to be an isolated case of a single overzealous deputy that did not reflect the general treatment of strikers within the village. The Poles, in fact, remained confident of Sheriff Harvey's good intentions to remain neutral in their dispute with the mill owners.

During the day pickets were on duty handing out pink cards, printed in English, that urged those working to join the strike. About 150 workers reported for work in Mill No. 3, with a few also on hand in the Bleachery. At noon when some workers went home for lunch, and again at the end of the day, they were taken from the mills in automobiles so they could not be approached by the pickets. No tension was apparent. The strikers handed their cards to those whom they could reach, while reporters noted that the pickets appeared good natured.[33]

Shortly before 2:00 p. m. that afternoon a triumvirate of strike leaders including Joseph Minszewski, Jan Baran and Józef Sypek visited the Oneida Bleachery to speak with Hobbs and Geissler, but were told that Hobbs had not yet returned. Soon after they left, however, officials at the Bleachery telephoned Sroka to indicate their willingness to meet again.[34] Later, when a reporter of the *Utica Observer* telephoned the Bleachery, Geissler told him that officials there were willing to meet with the strikers. "We are willing to do what is right by the employees," Geissler insisted. "We have always tried to do right by them and we want to do it now."[35] At least one group of officials were publicly committed to meeting with the strike committee.

The *Utica Saturday Globe* of July 22 contained profusely illustrated coverage of the strike that was generally favorable to the strikers. The photographs included several of women and children that could not help but effect the sympathies of readers on behalf of the strikers. The paper also took pains to assure its readers that everything was indeed peaceful.

"Unless one knew beforehand that there was a big strike on in New York Mills he would never imagine it by passing along the streets of that village these fine days, unless he happened to stray into the Polish Workingmen's Hall. The streets are scenes of peaceful quiet. Here and there one may see little groups of men, women and children on the steps and lawns, but they are all visiting or playing card games or reading. As is usually expected in such cases, there are no street orators hurling maledictions at mill owners, no threats, no disturbance. The mills are still and a Sunday quiet prevails. Some of the men are talking of having a parade, but the proposition excites little enthusiasm. The strikers simply gather at the hall and discuss the proposition calmly. It is their desire to confer with their employers and settle the matter satisfactorily and, if that cannot be done many of the men have declared their intention of seeking work elsewhere."[36]

The calm abated briefly about 5:00 p.m. when a villager named Ryczek, who previously bought some hay from the New York Mills Corporation, arrived at No. 4 to pick up his purchase. The night watchman refused to admit him, citing orders to let no one pass. Ryczek, he said, would have to obtain a special order from Superintendent Young before being allowed entrance. Ryczek went to Young, received the order, and returned once again to claim his purchase. The watchman agreed to allow him to pass, but a deputy sheriff now interceded, indicating that the watchman had no authority to admit anyone to the company's property. Once again Ryczek was turned away, but not before the situation escalated. As the *Utica Daily Press* reported, with some humor,

"It was now a question of authority between the watchman and deputy and it was argued so strenuously that the watchman struck the deputy twice and the deputy fought back and there was a lively scrimmage which ended in the deputy being fired. Mr. Rizek [*sic*] secured his hay and all went well. What amuses the strikers is that such elaborate preparations should have been made to 'preserve order' among the strikers and then to have the first row start among those who are hired to guard against outbreaks by the strikers."[37]

The oppressive heat which continued into Sunday, July 23, did not prevent members of the Polish community from scaling the hill to attend Mass at St. Mary's. There, they heard Father Fijałkowski, who consistently voiced support for his parishioners in their struggle against the employers, counsel them "to remain peaceable and dodge any trouble." If they remained peaceful, he assured them, "the strike would be settled to the advantage of all."[38]

The rest of the day the people spent lounging in the shade or enjoying the festivities of an afternoon picnic. The quiet calm of Sunday was indeed symbolic of the lack of activity that thus far characterized efforts to settle the strike. At a meeting in Union Hall at 9:30 a.m. on Monday morning Sroka called upon Minszewski for an update on the situation. The organizer indicated that no change had taken place over the weekend, but that he expected to meet with Hobbs later that afternoon following the latter's return from New York City. No progress at all was made in arranging a meeting with either the New York Mills Corporation or the Walcott & Campbell Spinning Company. He urged the strikers to stand firm, but to maintain a calm, peaceful attitude, remaining at all times within the bounds of law. By pursuing a peaceful course, he once again stressed, the strikers would gain the support of the public and eventually win concessions. He assured those assembled that no strike-breakers were being employed, while also announcing that he complained to Sheriff Harvey about the abuses of Deputy Alexander and obtained assurances that there would be no repetition. Minszewski urged all to remain either in the hall or at home, and to avoid being on the street so as not to provoke any disturbance. Sroka then took the podium to emphasize the need to remain unified and maintain a peaceful discipline. He counseled, the press reported, "against all attempts at force or coercion, and urged all to stand firm and avoid anything that might be construed as an act of lawlessness."[39]

In the afternoon a wedding reception took place at Union Hall. The formal wedding ceremony took place at St. Mary's at 9:00 a.m. uniting in holy matrimony Wojciech Widor and Agnieszka Zientara. The festivities began in the afternoon, in traditional Polish custom, with the attendants and other guests gathering at the bride's house. A procession wound its way down Main Street and up St. Stanislaus Street to Union Hall where an abundance of food and refreshments were on hand. It was a real community affair. The Polish band played, the guests danced, and everyone temporarily forgot about the strike and the rest of life's hardships.[40]

That evening two men working at No. 3 were heading home along Asylum Street [now Burrstone Road] when they encountered several strikers walking in the opposite direction. One of the latter offered a piece of bread to one of the two workers, who disdainfully threw the bread back, hitting the woman who offered it. The strikers, quickly picking up nearby sticks and stones, chased the man who threw the bread. No animosity was directed toward the other man. When asked by reporters for his opinion on this incident, Sheriff Harvey indicated that it was "nothing serious." Indeed, there was no further unrest that evening, and there is no indication that it was anything other than a minor clash set off by the abuse of the female striker.[41]

The following morning pickets were on duty when the mills opened, but there were no further incidents. During the day the strikers generally kept to their houses, tending gardens, caring for children, or cleaning their homes. The heat and humidity were oppressive, prompting several stories in the local newspapers including one about a man prostrated by the temperature.[42]

That afternoon several children began heckling a worker leaving one of the mills. In response the worker picked up a rock and threw it at the children, but missed them, hitting instead a pregnant woman who was passing by. Passersby took the woman to Dr. Jankiewicz for precautionary treatment, but her injury was apparently minor. The strikers went to the Justice of the Peace for a warrant against the man who threw the stone, only to be refused. Tempers increased, but Minszewski interceded to calm the situation. The authorities did nothing.[43]

At 8:00 a.m. on Wednesday, July 26, some sixty to seventy of the estimated 200 Syrians who were employed by the factories in New York Mills held an open-air meeting on the lawn across from Union Hall to discuss among themselves the issues precipitating the strike and the advisability of forming a Syrian union local. After electing a spokesman to represent their interests, several people spoke both for and against the strike and unionization, including one Syrian community leader from Utica who urged them to go back to their jobs. The vociferous speaker from Utica was apparently not one of the strikers, making his presence somewhat suspect. Was he, perhaps, an agent of the company attempting to promote dissension among the strikers? While his role is uncertain at this point, in the end the Syrians voted against unionization, charging their leader with informing the Poles that they, the Syrians, were willing to give up their union cards and go back to work. "The Syrians say they have no kick about the wages paid or treatment received," the *Utica Herald-Dispatch* reported.[44]

Indeed, most of the "Syrian" population was not really Syrian at all, but rather Lebanese. Much as the Poles had seen their homeland occupied by foreign powers, the Christian Lebanese suffered similar "economic poverty, political oppression and religious persecution" at the hands of the Ottoman Empire. In 1860 Druze Muslims conducted a widespread massacre of Christians throughout the areas that would later become Lebanon and Syria. Much as the United States offered a beacon of hope to Poles in the late nineteenth century, so too did the Syrian and Lebanese Christians look to America for a better, freer life. Some of the Syro-Lebanese population arrived in the Utica area between 1890 and 1915. Many of the Syro-Lebanese engaged in *tijara*, an Arabic term for "mercantile enterprise," becoming self-employed as dry goods merchants, restauranteurs, peddlers and opening other small businesses, while the rest generally sought employment in the various mills throughout the area. By 1903 there were approximately one hundred in the Utica area, with thirty-five already living in New York Mills. When this growing community erected St. Louis of Gonzaga Church in Utica, fifteen of the founding members were residents of New York Mills. Though their numbers were small by comparison to the Poles and Italians, the Syrian workers were important to the strike because many of them were skilled weavers, and because the show of inter-ethnic unity was important for the success of the strike. In the end, while a few crossed the picket lines, most remained loyal to the strikers.[45]

At 9:00 a.m. the Polish strikers convened a meeting in Union Hall, once again filled to overflowing. Several speakers addressed the group. In the longest oration, Minszewski reminded the strikers to avoid trespassing on private property, or doing anything which might provoke trouble. He cautioned that the owners, and perhaps the press, would surely blame the strikers for any disturbance that might occur, thus the only way to avoid losing public support was to stay off the streets and avoid anything that might give the appearance of provocative behavior. The atmosphere at the meeting "might have passed for a church service," noted the *Utica Herald-Dispatch*, "so quiet were the people in paying attention to the speaker."[46]

Following the Polish meeting, when strikers were asked about the decision of the Syrians to return to work they expressed disbelief. The general opinion among the Poles was that this was a ploy orchestrated by company agents. While the Syrians might indeed take other jobs in Utica or the surrounding area, they would surely not return to work in New York Mills so long as the strike lasted. Indeed, this appeared to be the case as over the next few days many of the Syrian strikers left the area to accept positions in nearby Rome and Oneida, but few entered the factories in New York Mills.[47]

That evening Minszewski left for New York City to confer with John Golden about obtaining a $4.00 weekly strike benefit for each union member.[48] Financial assistance from the national U.T.W.A. treasury was essential to the strikers, whose own resources could not possibly support a walkout of more than a few days. With the factory officials clearly playing a waiting game, financial support was needed soon if the strike was to continue.

On July 27 the New York Mills Corporation served a notice signed by Andrew Young on all of the Polish strikers occupying company houses announcing that they were to vacate their homes. It did not specify when they were to leave, thus strikers were advised to ignore the notice, which went only to the Poles, not to the French, Syrian or Italian strikers.[49] Not only was this an attempt to place further pressure on the strikers, but it was probably also an attempt on the part of the company to drive a wedge between the different ethnic groups, separating and isolating the Poles whom they regarded as the source of the labor unrest, by attempting to gain the support of the other groups.

That same morning, possibly in an attempt to divert public attention from the eviction notices, Young, general manager of all the facilities owned by the New York Mills Corporation, made his first public statement to the press. While he claimed to have no formal statement from the company, Young went on to tell reporters that a number of Poles and Syrians confided to him that they really had no grievances and were against going on strike, but were forced to walk out by the other strikers. Then, in an apparent attempt to influence the mercantile community in favor of the company, he noted that the loss of the payroll due to the walkout would place a heavy burden upon businesses in both New York Mills and Utica. Later, when queried by reporters, the local merchants repeated these fears, stating flatly that they wished the strike would end because the strikers were incurring large bills that would take a long time to repay.[50]

Young, continuing his comments, turned to the strikers' claims of low wages, pointedly asserting that the New York Mills Corporation "paid higher wages than were paid by cotton manufacturers in textile mills generally."[51] If they were paid such low wages, he asked rhetorically, why was it that they were able to purchase property and to send large sums of money to Poland for the relief of war victims? To emphasize his point, Young provided a portion of a financial statement that indicated some weavers earned as high as $16.00 to $20.00 per week in June. Skilled cutters earned as high as $18.00 to $21.00 per week in the same month. Young further stated that since 1911 wages increased by a total of about 25%, with some individual departments increasing by 50%, and that two raises were granted within the previous six months.[52]

As to the number of machines operators were required to tend, according to Young it was no greater than at most mills, and in fact less than some competing factories required. Further, the company not only installed new machinery that was easier and safer to operate, but also greatly improved sanitary conditions. "During the past two years the interior of the mills has been painted throughout. Ventilation and sanitation are being brought up to modern requirements," he proudly asserted in an attempt to solicit public favor.[53] A keen observer, however, might have noted that the implication of Young's statement about ventilation and sanitation "being brought up to modern requirements" clearly supported the strikers' claims that these were then below accepted standards. There is no evidence that the press appreciated the significance of this statement as support for the union's position.

But Young was not finished. The company-owned houses, he told reporters, were all improved by the installation of city water lines, painting, papering and renovations, while rents remained low at $1.50 to $2.00 per week depending upon the location of the house and the amount of garden space. "During the year 1915," Young stated, "the amount expended for repairs to the tenements greatly exceeded the amount received in rentals. The rents charged are very much less than at other manufacturing points and are considerably less than what mill operatives are required to pay in Utica."[54]

Young's statements were obviously intended to discredit employee grievances and create a more favorable public image for the company, the same tactic used by New York Mills Corporation officials during the 1912 strike. In point of fact, the company, under pressure not only from Local 753, but from the New York State Industrial Commission, made efforts to upgrade both the machinery and working conditions within its New York Mills holdings. Nevertheless, conditions were not nearly as good as Young led the press to believe. Many problems still needed to be addressed, as is evidenced by the records of the New York State Industrial Commission.

One example of what the Commission found during several visits to New York Mills can be seen by reviewing their inspections of Mill No. 1. There, when the inspections began in 1911, investigators found a series of poor health and safety conditions including such things as a lack of fireproofing, poor ventilation, inadequate fire escapes, and severe health hazards caused by dust and other airborne particles. Some of these conditions were addressed, not through the good will of the A. D. Juilliard Company, but by order of the Commission, with the installation of a sprinkler system, the enclosing of the single interior stairway with fireproof partitions, and other improvements. Yet as late as 1917 the four-story building was still not fireproofed. Although combustibles were on hand, investigators found that there was no fire alarm system, there was no exterior fire escape, and the single interior stairway, although enclosed with fireproof partitions, still lacked required doors over the various openings. A report of the State Industrial Commission found an "imperfect horizontal exit on each floor, except the first, consisting of bridges of wood covered with sheet metal." The doors to the bridges were fireproofed, but were not fitted with self-closing doors. Some were provided with springs, but upon inspection they were found to be "fastened back during working hours." The exits were described as "remote."[55] This deplorable state of rather basic safety precautions still existed six years after the tragic and infamous Triangle Shirtwaist Factory fire in New York City. Thus, Young's statements notwithstanding, the New York Mills Corporation could hardly picture itself as making serious efforts to insure the safety and well-being of its employees.

Young concluded by pointing to the many community improvements the company made in addition to the upgrading of its' housing. These included the laying of sidewalks, the planting of shade trees, and the providing of land for a new school house at nominal cost.[56] These were all contributions to the beautification and welfare of the village of which it could justly be proud. Yet, they did not speak to the main issues that the union raised.

The reporter for the *Utica Herald-Dispatch* concluded that "The attitude of the company seems to be one of waiting, but it is feared by American residents of the village that if the mills should start up with the Syrians, who it is said are nearly all in favor of going back to work, there might be a serious clash between them and the Polanders who are holding out."[57]

Naturally, some response to Young's statements was required if the strikers hoped to retain public support. Thus, Minszewski, addressing the question of wages, explained that it was true that there were two increases since January, but that during the recent depression wages were lowered to the extent that even with the two raises the wages had not yet reached the level they were at before being lowered. Several strikers further explained that wages were not paid until a particular job was finished, thus it was entirely possible that the records might indicate a pay of $20.00 or more for a particular week when, in actuality, the pay was earned over more than a single week. One weaver presented as evidence his pay envelope showing that for 60 hours of night work he received between $12.50 and $14 per week. They also maintained that while a few strikers who did make good money were willing to return to work, the number was small and the vast majority were committed to seeing the strike through to victory.[58]

While the press busied itself obtaining the statements and rebuttals of company and labor officials, Patrick J. Downey of the New York State Department of Labor arrived in New York Mills to confer with Young about the possibility of meeting with the strikers to negotiate a settlement to the walkout.[59] Downey's arrival was no doubt a cause for concern among company officials who remembered the pressure the State Board of Mediation and Arbitration placed upon the company to negotiate during the 1912 strike. Indeed, it appears that the arrival of Downey may well have led to an increase in the company's activities designed to force an end to the strike before State officials could be effective in mediating a settlement.

The very next day the New York Mills Corporation held a closed meeting of officials in the main office next to Mill No. 2 which included Chester A. Braman, the corporation's second largest stockholder. When asked by reporters for details, Andrew Young had no comment. It is almost certain that the meeting was a strategy session during which local company officials discussed with their superiors from New York City means by which they might force an end to the strike on their terms. Rumors held that the decision was made to begin evicting strikers from company housing on the following Monday.[60]

While the company officials huddled amongst themselves in the office next to No. 2, Downey met with the committee of strikers at Union Hall. The state mediator assured reporters that any settlement would be one acceptable to both sides, explaining that the Board "would act neutral in the matter and that justice to each side would be the aim of any action taken." With the formalities of introductions and preliminary statements completed, Sroka and the other members of the strike committee presented Downey with copies of the resolutions and demands adopted by the strikers. In support of their grievances, they showed Downey a collection of over 500 pay envelopes dated between February 1915 and July 1916 to document their case of low wages. In addition, several strikers stepped forward to relate personal experiences which further supported the other grievances of Local 753. A weaver asserted that he was responsible for 12 Draper looms and earned between \$13.00 and \$14.00 per week. Then, at the beginning of 1916 the company assigned him 16 looms, but, even with the additional machines his pay averaged only \$12.41 per week. A carder with a family of five presented a pay envelope for \$8.09 for 58 hours labor, from which \$4.00 was deducted for fines. Another envelope showed 63 hours of work with a salary of \$11.34.[61] When the presentation of evidence was concluded, Downey told the strikers that he would be returning to Albany later that day. He made it clear, however, that he wanted to be contacted if the strike lasted beyond Monday. If that proved to be the case, he promised to go to New York City to confer with Juilliard officials.[62]

The weekend passed quietly with no further moves made by either side. On Monday, July 31, Antoni Knutelski informed reporters that Minszewski was expected back from consultations in New York City that afternoon, and was thought to be bringing with him Jesse Walker, vice president of the U.T.W.A.[63]

The same day, Andrew Young, seen at his offices, told reporters that he had no statement to make regarding the strike.[64] Similarly, John P. Campbell, who returned to his office at Walcott & Campbell for the first time since the strike began, was immediately besieged by reporters. In response to their questions about the strike he appeared unconcerned, voicing the standard "company line":

> "I just returned from my vacation and am going directly back to the woods. I don't know anything about the situation, as I have not been here. Our employees walked out without any reason that I know of and we have had no conference with them either before or since the strike. I expect we shall be shut down for a good while, perhaps until September 1. We are paying higher wages than mills elsewhere. Some of our employees are getting $20 a week. When they get ready to return to work we may take them back, I don't know."[65]

At about 4:40 p.m. vice president Stefan Zamorytto called the daily meeting of strikers to order. To update those present, Antoni Knutelski explained the results of the visit of the state mediator, indicating that since the employers made no effort to negotiate a settlement to the strike he would telephone Downey in the morning. The strikers also discussed the necessity of raising funds for the support of their families, a concern that was growing deeper with every passing day. At this juncture Jan Pezdek, Stanisław Boduch and Józef Nowicki, village businessmen, all pledged themselves to support and stick by the strikers, providing assistance and credit wherever they could. Their assurances of support were met with warm applause. Then, Wojciech Nowak, a former president of the union, spoke of the conduct of the strike, congratulating the people on their exemplary behavior. Indeed, a reporter for the *Utica Observer* noted that "It would be hard to find in all the history of labor troubles a strike which has continued so long and has yet been so orderly."[66] Such was not to be the case much longer.

In the morning deputy sheriff Frank Tobin approached a line of picketers on horseback, demanding that they disperse. When they did not move quickly enough for him, he pulled his revolver, spurring his horse forward into the midst of the strikers, nearly trampling those nearest to him. "He gave a regular circus performance with his horse," Minszewski later commented, "whipping the animal when it balked at going among the people."[67] The incident passed, however, and the rest of the day remained quiet except for some "loud talking" and the "frequent mention of the word 'scab.'"[68]

Yet the day turned ominous for other reasons. The *Utica Daily Press* carried a story of a mysterious ailment afflicting three-year-old Pauline Karpiński of Utica, a malady local physicians thought to be infantile paralysis. The house and family were quarantined pending the arrival of an expert from Albany. Two additional cases were reported in Whitesboro, with at least two others in Utica soon thereafter. Similar outbreaks were reported in Rome, and across the state as the dreaded disease swept through the crowded urban areas spreading its crippling effects among the young.[69] Within days, the first cases were also reported in New York Mills, adding this malady to the many fears of village residents during that stifling hot summer.

The company was also active in its efforts to secure new workers. That afternoon a union officer indicated to reporters that he had information that the mill owners sent agents to other textile manufacturing areas to secure workers to reopen the New York Mills factories. Some non-union workers had already arrived in the village, he claimed, but this could not be verified and the paper reported no activity visible at the mills.[70]

About 7:00 a.m. on Wednesday, August 2, seven strike-breakers arrived by trolley car in front of Mill No. 1. As they began to move toward the bleachery where they were to finish some of the material left there when the strike began, they had to pass through a line of female pickets who greeted them with calls of "scab." One of the workers lagged slightly behind the rest. As he passed through the pickets a women reached out to him, placing her hand on his arm in an attempt to get his attention as she tried to dissuade him from entering the mill. Seeing this contact, Deputy John H. Barry ordered his men forward to clear a way for the employees. One of the deputies placed his hands on the woman to hold her away from the strike-breaker.[71]

Seeing the female striker "roughly handled," and fearing that she might be either hurt or arrested, Franciszek Trzepacz stepped forward to demand her release. When he did, Deputies Jacob Jones and Allen Phelps quickly announced that he was under arrest, while clubbing him with their night sticks in the process.[72] Stunned by the officers' clubs, Trzepacz fell to the ground. As he lay handcuffed on the ground, one of the deputies came by and, according to witnesses, "jumped on him with both knees and clubbed him until he was unconscious, in which condition he was lifted into an automobile."[73] Still unconscious, he was bundled into the back seat by Barry, Jones and Phelps where another witness later told of seeing him "pounded with a club after being placed in a automobile."[74]

Seeing Trzepacz's plight, Wincenty Wróbel rushed forward to help his compatriot. Deputies Howard Hutchinson and Charles S. Steele, both of Oriskany, met Wróbel with a flurry of clubs. In the altercation that followed, Steele was hit in the head with a stone he accused Wróbel of wielding. Wróbel was quickly arrested.[75]

Another man jumped to Wróbel's aid, and soon several people were engaged with flailing fists, clubs and stones. One of those involved wrenched Hutchinson's night stick from his hands and hit the deputy squarely over the head with his own weapon. As the striker fled, Hutchinson and Deputy Fred Schnurr gave chase down Main Street. Antoni Koziol was standing on the front porch of his home when the men approached. The striker ran up onto Koziol's porch and disappeared off the other side. As he ran past, Koziol reached out to pull a small child to safety lest she be trampled in the chase. The striker escaped. Apparently angry over the loss of his prey, Hutchinson then turned and arrested Koziol on charges of assault! Although completely innocent of any interference, Koziol did not resist. Despite this, witnesses later testified that he was punched in the jaw by one of the deputies as he was being placed in an automobile.[76]

The fracas ended suddenly when the two dozen deputies, now faced with a growing crowd of strikers estimated at between 200 and 300 people, drew their revolvers and threatened to open fire on the crowd. Trzepacz, Wróbel and Koziol were taken to the Utica jail under arrest, while several of the other strikers exhibited bruises and scratches from the altercation. Deputies Howard Hutchinson and Charles S. Steele were treated by Drs. Comstock and Mitchell of New York Mills, the former receiving two stitches and the latter one stitch in the scalp. Deputy Dewey Theobald of Whitesboro had two fingers on his right hand broken, while several other deputies also suffered scratches and bruises.[77]

The striker's were quick to issue a statement denouncing the actions of the deputies, characterizing them a blatant brutality. They maintained that the deputies attacked the pickets first, and that the officers continued to beat those arrested even after they were handcuffed and placed in automobiles. According to the union's version, the pickets gathered about 7:00 a.m. to see who would enter the mills. When the workers arrived by trolley the deputies ordered a path cleared. Then, according to the strikers, "The officers pushed the crowd and clubbed them when they did not move quickly enough to suit them. Then the people resisted, but they used no stones."[78]

Sheriff Harvey denounced the striker's account as entirely untrue. "There is nothing to it," he said. "They attacked our men and cut and bruised them with stones, and they were not going to stand there and submit to it without defending themselves."[79]

Later that same morning Deputy David Alexander, who was in the midst of earlier disturbances, rode through a line of pickets while on horseback. Witnesses swore that he used his whip on several girls in the crowd of picketers, but this incident also did not escalate.[80]

At a mass meeting of strikers in Union Hall that began at 10:00 a.m. and lasted until about 12:30 p.m., the events of the morning were on everyone's mind. In the absence of Jan Sroka, who was in Utica arranging for legal counsel for those arrested during the morning disturbance, Wojciech Nowak, president of the Polish Workingmen's Hall Association, presided. Nowak spoke for nearly an hour and one-half, being interrupted several times by remarks and applause from the audience. When called upon for information on his trip to New York City, and the possibility of financial aid for the strikers from the national U.T.W.A. treasury, Minszewski could not state positively that aid would be forthcoming. Rather, he expressed his deep concern over the morning's disturbance, indicating his belief that some of the deputies were "hot-headed" and "anxious to create trouble."[81]

That evening, those arrested were arraigned before Justice Fred G. Reinmann in New York Mills. District Attorney Fuller appeared for the prosecution and the Hon. James K. O'Connor, a former Utica judge, for the defense. Wróbel appeared with head bandaged and clothing stained with blood. The others had scratches and bruises on their faces. The three were charged with violating section 2000 of the penal code which precluded the use of force or violence to persons or property. Punishment for the offense was one to five years in prison, a fine of up to $1,000, or both. All pleaded not guilty, were released on $1,000 bail, and were ordered to appear in court the following week. Jan Kupiec and Agnieszka Wdowiak acted as bondsmen for Wincenty Wróbel; Tomasz Szlosek and Jan Sliski did the same for Franciszek Trzepacz; while Loren Soja and wife and Ramon Kozmeda and wife guaranteed bond for Antoni Koziol.[82]

On Thursday, August 3, Patrick J. Downey of the State Board of Mediation and Arbitration met with Andrew Young at the New York Mills Corporation offices next to No. 2 for "several hours." Downey characterized the meeting as preliminary, but productive, noting that Young was "most cordial" in his attitude. As a result of Downey's efforts, at noon it was announced that a conference between strikers and officials of the New York Mills Corporation would be held that same afternoon, the first such direct dialogue to take place since the strike began. Downey also noted that Jesse Walker, vice president of the U.T.W.A., was expected to arrive in the village to take an active part in negotiations, and that Louis Wiard, a member of the New York State Industrial Commission and chief of the Bureau of Mediation and Arbitration, was also expected on the following day. No meeting was scheduled with officials of the Walcott & Campbell Spinning Company, the feeling being that if the strike against the larger corporation could be settled the spinning company would follow suit.[83]

Walker arrived soon thereafter, as did Wiard. The two, together
with Downey, were present at the afternoon meeting of employers and
employees. Those who represented the company in the negotiations
were Andrew M. Young, general manager of the New York Mills Corporation, John Leiper, general superintendent of the New York Mills
facilities, and Alexander F. Hobbs, superintendent of the Oneida
Bleachery. Representing the workers were, Walker, Minszewski and
nine members of Local 753. The conference, the first meeting between
strikers and officials of the New York Mills Corporation in the two and
one-half weeks since the strike began, convened in the office at Middle
Mills and lasted from 2:30 p.m to 5:40 p.m.[84]   Commenting on the
meeting, the *Utica Saturday Globe* stated that "a conciliatory attitude
has developed in the strike situation," and predicted an early agreement
to settle the dispute.[85] The *Utica Observer* reported that the companies
offered to end the card system, pay time and one-half for hours beyond
fifty-four and for Sundays and holidays and to provide better working
conditions.[86]

On Friday, August 4, a morning meeting took place at Union Hall
to consider the settlement proposal negotiated with the assistance of
Downey, Wiard and Walker. Witnesses reported the attendance as
greater than any previous meeting. Despite the ever-present heat and
humidity, there were many speeches in an exceptionally long session.
As Walker explained at the meeting, the company agreed "to abolish the
so-called 'card system,' to promise to discharge any foreman who
applied abusive language to any worker and to promote employees
according to length of service."[87] The company also proposed replacing
the card system with an employment office where a bulletin board
would contain information on available jobs and people could apply for
positions. The company's proposal, in general, reflected the minor
concessions offered earlier by Hobbs, plus the willingness to abolish
the card system, but refused any increase in salary or concession on the
number of looms to be operated, both of which were regarded as
significant issues by the strikers. In his remarks, Walker noted that not
all of the evidence was on the side of the strikers and that he personally
felt some of their grievances were unfounded. Walker indicated support
for the strikers' attempts to obtain better treatment and an elimination
of ethnic epithets, but appeared unconvinced regarding the desire for
fewer looms to operate, which may also explain why the U.T.W.A.
was reluctant to provide strike benefits to the members of Local 753.
In the end, the strikers voted overwhelmingly to reject the offer, while
at the same time supporting the efforts of Walker and the strike committee to carry on further negotiations. Another conference with the
employers was anticipated for the same afternoon.[88]

During the day, rumors circulated to the effect that the New York Mills Corporation would attempt to resume operations the following Monday. Perhaps this was yet another attempt by the company to cow the strikers into submission. In any event, the *Utica Herald-Dispatch* reported that same day that some of the Syrian and Italian strikers found positions in other area businesses, while many of those who remained were ready to break with the Poles and return to work. The paper also expressed "some apprehension that an attempt to resume work in the mills with non-union help may lead to trouble and the hour for beginning work will be awaited with anxiety." Further rumors circulated to the effect that on Monday the New York Mills Corporation would also begin taking steps to evict strikers from company owned housing. The latter, surfacing as they did all in the same day, may well have been purposely started by the company to place additional pressure upon the strikers for a settlement. Whatever the motive, the newspapers feared the consequences should the mills open or evictions begin. The *Utica Herald-Dispatch* noted that "This is another cause for anxiety to those who are seeking to preserve peace and hoping for an amicable settlement of the dispute."[89]

The *Utica Observer*, however, expressed the belief that the strike would soon be over. "The only question to be settled now between the New York Mills strikers and employers is that of wages, and it is believed that a satisfactory decision will be arrived at in the conference that is being held this afternoon."[90]

At that meeting the dialogue between strikers and employers continued, focusing mostly on the issue of wages. The conference lasted from shortly after 3:00 p.m. to after 6:00 p.m. Once again it included Young, Leiper, Hobbs, Walker, Downey, and representatives of Local 753. Despite the earlier optimism, no agreement was reached. The position of the company continued to be that it had provided two salary increases since January and was paying very good wages. It could not afford any additional increase. Thus, the situation appeared, as the *Utica Daily Press* reported, to be "a waiting game."[91]

The next day, at a meeting in Union Hall, Jesse Walker reported to the workers that the company offered no new concessions. He urged the strikers to remain firm, but peaceful. He did not, however, offer any pledge of financial support from the U.T.W.A. treasury. Following Walker's address, Jan Sroka took the podium. "In heated terms," according to a reporter who witnessed the event, "he told the strikers to stick by their demands. He pointed out that it would be cowardly for the Polish people to go back to work. If the Assyrians, French and Italians wanted to go back he said to let them go unmolested, but that the Polish people should stick to what they started out after."[92] Given the firm attitudes of the two sides, it is little wonder that the *Utica Herald-Dispatch* reported "The situation amounts to a deadlock."[93]

The lack of any offer of a wage increase by the company, coupled with Walker's refusal to offer strike benefits from the national U.T.W.A. treasury, were certainly not good news for the strikers. At this point, the offer of a small increase might well have led to a quick settlement. But the company remained firm and Walker, with apparent misgivings of his own, was equally evasive when asked for U.T.W.A. support. Further bad news came from the *Utica Herald-Dispatch* which reported that:

> "It is regarded as significant that the Italians, Syrians and French operatives, many of whom were conspicuous among the strikers early in the strike, no longer are attending the meetings. Only the Poles gather in the hall and the business is transacted almost entirely in their language. The speeches in English of Vice President Walker have been the chief exceptions lately. Absence of the Syrians, Italians and French from the meetings gives support to the rumor that those people, about 550 in number, no longer are in accord with the Polish strikers, but are disposed to return to work."[94]

The paper further explained that

> "There is a deep racial prejudice between some of the nationalities in the village, which has stood in the way of united action. The people of Latin blood do not mix amicably with the Slavs. If the Latin operatives are given assurances of protection, there were signs today that they would go back to work, and if they do, it will mean a severe if not fatal blow to the strike."[95]

The paper also speculated that a number of the Poles who were not union members would opt to return to work once the factories resumed operations.[96]

With the situation obviously deadlocked, Downey and Wiard left on Saturday afternoon for Albany, while Walker, without promising any aid to the strikers, returned to the U.T.W.A. headquarters in New York City. Local 753 was left to its own resources. In this moment of need, the strikers' resolve may have been strengthened by a story that appeared the same day in the *Utica Saturday Globe*. Titled "Garment Workers Win," it detailed the success of the garment workers in New

York City in obtaining increased wages and better working conditions through a lengthy strike against their employers.[97]

In its August 6 edition, the *Utica Sunday Tribune* reported that the New York Mills strike, now nearly three weeks old, cost the strikers some $50,000 in lost wages. The press further reported that all efforts of the past week to resolve the strike proved unsuccessful, with the result that the situation was deadlocked. The paper further opined that

> "The developments of the last few days of the struggle seemed rather in favor of the companies. The union appears to have been weakened by the withdrawal of a large number of Syrian, Italian and French operatives, who at the beginning of the strike declared that they would stand with the Poles to the bitter end. For some reason, the people of those three nationalities no longer attend the meetings of the strikers and there are persistent reports that they intend to go back to work as soon as they are given a chance."[98]

With the situation seemingly growing more critical by the day, the strikers arrived at St. Mary's that Sunday morning to worship and seek Divine assistance for their efforts. Key to the success of the first strike was the support of Fr. Fijałkowski, the spiritual leader of a people deeply committed to their religious beliefs. Yet, the *Utica Observer* reported that Fr. Fijałkowski "is viewing the situation from a neutral point of view. He stated today that he was of the opinion that the strike would not last long and that there would be no trouble. ... The Polish people attend church every morning and Father Fijalkowski has advised them to be orderly whatever they do. Mediation would be welcomed by Father Fijalkowski as a good way to settle the strike. He said that the settlement of the strike depended, of course, upon what attitude the company took toward the situation. If the two parties could agree on a disinterested committee, acceptable to both, to settle the situation it would be more satisfactory, quicker and more equitable to all."[99]

As the strike lengthened, Father Fijałkowski increasingly became a man torn between many forces. On the one hand Myśliwiec sought his offices to influence a settlement on behalf of the company, and Fijałkowski could ill-afford to lose the financial contributions of the company to his parish coffers. At the same time, the longer the strike lasted the less money his parishioners would have for their families or the support of the church. As a cleric, Fijałkowski had to be concerned with the financial stability of his parish, as well as the preservation of the peace. He was clearly in a very difficult position.[100] "He tried to mediate and bring peace and to bring them together," Bertha Kozak recalled. Yet his sympathies were clearly with his parishioners. While preaching peace, he also counseled them to remain unified. *Jedność* [unity] remained his theme, as it was in 1912.[101]

Everyone waited with apprehension for Monday morning, the citizenry fearing an outbreak of violence should the mills attempt to reopen, while the strikers feared the showdown of force that might lead to defections from their ranks. Before the day was out temperatures between 95° and 110° were reported throughout the area. The thermometer at Seneca Square in Utica reached 111° in the afternoon, while that at police headquarters read 104°, and some citizens reported readings as high as 115° in the sun. A brief heavy rain shower around 11:00 a.m. brought momentary relief, but failed to mitigate the afternoon temperatures to any appreciable extent. The extreme humidity made moving about or cooling off all the more difficult. That night many people slept on porches or lawns to avoid the intense heat that accumulated indoors during the long afternoon hours.[102]

The tensely awaited Monday morning soon arrived, but to the relief of both citizens and strikers the rumored attempt to resume manufacturing operations did not materialize. "The opinion of the strikers," noted the *Utica Herald-Dispatch,* "was that the company had been bluffing and that talk of reopening the mills had been intended to influence the employees."[103] Later in the day additional good news for the strikers arrived when reporters spoke with Benjamin Shiro to inquire about the intent of the Italians if the strike continued. Shiro, the Italian union leader from Utica, expressed the belief that most would remain loyal to the strike. "I have talked with a few of the Italian textile workers in the last few days and they assured me that they would not return until a satisfactory agreement were reached," Shiro stated.[104] When asked about the Italians' lack of attendance at union meetings, Shiro explained that their absence was no doubt due to the fact that most lived in Utica and it was simply inconvenient for them to travel to attend all of the meetings. While some might choose to return to work, Shiro remained confident that the majority would stay out.[105]

Similarly, Antoni Knutelski stated that he was sure the Syrians would remain on strike until an increase in wages was attained. "The report that they were going to desert the union," he told reporters, "originated with the mill owners and was calculated to weaken the organization."[106] The fact that the mills did not resume work was a major boost to the strikers' morale, as were the comments of Shiro regarding the continued loyalty of the Italian strikers. Knutelski and the other strike leaders grasped at these facts, emphasizing their importance to the press in an effort to revive both the spirits of the strikers and the donations of sympathetic citizens.

In the evening, Wincenty Wróbel was arraigned before Justice Reinmann on charges of riot. The hearing, held in a "stifling hot" office at an old soap and candle factory located near the canal bridge in Yorkville, lasted two and one-half hours. About fifty strikers jammed the room, with twice that many outside unable to get in. "Coats and collars were discarded in the interests of comfort," noted the *Utica Daily Press*.[107] The prosecution, represented by Assistant District Attorney William Rose Lee, contended that Wróbel assaulted Deputy Hutchinson after approaching him with a rock in his hand. The prosecution swore in as witnesses Deputies Hutchinson, Charles S. Steele, Fred Schnurr, G. Allen Phelps, and John H. Barry, and one mill employee, William Decker. In his defense, Wróbel, represented by J. K. O'Connor, explained that he saw men holding clubs over a woman's head and, not knowing that they were deputies, he asked the men not to strike the woman. When he did so the men turned upon him and knocked him down. Witnesses attested to the fact that Wróbel was rapped on the head with a club and arrested. Hutchinson maintained that Wróbel had a stone in his hand, an accusation Wróbel denied. Witnesses for the defense included Antoni Koziol, Frederick Fox, Stanisław Chamelik, Walenty Markut and Jan Fugrał. Trzepacz and Koziol waived their hearings, deciding to await instead a formal trial.[108]

The strike completed its third week on Tuesday, August 8. That evening hundreds of cards were passed out among the strikers to bolster their determination to hold out until their demands were met. In large black type, the heading on the cards read "Beware!! Don't Be a Scab!" Then, underneath in normal print,

> "You are warned hereby not to work in the mills of The New York Mills Co., the Oneida Bleachery and The Walcott and Campbell Co.
> The strike has broke out in the above mentioned mills. You should not work there. It is the greatest shame for you to do so. We are fighting for better conditions of life. We want better wages. We want better treatment of workers in the mills, as we are human beings. We want abolition of the card system. We want better condition of work. We want nothing else but what we have a right to get. Your place as our brother worker is in the ranks of strikers. Help us. Sympathize with us. Be a man. Be an American. Don't be a scab!"[109]

Negotiations continued on intermittently, though with no progress in breaking the deadlock. At a strike meeting on the morning of

August 9 Minszewski urged the Poles to become citizens as soon as they could, explaining that their rights could best be obtained by becoming citizens and speaking English. Following his remarks, an open discussion continued until nearly 12:30 p.m. During this time anyone who wished to speak could rise and address the issues involved in the strike. Some spoke about the number of looms they were required to run, claiming that they could make more money with ten looms than others did with sixteen. Others, however, felt that the differences in earnings might result from the difference in the degree of skill between workers. The question of wages also brought forth considerable discussion as the primary point of disagreement remaining. Described by reporters as "a free-for-all discussion" in which "nearly every one took part," Minszewski pronounced the meeting to be the "best yet held."[110] Although no consensus was reached on the number of looms to be managed, the meeting did provide a good forum for the venting of frustrations, while at the same time reaffirming both the strikers' demand for an increase in wages and their will to continue the strike.

During the day there were further rumors to the effect that the company would attempt to restart the mills, but no official statement. A company spokesman did offer the information that some 150 Italians were ready to go back to work, but a union officer refuted this, saying that those who wanted to go back to work had secured employment elsewhere. Similar discrepancies existed for opinions on the Syrians, while no one knew what guess to make regarding the French.[111] Union officials, however, continued to fear the opening of the mills because it might lead to a show of strength that would see some strikers return to work. Apparently, they were not entirely convinced that the Italians and Syrians would stand by them, or that the non-union Poles would either.

At 7:00 a.m. on August 10 Mill No. 4 in the Upper Mills began operations. The company, fearing violence, Deputy John H. Barry in charge of some thirty other special deputies ringing their property and placed fire hoses at the ready to be used on the strikers if necessary. The company also hired a Utica photographer to take pictures of any disturbance. He was prominently visible with his camera set up so as to focus on the main gate to No. 4. "A machine gun would not have been any more effective in keeping the strikers at a distance," reported the local press. "At the sight of the camera they hurried to get out of range of the instrument."[112]

Several hundred strikers were present, but they remained across the street from the mill and no violence occurred. When a street car arrived with workers, the crowd laughed and jeered, but Minszewski quickly stepped among the strikers and silenced even this brief expression of disgust. Only about a dozen strikers returned to work, a fact that union officers considered a major victory.[113] The *Utica Herald-Dispatch* reported that

> "The chief development of the morning was the proof that the strikers are holding together. It had been persistently rumored that the Italians, French and Syrians would desert the Poles and go back to work if given a chance. They had the opportunity this morning, but very few grasped it. Out of about 100 persons who entered the mill, it is said that the majority are foremen or their assistants and English-speaking workers who had taken no part in the strike and do not belong to the union."[114]

Nevertheless, company officials expressed themselves as pleased with the day's activities. The mill was reopened peacefully and, by the company's count, some 150 people reported for work, about one-half of the mill's normal workforce. They further stated that now that the mill had reopened peacefully, more defections would soon occur from the strikers' ranks. Reporters said the strike-breakers included mostly Italians, English, and a few French. The Poles and Syrians stayed out, while most of the Italians appeared to be from Utica, not from amongst the ranks of the Italian strikers.[115]

"There were considerable heated discussions in Polish, but nothing further than talk."[116] The only disorder occurred with the arrests of Agnieszka Soja for throwing a rock at a female employee leaving the mill for lunch, and Władisław Czerniak charged with interfering with an officer during the disturbance on August 2. Soja pleaded guilty and was given a six months suspended sentence, while Czerniak was fined $5.00.[117]

The following day Mill No. 4 continued operations with the company reporting the return of more workers, a total of some 200 in number. Union officials maintained that the workforce included only bosses and "mainly unskilled Italians from Utica" who would be "of little use to the company" because they were unfamiliar with the equipment or textile operations. "Yesterday I counted the people who went into the mill," Minszewski told reporters, "and there were about 50. These included all the bosses, second hands [foremen] and machinists from mills Nos. 1, 2, and 3, seven American women and girls, nine Italians and two Syrians. The Syrians soon came out and went away. The Italians were all from Utica and among them were two or three strikers. That was all." Minszewski went on to explain that "I understand the company has had agents in Utica hiring Italians, no matter what their trade is, or whether they have any trade. Those strike breakers know nothing about textile work and will spoil more material than they will make. When it comes to starting the spinning and weaving rooms, the companies will find that such help will be worthless, so we are not worried." As to the strikers, Minszewski flatly stated that "they would die of hunger before they would return without more pay."[118]

Minszewski also told reporters that he protested to Sheriff Harvey regarding the conduct of Deputy David Alexander, his second complaint about this particular officer. It seems that during the day Alexander ordered the driver of one of the cabs, hired by the company to transport strike-breakers, to drive through a line of pickets, and on another occasion to direct his vehicle at a group of strikers sitting on a wood pile. "I heard the orders given with my own ears," Minszewski maintained. "I was there to preserve order, but I told the officer in command that, if such methods were continued, I would not be responsible for anything that might happen."[119]

The day was, however, crucial because of another event that took place. With the strike more than a month old, and no financial assistance forthcoming from the national offices of the U.T.W.A., the strikers were in desperate need of food, supplies and financial assistance. Their efforts in the local towns and villages netted some donations, and many of the local merchants in New York Mills extended credit, but they desperately needed the support of organized labor for their holdout to continue. Thusfar the largest labor organization in the area, the Utica Trades Assembly, was somewhat skeptical of the strike and offered little support. Now, with the violence that occurred and the threats to evict the strikers from their homes, the Assembly was willing to investigate the dispute for itself before making a final determination on whether or not to offer support. Thus, on this day it sent a committee to visit Andrew Young to obtain the company's side of the dispute. "It is understood," the *Utica Herald-Dispatch* stated, "that upon the report of this committee, the assembly will decide whether or not to lend financial aid to the strikers."[120]

The company also realized that the strikers needed assistance to survive. When Patrick J. Downey visited the A. D. Juilliard offices in New York City during the week he met with a flat refusal of any wage increases.[121] The company was determined to smash the strike, and in the process the union, before the strikers could obtain outside support sufficient to prolong the walkout.

To place additional pressure on the strikers, on Saturday, August 12, the company served legal notices on some of the strikers who lived in company-owned houses that they must vacate them within one week, on or before Saturday, August 19.[122] Sensing that a critical stage had been reached, A. D. Juilliard officials were about to increase the pressure further in an attempt to administer the *coup d' grâce* to the strike and the union. As the *Utica Herald-Dispatch* concluded, "It seems to be a question of endurance."[123]

The New York Mills Corporation's plan was self-evident; it was attempting to put pressure on the strikers to concede. First by reopening No. 4, and now by issuing specific orders to vacate company owned housing. "We are prepared for a long battle," one of the strikers told reporters, "and we will not go back to work until an increase is granted."[124] To back this up, strikers announced that the Utica breweries donated $250 for the strike fund, while strikers who obtained other employment agreed to donate a portion of their earnings.[125] There was still no word from New York City, however, on whether the U.T.W.A. would provide financial support. Such aid usually began after the second week of a strike, yet by the end of the fourth week there was still no commitment on the part of U.T.W.A. officers to provide the necessary benefits.

When No. 4 reopened after the weekend on Monday, August 14, the number of people reporting for work increased significantly over the previous week. They included some Syrians and, for the first time, three Poles who broke ranks with the strikers and returned to work. Estimates placed the workforce at between 200 and 250 men and women, not far short of a full compliment for No. 4. All of the finishing and dying machines were operating, and company officials announced that cutting, dressing and packing operations would soon be resumed. The Oneida Bleachery also reopened with a small crew including several Syrians. It was reported that the company had agents in surrounding communities looking for workers and that it paid these agents $2.00 each for every worker they signed.[126]

In another escalation, the New York Mills Corporation sent notices to the Syrian and Italian strikers to vacate their company-owned homes by the following Saturday.[127] Until this point the company focused on the Polish strikers in an apparent attempt to cause schisms between the various nationalities. Now, those who stood with the Poles would suffer the same consequences.

August 15 is celebrated in Poland as the feast of the Assumption of the Virgin Mary. It is also a celebration of Mother Earth, and a typical scene in rural Poland witnessed women carrying grains, vegetables, fruits, herbs and flowers to church to celebrate a bountiful harvest.[128] In New York Mills it was an especially important occasion because of the community's tie to St. Mary, the patroness not only of Poland but of their own parish. On this day the Poles took time out to celebrate the occasion with Mass, a procession and the usual community activities associated with the Old World holiday. They did not, however, neglect their worldly situation completely.

Fund-raising activities continued, even at the religious celebrations. During the day Antoni Knutelski showed reporters "a dozen or more papers with over 100 names pledging amounts totaling $263.25" in donations for the support of those on strike. Reporters noted that "The strikers have been canvassing for the past two weeks and they claim they have secured much encouragement everywhere they have been, and especially in Utica, where the largest contributions have been received." Two members of Local 753 went to the textile districts in Massachusetts to solicit further aid. Stanisław Noga and Kazimierz Wróblewski, co-chairs of the fund-raising efforts, announced plans to establish a kitchen in Union Hall to feed any strikers who might be evicted and to make arrangements for them to be taken in by others.[129] Indeed, the spirits of the strikers appeared to be running high. With contributions beginning to increase, the strike leaders felt confident they could hold out until final victory. Nevertheless, to insure the continued loyalty of their members they decided to hold mass meetings every day, rather than every two days as they had been doing.[130]

The trolley cars arriving in New York Mills from Utica on the morning of August 16 were filled with Italian workers, said to number some 255 in all.[131] "The report that a full force of men are at work in Mill No. 4 is false," Knutelski told reporters, also noting that a report stating the Oneida Bleachery had reopened was false. He insisted that not more than eight members had deserted the union since the strike began, and that none of these were Polish. Knutelski also stated that as of that morning, August 16, only about 180 people entered No. 4, while just ten were at work in the bleachery, six of the latter Syrians. Two of these were former strikers and four were from Utica. He further explained that the remaining workers were machinists and others who were never on strike.[132]

That evening Józef Myśliwiec went to the Rose Lawn, a hall in New York Mills owned by Józef Smoła where members of the Polish community frequently gathered for an evening drink. Soon words were exchanged between Myśliwiec and two Polish strikers angered that he had remained at work in the mills. An argument ensued, quickly leading to blows. Deputies intervened, arresting the two strikers, Piotr Kantor and Jan Kowal, and charging them with assault and violation of Section 720 of the penal code respectively. The two strikers were taken to the Utica jail. Myśliwiec was not detained.[133]

There was a meeting of Polish and Syrian strikers that same evening that resulted in a new agreement between the two groups that jointly declared their intentions of continuing the strike. Some who attended had already gone back to work, but pledged to stay out hereafter.[134] Yet, ethnic tensions remained high as A. D. Juilliard continued to import Italian strike-breakers from Utica. The *Utica Observer* reported that strikers in New York Mills claimed that "the Italian people from Utica who are going to work at the mills are doing so partly out of natural enmity toward the Polish people." Most Poles in New York Mills traced their origins to Galicia, the Austrian section of partitioned Poland, thus their relatives at home were drafted into the Austrian army during World War I and were often sent to the Italian front to fight against the relatives of those acting as strikebreakers. The Poles believed this wartime situation greatly influenced the Italians' attitude during the strike. "These people are the enemies of the Italians in the European war and this factor is said to influence their attempt to break the strike," explained a reporter for the *Utica Observer*.[135]

An estimated 400 workers reported to Mill No. 4 on Friday morning, August 18, most of whom were Italians commuting from Utica. The strikers professed to be unconcerned because the finishing operations in No. 4 could not hope to operate very long without the reopening of the other mills where the fabrics were initially made. Union leaders insisted that the finishing department would soon run out of material, and that the weaving and spinning operations in the other factories could not possibly be restarted without experienced operatives. As the workers left the factory that evening words were exchanged between pickets and strikebreakers. The Italians "made up faces," and the Poles responded with a barrage of rotten apples.[136]

During the week newspaper coverage of the strike dropped off markedly, while taking a turn in favor of the company in that stories began to stress the number of people going back to work and the opening of new operations. Also, other news began to dominate press coverage. Utica was under quarantine because of the outbreak of infantile paralysis. No children were allowed to enter or leave the city beginning on the evening of Friday, August 18.[137] In Europe, the "Great War" dragged on with mounting destruction matched only by the toll of dead, maimed and destitute.

On Saturday, August 19, the New York Mills Athletic Association held its annual field days. It was reported that there was a large turnout, but whether the Poles attended is unknown. What is known is that the Polish band declined to play at the event as it was sponsored by the company.[138]

The same evening a hearing was held before Justice of the Peace Nelson in Washington Mills regarding the first two cases of eviction of tenants from company owned housing. The company argued that the occupants had no leases and were merely weekly tenants, thus they could be evicted at any time on a week to week basis. The tenants, represented by George M. Speaker, argued that the company lacked sufficient grounds to evict the tenants, insisting that they were entitled to thirty days notice before vacating. Speaker also moved that the trials be held closer to the tenants' residences as the long journey to Washington Mills constituted a hardship on the tenants and their witnesses. His motion was denied, and in each case the court found in favor of the company, ordering that the tenants be evicted.[139]

The strike was about to enter a new and dramatic phase. With the mills now back in operation, if only on a very partial basis, the strikers feared the company would gradually increase its work force by hiring people from outside the area until full operations could be resumed. Appeals to the United Textile Workers of America for financial assistance met with evasion. The Utica Trades Assembly was investigating the situation, but no significant aid appeared forthcoming in the near future. Some donations were received, but they could hardly be expected to support nearly 1,500 strikers for any length of time. And now, the legal path was cleared for the eviction of strikers from company-owned housing. The situation was indeed critical.

Chapter 8

A Fight to the Finish

The new initiatives to open the mills and evict the strikers were serious blows to the union's efforts that called for immediate response. Of prime importance, since the mills were already reopened, was the need to dissuade additional workers from accepting employment in New York Mills. Representatives of Local 753 lobbied among the Syrian workers, most of whom appear to have remained loyal, while others concentrated on the Italians. Although some Italian strikers returned to work, the most immediate problem for the union was the constant arrival of new Italians in Utica, many of whom did not understand English, and virtually all of whom knew nothing of the strike or the general struggle of American labor for recognition. Poor and in need of jobs to support themselves and their families, these new arrivals were willing recruits for A. D. Juilliard's roving agents who sought to use one immigrant group against another. This was the most difficult source of strike-breakers to eliminate. To address this problem the union planned to publish notices in the Utica newspapers to inform the area's Italian community that the strike was still in effect and they should not seek work in New York Mills. In addition, a meeting of non-union Italian employees was held at 315 Nichols Street in East Utica on the evening of August 22. There, with an estimated crowd of some seventy-five to one hundred Italian strike-breakers on hand, Florio Vitullo of Utica called upon his compatriots to quit their jobs in New York Mills and support the strikers in their efforts to win better wages and treatment.[1]

These efforts became all the more urgent following a conference between strikers and employers on the morning of August 23. In a meeting that lasted from 10:30 a.m. until noon, a committee of twelve strikers met with Young, Campbell, Hobbs and Leiper at the office near Mill No. 2. Jan Baran acted as spokesman and interpreter for the Polish members of the strike committee, while Józef Myśliwiec acted in the same capacity for the company officials. During the course of the meeting Young indicated to the strike committee that the mills would continue operating and that he expected to hire non-union workers to reopen the other factories. At one point he specifically mentioned that he could obtain Syrian workers, but the Syrian member of the strike committee raised an objection, challenging the assertion that his people would break ranks and go back to work. The company officials appeared to the Poles to be somewhat surprised that the strike committee did not drop any of its demands. Young apparently dominated the conversation with lectures on how the company was planning to reopen and assertions that it would not offer any compromises on the major issues of the strike. After this continued for some time, a member of the strike committee stated that the committee did not come to the conference to hear Young speak, but "to do business." Hobbs, perhaps trying to lower tensions, expressed his reluctance to hire strike-breakers, while indicating that he would welcome the strikers back to work. But the employers remained emphatic in their refusal to consider any increase in wages, thus nothing of consequence was accomplished.[2]

Not to be outdone by its larger neighbor, the Walcott & Campbell Spinning Company announced it would be reopening its plant on the following Monday, August 28. It also notified its striking employees that any who did not report for work would be required to move out of their company-owned houses. This was expected to be a real test of the union's strength since the union maintained that the spinners employed by Walcott & Campbell were loyal to the union, and that inexperienced workers could not successfully operate the machines. Walcott & Campbell officials, on the other hand, expected that enough strikers would return to enable them to resume operations. In a prepared statement, John Campbell claimed that his company expected to be operating at full capacity in every department except for the weaving of new materials, which would not begin for some weeks due to a backlog in the finishing operations.[3]

The strikers received a small boost later that day, August 25, when Minszewski returned from Adams, Massachusetts, with the news that two Polish union locals there were sending checks for the assistance of the strikers. In addition, thirty businessmen from New York Mills pledged a minimum five dollars each per week to the strikers' relief fund.[4] These contributions were welcome additions to a fund that relied exclusively on the small contributions of individuals and union locals to provide assistance to families without incomes for over six weeks.

At about 7:00 a.m. on the morning of August 26, Minszewski strolled down Main Street in New York Mills with two women strikers when two deputies "pounced upon him at the instruction of the mill officials" and "used their clubs on him." Witnesses placed Andrew Young at the scene, but whether he had any direct role in Minszewski being accosted is doubtful. In any event, the attack was a brief one, ending when Deputy Sheriff Barry arrived on the scene.[5] The names of the two deputies who attacked Minszewski are unknown, but they may well have been among the several company bosses sworn in by Sheriff

Harvey at the beginning of the strike. This small group of officers were continually involved in minor disturbances throughout the strike, leading union officers to the conclusion that they were trying to provoke some outburst that could then be blamed upon the strikers to portray them as lawless radicals in the eyes of the public.

That same afternoon a hearing involving the eviction cases of ten strikers was held before Justice of the Peace Nelson in Washington Mills. George M. Speaker again represented the strikers, with attorney James F. Hubbell employed to present the company's arguments. The company asked that summary evictions be ordered for fifteen tenants occupying company-owned housing. Three cases were handled, with the remainder being postponed until the next morning. Speaker argued that the company had not given the required thirty day notice to vacate. Hubbell argued that only one week notice was required since rental was on a weekly basis, and in any case that more than thirty days elapsed since the first notice to vacate.[6] Once again the court ruled in favor of the employers. The eviction orders continued.

On the morning of August 28 the Walcott & Campbell Spinning Company reopened. The *Utica Herald-Dispatch* reported that "a considerable number of operatives went to work amid scenes of suppressed excitement."[7] In an effort to dissuade those entering the mills, the strikers posted large signs in English announcing that a strike was still in progress. Some thirty deputy sheriffs were on hand to maintain order, but the picketers stood by silently and watched the strike-breakers enter the mills, making no attempt to interfere with their entrance other than an occasional shouted remark. The strike-breakers were primarily English and Italians, most of the former from New York Mills and the latter from Utica. Polish union officials insisted that none of their strikers returned to work, a position the Utica newspapers felt to be "substantially true."[8]

Following the opening, John Campbell released an official company statement to the press:

"The Walcott & Campbell Spinning Company is now running practically full time in every department. Some departments are overfull. All of the American people employed by us are working and nearly all of the Italians. Some of them are from Utica.

We have more help than we need and some we do not know what to do with. The finishing works and the Oneida Bleachery are filled up with every hand needed.

There are only two cotton mills to start and it is not necessary for them to start for six weeks yet. They wont be started because we have enough unfinished cloth on hand. We don't care to do any weaving for six weeks yet.

We are getting up now almost to our normal production of finished cloth.   Our mills are working full capacity.

There are about 1,000 working in the mills altogether.   We are paying more wages than any other place in this locality.   Since the first of February we have increased our wages on an average of 15 per cent.   In the past few years an increase of nearly 40 per cent has been made in the wages by us.

The principle thing the corporation needs now is more house room."⁹

Naturally, the strike committee viewed the reopening of the spinning operations as a serious blow. That morning a meeting in Union Hall was "filled to overflowing." None of the Poles present expressed any inclination to go back to work without an increase in wages. Sroka emphasized the familiar refrain to remain calm, not to trespass on company property, and to create no disturbances. Although nothing in particular was accomplished at the meeting except for a show of solidarity, the strikers successfully obtained positive media coverage after the meeting adjourned. Noting the presence of reporters, several strikers produced pay envelopes dated 1916 indicating that their pay fluctuated from week to week, the average since January of that year ranging from slightly less than $9.00 per week to $11.00 per week for between fifty-four and sixty hours. Reporters noted that the higher wages of $12.50 to $16.00 were usually for weeks in which the work load was sixty-four to seventy-two hours.¹⁰ As a result, the public read information that seemed to contradict the statements of Young and Campbell. The brief coverage they received, however, was small compensation for the reopening of the spinning company or the events about to transpire.

On the following day, Tuesday, August 29, the evictions began. Acting under the orders of Deputy Sheriff John H. Barry, Deputies Alexander and Comstock and thirteen other men, including some Italian strike-breakers in the employ of the New York Mills Corporation, evicted seven families, six from company houses on Asylum Street and one from a company owned tenement opposite Mill No. 4 on Main Street. Deputy Alexander directed the actual evictions. SIgnificantly, these took place in the Upper Mills where most of the Anglo-Saxon workers lived, not in the Lower Mills where Poles predominated, and where a much larger crowd of hostile onlookers could be expected.¹¹

The first two houses, those of Józef Satera on Main Street and Józef Burysz on Asylum Street, contained nineteen people, eleven being members of the two families and the other eight being boarders. As the tenants looked on, the sheriff's deputies directed their assistants to carry the people's belongings outside where they were "dumped in a pile on the sidewalk in front of the buildings."[12] In one instance, reporters observed that "A kitchen stove was carried from one of the houses during an eviction late Tuesday afternoon and placed at the roadside. An energetic Polish wife promptly started a fire in the stove and cooked supper for her husband and children."[13] An additional five families were evicted that afternoon, and over the next two days, including the families of Jan Łopata, P. Bachara, J. Wiatr, Grzegorz Młynarski, Ludwik Korzec and J. Karuza. There was a threat to "get even" with Alexander, but little other disturbance.[14]

One of those evicted was Jan Chrzan who was sick in bed when the deputies arrived. Chrzan was taken to a barn owned by Bronisław Sliski that was prepared to receive those evicted if the occasion arose.[15] Officials of the New York Mills Corporation later denied that any ill people were evicted, but a reporter for the *Utica Observer* who witnessed the incident wrote that "A young man, ill with tuberculosis, was carried from one of the houses during an eviction late Tuesday afternoon and placed at the roadside. Hundreds of strikers grouped around him there, and his eviction under the circumstances named caused a very bad feeling."[16]

The eviction of the strikers from their homes was a public relations bonanza for the union, an event that the strike committee was prepared to use to its fullest advantage. Prior arrangements were made against such an eventuality. The women and children were taken in by neighbors, who also provided room to store the evicted families' belongings. The men were housed in tents erected on a plot of land owned by the Kozaks and donated to the union for just such an eventuality, in Józef Smoła's hall, or in Sliski's barn. The use of the tents was donated by Group 320 of the Polish Falcons, which also provided financial assistance.[17] But the removal of those evicted to temporary quarters did not take place until the strikers took full advantage of the scene to curry public support. A photographer was on hand to document the evictions as evidence in later legal actions, while members of the strike committee moved about deploring the action to the many reporters who descended on the village.[18]

The strikers asserted that the significance of the evictions was to emphasize their determination to remain firm in their demands even at the risk of being thrown out into the street. The mill owners, on the other hand, complained to reporters that no one who was sick was

Workmen piling the possessions of those evicted alongside the street.
Note the deputy cradling a shotgun in the background to the left.

Ze Strajku w N.Y. Mills. Strajk rozpo-
czął się 18 Lipca 1916. Czysty dochód na
Strajkierów.

View of the N. Y. Mills Strike. Started
July 18-th 1916. Benefit for the poor
Strikers.

Evicted from her home, this woman is busy
preparing her family's dinner on a streetside stove.

evicted, and that the claim made by the strikers was simply done to obtain public sympathy. Company spokesmen insisted that in any cases where illness was claimed two physicians were sent to investigate and, if the tenants were really found to be ill, they were not evicted. In the case that the strikers complained about, the company spokesman indicated that no illness was claimed at the time of the eviction, and that the man now claiming to be ill could not even be identified as a resident of that house.[19]   According to reporters, the company spokesman "concluded his statement by emphasizing the fact that the company was not indulging in the old-fashioned rough-shod methods in evicting the tenants and that there was no desire to work unnecessary hardship; that no evictions would be made in bad weather; that the company had gone so far as to provide bags for coal and wood removed in order that it might not be scattered and lost, and that persons actually ill are not disturbed." The mill owners also denied that anyone was carried from a house sick in bed, but said that a man climbed into one of the beds after it had been removed from the house.[20] Nevertheless, on the orders of the town health officer one of the evicted families was returned to their dwelling when a case of *infantile paralysis* was discovered in an adjoining residence.[21]

Feelings of anger and frustration ran high that afternoon as the strike-breakers headed home from work. Here and there strikers paused to watch grimly or hurl taunts of "scab" as they passed. Astian Carom, one of the Syro-Lebanese strikers, stood near Main Street jeering at the workers as they departed for Utica on the trolley cars. Caught up in her own emotional rhetoric, she threw a tomato that hit a female trolley rider, for which she was immediately arrested, charged with violating Section 720 of the Penal Law. Soon after, Agnes Kadian was arrested on a charge of using "abusive language." Kadian later pleaded guilty and was fined $3.00, while Carom posted a $30 bond and was released pending trial.[22]

The evictions placed an additional financial and logistical burden on the hard-pressed strike committee of Local 753. That night a delegation of strike leaders met with a special committee of the Utica Trades Assembly to solicit funds for the support of the strikers. Meanwhile, at another meeting in a hall on the corner of Jay and Nichols Streets in Utica, a group of Italian civic and labor leaders met to discuss means of aiding the strikers in New York Mills and preventing their fellow Italians from acting as strike-breakers. Several speakers urged those present to avoid New York Mills so long as the strike lasted and to exert pressure on their friends to avoid the village.[23] It appears that the leaders of the Italian community, including the Sons of Italy, were firmly behind organized labor, expending considerable effort to keep their countrymen from breaking strikes both in Utica and New York

M Sobieraj 239	23			
J. Fijespring 241	25	Evicted Sept 13 - 1916		4-12-14 2-
A Szcze fini 242	27	" Oct 6/16		6-17-14 6-13-14 2
M Wolak 243	28			12-27-15 13
A Prijmai 244	26	Evicted Oct 6/16		
M Gadziala 245	24	" Sept 20-1916		3-6-15 1- 12
C Tunelis 246	22			
P Krajik 247	20	" Sept 21-1916		1
M Jill 248	18	Evicted Sept 21-1916		2-

A part of a page from the A.D. Juilliard Rent Rolls
indicating some of those evicted.

The tent encampment erected on Kozak's property
to house some of those evicted from their houses.

Mills. The difficulty appeared to arise from newly arrived, unemployed Italians, unaccustomed to the ways of America, unions, and labor strikes, and badly in need of jobs. Since most of these people were new to the area, and therefore unassimilated into the social and economic infrastructure of Utica's Italian community, the pleas of civic leaders meant little to them when faced with the necessity of finding immediate employment. The jeers, ethnic epithets and other ill-treatment they received in New York Mills most likely hardened them against the Poles and the union cause, and may even have eventually dampened the enthusiasm of Utica's Italian leaders for the struggle of the Poles.

On the following evening, August 30, an eviction trial was held before Justice Reinmann in Yorkville. This was the first eviction case heard in the Town of Whitestown, encompassing the Lower and Middle Mills where most of the Poles actually lived. The others were all from the Upper Mills, thus they were heard before the Justice of the Peace in Washington Mills in the Town of New Hartford. Attorney George M. Speaker, representing one of those to be evicted, once again argued that the tenants were entitled to thirty days notice of any planned eviction, but received only a one week notice. Attorney James F. Hubbell, acting for the company, maintained that seven days notice was all that was required since rent was paid by the week, and that regardless, the tenant in question had in fact received thirty days notice since the time of the first notice to vacate that was ignored by the strikers. The trial resulted in a hung jury that, although it did not provide any relief to those evicted, was regarded as somewhat of a victory by the union since it was the first time an eviction case was actually placed before a jury, and the first time the verdict did not go against the strikers.[24]

While the trial was being held, Minszewski met with the strikers at Union Hall to urge them to remain calm and to assure them that he was making efforts to find assistance for them. He urged them not to accept positions in Utica mills, as some suggested, for fear that if they did so unemployed workers from Utica would then be retained by the factories in New York Mills. Further, he also indicated that English and Italian-speaking union organizers would soon be sent to Utica in an attempt to strengthen unionism and support for the New York Mills strikers among those groups.[25] But he was unable to announce what the strikers sought most; the U.T.W.A. national office remained unwilling to back the strike with financial assistance.

August 31 saw the eviction of several families from the area of Asylum and Main Streets. Between 5:00 and 6:00 p.m., a large group of strikers gathered on Asylum Street, adjacent to Mill No. 4 and the site of most of the recent evictions. Feelings of anger and frustration ran very high, the crowd's emotion fueled by the sight of personal belongings of their friends and relatives piled in the open air along the sidewalks. As the strike-breakers began to leave on the completion of their day's work in No. 4, the Poles pressed forward with jeers and shouts of "scab," but Detective Barry and some of his men intervened to prevent them from approaching the waiting trolley cars. The strikers halted at the corner of Asylum and Main Streets, but continued to hurl insults at the departing strike-breakers. Deputy Barry, who later claimed that the strikers appeared to "surge forward," ordered the fire hoses turned on the crowd to prevent them from attacking the strike-beakers. Heavy streams of water shot across the street, blanketing the strikers and forcing them back from the road. While some sought cover, others, infuriated by Barry's actions, replied with a barrage of sticks and stones. One missile went through a window on a passing trolley, sending shattered glass in all directions. Some of the sharp splinters struck Joseph George, a Syrian who lived on Bleeker Street in Utica, inflicting a cut on his forehead, while other bits slightly injured an unidentified Italian girl sitting nearby. George was taken to the office of Dr. H. M. Mitchell where his wound was closed with one stitch, while a young girl was arrested for throwing the stone.[26]

Later that evening Minszewski visited the Labor Temple near the corner of Charlotte and Devereux Streets in Utica to speak with several members of the Utica Trades Assembly. When he emerged from the meeting about 9:00 p.m., three men lay in wait for him. As he reached the sidewalk and turned to walk down the street, one of the men waved a handkerchief as a signal. The others rushed forward, seized Minszewski by the arms and dragged him toward a waiting automobile. "You stay away from Labor Temple," one of the three commanded. Caught by surprise, the labor organizer cried out "Help me! Help me! Help me!" and "Murder! Murder! Murder!" As he shouted, his assailants began punching him in an effort to silence his cries for help, pushing him at the same time into the back seat of the waiting automobile. Hearing the pleas, A. L. Waldron of Trenton, New Jersey, came out of the nearby Elks Club, assuming that a crime was in progress. Waldron approached the car to offer his assistance, but was greeted by an automatic pistol and an order to stand clear. Within seconds, others began arriving on the scene.[27] "For a time," the *Utica Daily Press* reported, "it appeared as though a regular western hold-up was being committed."[28]

As it turned out, the mysterious men included John H. Barry, Frank Turck and Allen Phelps, all of whom were employed by the New York Mills Corporation before being appointed as special deputies. The three whisked Minszewski away in their automobile to the Utica jail. When members of the Trades Assembly finally discovered what happened, they were "indignant" over Minszewski's arrest and the manner in which it was accomplished. The Assembly immediately retained former City Judge James K. O'Connor to investigate the situation and to represent Minszewski. O'Conner obtained statements from Horace V. Durant, Lincoln Patten and A. J. Horohoe, all of whom witnessed the affair and assumed from the conduct of Barry, Turck and Phelps that a crime was in progress. In fact, the witnesses alerted Utica city police who responded, but arrived shortly after Barry's automobile drove away. After interviewing those who witnessed the incident, O'Connor went to the Utica jail along with several members of the Trades Assembly to demand Minszewski's release. O'Conner argued that the labor organizer was arrested illegally without a warrant, and was held illegally without due process of law. Sheriff Harvey replied that Minszewski was charged with a felony for inciting the "riot" at No. 4 earlier that afternoon.[29]

At 1:45 p.m. on September 1, "in the ancient, tumble down Town Hall of Washington Mills," Minszewski was arraigned before Justice of the Peace William E. Nelson of the Town of New Hartford on a charge of riot. Labor leaders from Utica and New York Mills jammed into the small room where "A bitter verbal tilt between Mr. O'Connor and Justice Nelson held spellbound the crowd of 20-odd men that were lined about the walls of the little room."[30] Affidavits sworn by Joseph Cheres, Joseph A. Kelly, John H. Barry, Fred Anderson and Ira A. Goodness were read into the court record, giving the deputies' version of the afternoon "riot" and Minszewski's part in it. The affidavit of Fred Anderson, similar to the rest offered by the prosecution, read in part:

> "That deponent was stationed with four or five other special deputy sheriffs near the corner of Asylum street and Main street in New York Mills, New York, under the direction of John H. Barry; that some 200 to 300 Polish people assembled on and near Asylum street, and when the employees of the New York Mills Corporation at its mill known as No. 4 left their work in said mill, said crowd of Polish people advanced down Asylum street toward said employees.
>
> That dependent and said other deputies were directed by said Barry to hold back said crowd near the corner of Asylum street and Main street until said employees had an opportunity to board said cars; that deponent and said four other deputies did hold back said crowd for about five minutes.
>
> That the Joseph Mniszewski [sic] pushed through between two of said deputies, although one of said deputies commanded him to keep back in said crowd, and advanced for a distance of about 20 or 25 feet in front of said crowd, and then turned toward said crowd and gave a slight movement or signal with his hand; that immedi-

ately the said crowd gave a loud yell and rushed through
and past said deputies toward said street cars and employees of said New York Mills Corporation, and at the
same time persons in said crowd began throwing bottles,
stones and other missiles at said cars, employees and
deputies. That then a hose was turned upon said crowd,
which caused it to disperse."[31]

Following the reading of the affidavits O'Conner moved for the
prisoner's release on grounds of insufficient evidence. The motion was
summarily denied, whereupon the former city judge complained bitterly
that "there had been no deliberation on the affidavits." O'Connor
further protested that the men who arrested Minszewski did so illegally,
on their own authority, without any warrant for his arrest having been
issued, and that they acted improperly by beating the prisoner before
forcing him into the automobile. All of these objections were over-
ruled, with Minszewski being released on $1,000 bail and ordered to
appear before the Grand Jury.[32]

Faced with a lack of substantial financial assistance, their own
resources and the funds of Local 753 long since expended, the strikers
not only witnessed the reopening of some of the mill operations, but
also the importation of large numbers of strike-breakers, the defection
of a few of their own members, and the eviction of families from
company-owned housing. Their victories were few, confined to the
offer of small financial donations from individuals or union locals,
while their chances of success dwindled with every passing day. Indeed,
the strikers' situation was desperate. Though still defiant, many
thought of leaving the village to find work elsewhere, while others were
reduced to living in tents on whatever donations could be secured. They
could not know it then, but the arrest of Minszewski, particularly the
manner in which it was carried out, proved to be a turning point in the
strike.

Outraged by the treatment of the union organizer, the Utica Trades
Assembly held a special meeting chaired by its president, Stephen S.
Dwyer, on the evening of September 1.[33] Minszewski addressed the
group, giving the history and reasons for the strike in New York Mills.
Father Fijałkowski followed, speaking on the conditions in the village.
"Fijałkowski's sympathies are with the strikers," the *Utica Daily Press*
reported. "He expressed his sorrow that women and children are made to
suffer, and requested the assembly to protest against the actions of the
deputies which he said he himself witnessed."[34] Judge O'Connor delivered an address on the strike and the arrest of Minszewski. "The judge,"
the press reported, "commented in sarcastic fashion on the 'flimsy' case
against the organizer, and said that the mill owners wanted to get him

out of town."[35] The reporter for the *Utica Daily Press* later wrote that "The delegates at the meeting expressed indignation at the treatment of the strikers and are so aroused that, while they have been quiet in the matter up to this time, they will now take an active part."[36]

Before the meeting adjourned, the Assembly adopted a resolution to Sheriff Harvey deploring the arrest of Minszewski and appointed a committee consisting of Madison G. Roberts, John J. Conway, Michael Walsh, Father Fijałkowski and Joseph Minszewski to present it to Sheriff Harvey. The resolution read as follows:

"Whereas, The spectacular arrest of Organizer Joseph Minszewski of the United Textile Workers, pulled off in the vicinity of the Labor Temple, was evidently done with the intention of discrediting organized labor, and, whereas we are in possession of facts which tend to show that certain mill owners hereabouts are desirous of driving said organizer away from this vicinity, because of the success of his efforts in organizing textile workers. And, whereas, certain men in the employ of said mill owners are holding commissions from the sheriff of Oneida County and are doing their best to create trouble every day and then charge the strikers with rioting.

Resolved, That because of the unlawful and high-handed methods in the arrest of Organizer Minszewski and the hostility displayed by them against organized labor without any just excuse or reason, we demand that the sheriff of Oneida County revoke the commissions as deputies, issued by him, to John H. Barry, Deputy Turck and all others who took part in the brutality displayed toward Organizer Minszewski on August 31."[37]

The Trades Assembly also appointed a committee to solicit funds and other forms of relief aid for the strikers, and "to observe conditions nightly at New York Mills, when the mills close and with authority, if any unlawful act is committed, to swear out warrants." This committee consisted of W. O. Jones, Jacob Stahlhofer, Theodore Crist, T. J. Carroll, Edward Martin, John J. Conway, Michael Walsh, C. Sorensen, A. Rosenthal, James Largay, Owen McRorie, Fred Nelson, John A. Grecker, Madison G. Roberts, Isadore Karn, Otto De Comaine and Mr. Strobel. The Assembly delegated an additional committee consisting of Benjamin Shiro, S. Fedeschi, Theodore Crist and William Colwell to visit the Sons of Italy and urge them to influence their members not to work as strike-breakers in New York Mills.[38]

Given the events of the previous two days, tensions were high on September 1. That evening, as the factories closed down and mill operatives began to leave Mill No. 4, the Italians, no doubt tired of the jeering taunts of the strikers, declared their intention to stage a defiant parade through New York Mills on their way home to Utica. They were apparently dissuaded from doing so by sheriff's deputies who insisted that they take the trolley cars. The *Utica Daily Press* reported that "they objected strenuously" to this, insisting that they wanted to parade through the village.[39]

As the loaded cars left the mill, deputies rode along behind them in separate automobiles. Here and there along the way words were exchanged between the Italians and Poles they passed along the street, some of whom were reported as "beating on tin cans and making a general hullabaloo."[40] As the trolleys passed the corner of Main and St. Stanislaus Streets in the heart of the Polish residential area, the jeering continued and witnesses claimed that some children began hurling stones at the trolleys. At this, the trolley cars immediately stopped and a large group of Italians "swarmed out of the cars like so many ants," charging upon the few Poles lingering nearby. "Men and women were armed with sticks, some of them as long as canes and about the size of a patrolman's night stick, while in the other hand quite often could be located a rock. Undaunted the Italians sailed in with a cry of 'No can licka Italianos.'"[41]

Caught by surprise and outnumbered by the onrushing Italians, the Poles escaped up the hill past Union Hall. The Italians followed, with many of their number turning abruptly to enter Union Hall as the group rushed past. Inside were several Poles working on the scenery for a forthcoming theatrical production. Hearing the Italians approach, most escaped upstairs where they locked themselves in an office. Franciszek Ziober and Jan Solnica concealed themselves behind some of the scenery, but were discovered by the mob, "cornered and beaten unmercifully."[42] Deputy sheriffs finally intervened to prevent the Poles from being killed and some twenty Italians were herded out of Union Hall and back down the hill. Some of the Italians returned to the trolleys, while the rest paraded away on foot as they originally planned, protected as the did by the Sheriff and his deputies.[43]

Ziober was taken to Dr. Mitchell's suffering from three serious scalp wounds requiring several stitches to repair, as well as assorted scrapes and bruises. Solnica was also treated for various bruises and scalp wounds.[44]

"It would seem as though the situation is getting a little too strong for the sheriff's department," the *Utica Daily Press* opined, "and if matters continue along the same strain the militia will have to be called out in order to prevent the loss of life which must follow if men and women are going to walk the streets with clubs in their possession. Race feeling is even higher than that of the strike."[45] "It is no longer a strike," a village resident told the *Utica Observer*, "but a spirit of race hatred between the Italians and Polish people that exists there."[46]

The newspapers generally credited sheriff's deputies with preventing the situation from turning into a real tragedy, but the strikers offered another version of the incident in a statement issued by spokesmen Antoni Knutelski and Jan Kwieciński:

> "About 10 minutes to 6 Friday evening there came five cars with Italian strike-breakers. Two cars passed on the way to Utica. The third car was chased by Deputy Sheriff Barry in an automobile, who called to the motor-man to stop. The motorman stopped the car and Barry called to the Italians to come out of the car. They got out and Barry sent them to Labor Temple. He waved his hand and ran with the strike-breakers to the private grounds of the temple. The Italians had pieces of iron pipe, clubs, etc., in their hands. In the middle of the road to Labor Temple the Italians stopped and turned and made as though to return to the car, for the motorman was whistling to them to come back. But Mr. Barry called to them and led them to the temple. Mr. Barry ran into the hall and called to the Italians behind him to follow.
>
> Mr. Young and Mr. Lippert then came along and other deputies. They stopped in Main street and left their automobiles so that they blocked the street so the Polish people could not run that way. Mr. Young shouted to the Italians to come, and lead the way to Labor Temple. Mr. Young started to go to the temple, but changed his mind and walked back. Mr. Barry went to the temple and on the stage, where there is some scenery. Eight Polish men had been in the hall, but six ran upstairs to the secretary's rooms and went into one room and locked the door. Two men were behind the scenery on the stage. Barry found one man, John Solnica, and shouted to the Italians, 'Come on, boys, here is one of them.' Barry got hold of Solnica by the neck and punched him. The Italians hit him with the iron pipes and then they put him out of the temple and into an auto, and he was taken before Justice Raymond.
>
> When the rush started, a Pole came to the temple to see what the trouble was about, and an Italian saw him and shouted, 'Boys, here is another.' They hit him and

made three holes in his head, hurt his back and broke his nose. Dr. Mitchell dressed his wounds, and he is in bed and can not move, very sick.

The secretary, who had gone out of the temple, now returned, and the Italians took hold of him. They did not hit him, but called to Officer Turck. Mr. Turck looked at him, but did not hit him, but let him go, after putting his revolver right in front of his face.

In Yorkville the deputies took all the clubs and knives from the Italians and took them back to Mill 3, where they had been distributed to them."[47]

It was surely no accident that Barry, a detective in the employ of the New York Mills Corporation and the man who instigated the arrest of Minszewski, was also active on the scene of this latest "riot." Nor does it appear accidental that the other two deputies mentioned prominently as being on the scene were Turck and Phelps, accomplices of Barry's in the Minszewski arrest, who were also involved in earlier confrontations with strikers. It is also interesting that none of the Italians were arrested or charged with "riot," despite the fact that they were clearly the aggressors and invaded the private property of the Union Hall, while Poles continued to be detained and charged under less overtly violent circumstances.

Kilka z pogubionych narzędzi, podczas napadu włoskich łamistrajków na Salę Robotniczą w N.Y. Mills, N.Y. 1 Września 1916 Dochód na strajkierów.

Several weapons left by Italian strike-breakers during the atack on Labor Hall New York Mills, N. Y. Sept. 1st 1916 Benefit for the Strikers

Some of the weapons used by the Italian strike-breakers in their assault on Union Hall, September 1, 1916.

The arrest of Minszewski and the subsequent disturbances were viewed as serious by the U.T.W.A., which sent vice president Jesse Walker scurrying back to Utica to investigate. He arrived on the afternoon of September 2. A conference was held at the Hotel Utica at 11:00 a.m. on Sunday morning, September 3, at which Walker met with Young, Leiper and Hobbs, along with Madison G. Roberts, Michael Walsh and John J. Conway representing the Utica Trades Assembly. The meeting lasted over three hours, with representatives of the companies remaining firm in their refusal to offer any increase in wages. Consequently, no progress was made.[48] Nevertheless, the strikers received substantial and welcome support when Walker announced to reporters that "On account of the methods used in arresting our man Minszewski, we feel that it is necessary now for the international union to get into this fight and we will from [now] on give financial assistance to the strikers. And we intend to organize the entire trade of textile workers in this district, thus strengthening local conditions in the United Textile Workers' ranks."[49] The strikers finally obtained the financial backing they so desperately needed.

That same Sunday Jan Chrzan, the member of Local 753 evicted from his company-owned home despite protests of illness, died of tuberculosis. Since his eviction Chrzan lay in a barn on a farm owned by Jan Sliski off Asylum Street. Now, his body was placed in a coffin amongst the hay in the middle of the barn, his eyes covered with coins in an old Polish tradition, as people came by to pay their respects and offer small donations to the family. These obligations completed, union members carried his casket down Asylum Street and along the length of Main Street in a public procession to Union Hall where it lay in state. The following Wednesday a solemn funeral was held beginning at 8:00 a.m. in St. Mary's Church. After the funeral Mass another long, somber procession of some 700 mourners, headed by the village's Polish band, marched through the streets to the Polish cemetery in Yorkville to witness the interment of the body. The union paid a death benefit of $75.00 to provide for funeral expenses.[50] In death, Chrzan became a martyr, a symbol of corporate oppression and cruelty that created great public sympathy for the plight of the homeless strikers.

September 4 was Labor Day. By that time eviction notices were served on over 100 families in New York Mills. Local 753 hoped to have 1,000 people marching in Utica in the annual Labor Day parade to emphasize its unity and to solicit donations. James P. Holland, president of the New York State Federation of Labor, made a lengthy speech in which he commented on the general condition of labor in the state, the attempts by some employers to take advantage of or circumvent the new law limiting the labor of women and children to fifty-four hours

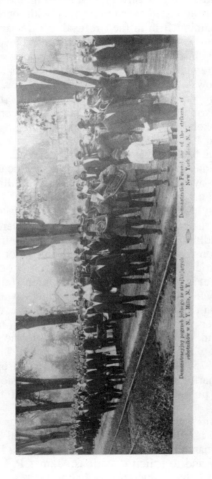

The funeral procession of Jan Chrzan. The Polish band leads, followed by union officials, the casket, and hundreds of mourners.

per week, and other similar items of immediate interest to labor in general.[51] Toward the end of his address he commented briefly on the New York Mills situation, noting that "if labor men acted like the fellows who arrested the textile organizer at Labor Temple last week, they would be arrested as thugs and put in State's prison." He concluded by condemning the inequitable administration of justice, asserting that "it's pretty near time the judges of Utica got busy."[52]

On the morning of Tuesday, September 5 the factories in New York Mills reopened after the long weekend. To prevent further violence, Sheriff Harvey, who suspected that the strike-breakers might be arming themselves, ordered his men to search all of the incoming trolley cars for weapons. By the end of the morning, deputies confiscated more than a dozen weapons from strike-breakers heading into the village, including razors, sharpened files, scissor-halves and heavy bolts.[53]

The following evening Mrs. Sara Conboy, secretary-treasurer of the U.T.W.A., spoke at the Labor Temple in Utica in support of Union Label Promotion Week. "The union label to trades unionists is just as sacred as the cross to Christianity," asserted Conboy in her lusty speech. "Let us not be trade unionists in name only. If you demand the label they'll give it to you."[54] She then turned her attention to the strike in New York Mills, noting that the cause was "worthy of help," and promising that the international U.T.W.A. would provide financial aid to the strikers.[55]

To this point, A. D. Juilliard officials expected the strikers to be crushed as they ran out of funds and either came back to work or left the village. When the State Board of Mediation and Arbitration became involved in the case, Juilliard officials decided to place additional pressure on the strikers by evicting them from their homes in an effort to force a quick submission. Now, with pledges of support from the U.T.W.A. and the Utica Trades Assembly, the company realized that the strikers might be able to hold out indefinitely. Thus, they increased the rate of evictions in the hope that if the strikers were not forced to return before assistance arrived, they would at least be out of the way and their places could be taken by others whom the company's agents were busily recruiting.

On Wednesday, September 6 the evictions resumed, again in the Upper Mills area. Over the next two days the families of J. Zytowski, F. Warchałowski, S. Goodyear, P. Borys, J. Topór, J. Kułaga and F. Burysz were all removed from their homes. During the process, Bronisław Borek was arrested for throwing a stone through a window at 30 Clinton Street. He spent the might in jail. To discourage those evicted from damaging the company's property, officials adopted a policy of only evicting one family at a time from its two-family residences. If one family remained, company officials reasoned, those evicted would be less likely to damage the property. The strikers also developed some methods of non-violent resistance. As word spread that the deputies and their assistants arrived to begin more evictions, the strikers heaped coal into their stoves, starting as hot a fire as they could despite the warm August and September weather. By doing this, the men assigned to evict them were unable to lift the hot stoves until they cooled down, thereby stalling the evictions and limiting the number of families that could be moved out in one day.[56]

September 8 is celebrated in Poland as the feast of Our Lady of Sowing and the Birth of Mary. In the rural agricultural communities it was tied to the time when the winter crops were sown.[57] On this date company officials renewed efforts to undermine the unity of the strikers by spreading rumors that the union organizer and Local 753's officers were needlessly prolonging the strike because they were profiting from it. Union officers vehemently denied these charges, asserting that the accusations were probably circulated on purpose to make it more difficult for them to raise funds to assist the strikers. Yet, the rumors became so persistent that the parties in question, Jan Sroka, Antoni Knutelski, Kazimierz Dziedzic and Joseph Minszewski, felt it advisable to swear out an affidavit to present their formal denial of the charges. Thus, before notary public George M. Speaker, they signed a document indicating that they,

> "duly sworn, depose and say that the first 3 above-named are officers of the New York Mills, Local No. 753, United Textile Workers of America, and the last named is a duly authorized organizer of United Textile Workers of America, with headquarters in New York City; that it has been reported to the above-named that the duly authorized collectors of funds for the benefit of the striking members of said New York Mills Local have learned from business men from whom they have solicited aid, that a report has been spread broadcast that the said officers and organizer receive large salaries from the funds of said local, and from the money subscribed to help the strikers.
>
> Dependents say further that not one of said officers is paid or receives anything by way of salary or otherwise for his services rendered for or during the strike; and that the said organizer receives only his regular compensation, which is paid to him by the United Textile Workers of America, and none of which is paid by the New York Mills Local.

Depondents say further, that they are informed and verily believe that all stories as to pay they are alleged to receive emanate from the New York Mills Corporation, and are maliciously circulated for the purpose of lessening contributions to the strikers' fund and for the purpose of discrediting the officers of the local.

Depondents say further, that said New York Mills local has three auditors, chosen for one year, who audit the books and accounts of said local every three months, and that no such use of the funds of said local is made, or would be permitted.

Deponents say further, That all funds collected by and donated to the New York Mills local are used for the purpose of relieving the needs of the members of said local, and are paid out in benefits, and for necessary expenses in defending its members when unjustly arrested, and for protecting its members from being evicted from their homes, and thrown into the streets, with no place to go, and with no other city or town open to them and their children, because of the prevalence of infantile paralysis and the strict quarantine maintained in all directions.

John Sroka , Pres.
Antoni Knutelski, Secy.
Kazimierz Dziedzic, Treas.
Joseph Minszewski[58]

On Tuesday evening, September 12, the Utica Trades Assembly held its regular monthly meeting at which it decided to donate $200 of the $741.75 raised through the Labor Day celebration activities to the strikers in New York Mills. Also, the committee sent to present the demands of the Assembly to Sheriff Harvey reported that Deputies Barry and Turck had been suspended. Interestingly, of all the Utica news-papers, only the labor-oriented *Utica Advocate* carried this important piece of information that lent credence to the strikers' complaints.[59]

During the first two weeks of September, legal orders were issued for the eviction of some forty additional families, while about twenty-five families were actually evicted. Several appealed.[60] Among those evicted between September 11 and September 14 were the families of Jan Wąż, Józef Zientara, Wacław Czerniak, Jan Misterka, Stanisław Trzepacz, Jan Fila, Roman Wójcik, Stanisław Misterka, J. Sambor, Jan Swierat, Jan Łabuz and Józef Chrabąszcz. In addition, J. Houle moved out voluntarily on September 9. A review of the rent rolls of the New York Mills Corporation indicates that nearly all of the names of those evicted were Polish, with only a few such as the Englishmen Sheppard and Goodyear, and the Frenchman Houle being non-Poles.[61]

By mid-September the oppressive heat of the summer months began to give way to cooler evenings. With winter weather not far off, the problem of caring for additional homeless families became more acute. More than fifty families were actually evicted by this time. The impact of this among the Polish community was felt everywhere. The first two evictions on Asylum and Main Streets in August resulted in nineteen people being left homeless. Although all of the households were not this large, when one considered the family members and boarders affected by each eviction, the removal of fifty families must have left well over 300 people homeless. Smoła's hall was filled with people, as was Sliski's barn and the tent encampment set up on Kozak's property. Individual families who owned their own homes also opened their doors to those in need.[62] "I don't remember how many people would come into the house and stay because they had no other place to go," Bertha Kozak recalled. "Mother used to cut bologna, she was such a good hearted soul, she'd slice the bologna and have them come and make a sandwich for themselves."[63]

Another of those who owned his home, opening it to those evicted, was Kazimierz Dziedzic. The wood-frame structure on Floyd Street had a kitchen, dining room and two bedrooms on the first floor, four bedrooms on the second, and an open attic above. As more and more strikers were evicted, Kazimierz and his wife Katarzyna moved their three children — Michał, Helena and Bronisław — into a single bedroom with them, while the other first-floor bedroom was reserved for several young, unmarried girls. The second-floor bedrooms housed Dziedzic's in-laws, two uncles, and four men evicted from the mills. The attic floor was crowded with beds and mattresses accommodating several other men. Conditions were crowded, but it was the only alternative for those evicted.[64]

Families were often split, women and men housed in different locations and children sometimes taken in by still other neighbors. Józef Myśliewiec and those who remained at work paid their rent and occupied their homes throughout the strike.[65] Once the other homes were vacated, the company attempted to move its newly-hired strike breakers into the buildings. Ferris George, a non-striking Syrian worker at No. 3, moved into one of the vacated homes on Asylum Street, while some of the Italian strike-breakers took possession of other residences in the Upper Mills area.[66]

The large number of people to be fed, sheltered and clothed, coupled with the fact that financial assistance was so long delayed by the U.T.W.A., led to a real crisis in mid-September, before the newly-won aid from the international union and the Utica Trades Assembly arrived. The rumors the company started about union officers profiting, together with the evictions, caused dissension to spread within the ranks of the Polish strikers. Some began to waiver. Two Polish strikers went back to work in September, and others certainly waivered under the increasing financial and other pressures.[67]

In other cases, strikers argued over the allocation of the meager assistance that was available. One day the strikers lined up to receive their respective shares of the donations received during the week. When Kazimierz Dziedzic heard his name called he stepped forward, but before he could receive his allotment a voice called out from the crowd in objection "He is a *dziedzic*, he does not need help!" The English translation of the word *"dziedzic"* is "lord" or "property owner," thus, the disgruntled striker used this play upon words to express his resentment that someone who owned his own home should be seeking aid when those evicted were in more need. The person who objected did not realize that Dziedzic had mortgage payments to make and extra expenses that his family incurred in providing food and shelter for a large number of those evicted from the company housing. Nor did he know that Dziedzic, who was also on strike and receiving no wages, was forced to secure a personal loan at a Utica bank to support his family. Nevertheless, such bitterness and dissension began to plague the strikers in these times when donations to the relief fund could not meet the demand for support.[68]

The company was not without knowledge of the strikers' desperate situation, nor was it oblivious to the fact that once aid from the U.T.W.A. and the Utica Trades Assembly began arriving such dissension would be less likely. It determined to focus even more pressure on the already beleaguered leaders of Local 753. On September 20 the *Utica Herald-Dispatch* reported that officials of the New York Mills Corporation filed suit against Jan Sroka, Antoni Knutelski, Jan Nowak and Jan Solnica for organizing a conspiracy to promote a strike among workers in the company's mills, thereby preventing their operation and damaging its business. The suit sought $25,000 in damages, alleging that the four mentioned defendants were not in the employ of the New York Mills Corporation at the time of the strike and were thus not attempting to increase their own wages. Hon. James K. O'Connor, representing the defendants, quickly informed reporters that the suit was simply an attempt to intimidate the labor leaders.[69] It is interesting to note that on the one hand the company argued it was losing money and could not afford to raise wages, while on the other hand it stated in its legal action that the leaders of Local 753 were responsible for a loss of some $25,000 in profits during the first two months of the strike. The contradiction was obvious.

Examples of the Postcards Sold

Strajku w N. Y. Mills. Strajk rozpocz. Lipca 1916. Czysty dochód na straj-kierów.

By S. Kaczowka

View of the N. Y. Mills Strike. Start July 18th 1916. Benefit for the po Strikers

Ze Strajku w N. Y. Mills. Strajk rozpocz. 18 Lipca 1916. Czysty dochód na straj-kierów.

By S. Kaczowka

View of the N. Y. Mills Strike. Started July 18th 1916. Benefit for the poor Strikers

to Raise Funds for the Strikers

Z życia strajkujących robotników w New York Mills N. Y., 18 Lipca 1916. Dochód na strajkierów.

View of the strikers life at New York Mills, N. Y., July 18th 1916. Benefit for the Strikers

Z życia strajkujących robotników w New York Mills N. Y., 18 Lipca 1916. Dochód na strajkierów.

View of the strikers life at New York Mills, N. Y., July 18th 1916. Benefit for the Strikers

That same morning Mill No. 2 reopened with about 200 workers, most of whom were described as Italians and Syrians, with a few Anglo-Saxons. The Syrians and Anglo-Saxons together were said to number about forty percent of those employed. A large crowd of strikers was on hand to watch, along with several sheriff's deputies, but no trouble developed.[70] The company hoped the reopening of No. 2 would encourage additional strikers to return to work, but this does not appear to have been the case.

In fact, given the recent violence, the evictions, and the rough treatment accorded Minszewski during his arrest, both public opinion and the support of other labor organizations were already turning in favor of the strikers. Local No. 425 of the International Association of Machinists voted a contribution to the relief of the strikers, as did Bakers Local No. 14, at whose meeting a committee from New York Mills spoke. Sheet Metal Workers' Local No. 23 "pledged its moral and financial [support] to the striking textile workers in New York Mills," along with making "a liberal donation."[71] Other groups followed, while the general public was quick to purchase copies of postcards sold by the strikers to raise money. The cards featured photographs of the evictions with captions in both English and Polish.

On September 21 two new cases of infantile paralysis surfaced in New York Mills. The New York Mills Corporation donated the use of a large house it owned on the corner of Main Street and Campbell Avenue as a temporary hospital to handle the four cases thusfar reported. In announcing this, Andrew Young pledged to allow the village the free use of the building during the epidemic and dispatched a group of workers to clean the building and make it ready for use. He further pledged to cease all evictions of Polish workers until the epidemic ended. A committee was established to seek supplies for the hospital, and plans were announced to have a physician visit all of the homes of the Polish workers to identify any additional cases of the disease among Polish children.[72] Whether this was done to try and regain the sympathies of the public is uncertain. Regardless, it did relieve some of the tension apparent throughout the village at that time. It is interesting to note, however, that while Young pledged to end the evictions until after the epidemic was over, the records of the New York Mills Corporation indicate that despite the spread of infantile paralysis and the now frosty evening temperatures, the evictions continued. The families of Marek Hałat, Stanisław Kowal and Stanisław Kumurek were evicted on October 3, while those of Józef Głód, Jan Soja, Andrzej Miodunka, J. Zalewski, Władysław Szczerba, Andrzej Kiljan [Killian], Józef Kulpa, Michał Miga, Wacław Nogaś, S. Sheppard, J. Kukułka, J.

Sułkowski, J. Zieman, S. Prymas, A. Szczepański and Jan Szymański were all thrown out on October 6.[73]

On the same day that Young made his promise, September 21, Sara Conboy arrived in New York Mills with the first financial contribution from the national headquarters of the U.T.W.A. Her appearance greatly strengthened the resolve of the strikers, as did the arrival on the following day of Dante Barton, a member of the New York State Industrial Relations Commission who came to the village to observe the situation at first-hand and to report to the Commission on what he found.[74] Not only was the U.T.W.A. now offering financial assistance, but State labor officials were beginning to take a more active interest in settling the strike.

On October 14, John Barry, Frank Turck and Allen Phelps were tried before Judge Fred E. Lewis on charges of assault preferred against them by Joseph Minszewski. In the presence of a large crowd, the Honorable James K. O'Connor, acting as Minszewski's attorney, opened by reading the details of the complaint and the chronology of events of the evening, noting that Minszewski was "beaten and dragged into an automobile." He closed by pointing out that his client was apprehended by the three on charges of riot, despite the fact that he was alone at the time and the legal definition for riot required that three or more persons be involved. Elfio Troja, Horace U. Durant, Mrs. Kate O'Connor, Mrs. Edith Knapp and Mrs. Cornelia Tyrrell all appeared as witnesses to testify that the three defendants used "harsh methods" while arresting Minszewski on August 31. Elfio Troja, an undertaker, testified he heard a man calling "Help me! Help me! Help me!" When he arrived at the scene he saw several men in an automobile and another man approaching it. As he neared it, one of the men in the car stuck out a gun, shouting "Move another step and I'll shoot you dead!" He further testified that "The men in the auto were striking another man they had there. Each one of them struck the other man at least six times. I thought it was a hold-up and went back to the store. The auto came down Devereau [sic] street and stopped in front of my place. I supposed they were after me, but the auto went down Devereau [sic] street." Troja identified the man who held the gun as Turck.[75]

Horace U. Durant also testified, but had difficulty identifying the defendants. "They were dressed shabbily that night and they look somewhat different now," he testified, but he identified them nonetheless. Durant swore that prior to the attack Barry and Turck stood beneath the window to his residence and he heard Barry say to Turck, "You see you do your work and do it right and I'll take care of the rest." Durant said he was watching the men as Barry gave a signal when Minszewski came down off the steps to the Labor Temple. He further testified that Barry's accomplice grabbed Minszewski and said "You'll not go back to Labor Temple again." Then he heard Minszewski shout "Help me!" three times, whereupon the man who grabbed Minszewski punched him several times, pushing him bodily into the automobile. He swore that he saw the men in the automobile strike Minszewski several times before they drove away.[76]

The defendants were represented by former District Attorney Emerson M. Willis. Despite the evidence presented by the various eyewitnesses, the jury deliberated only sixteen minutes before returning a verdict of not guilty.[77]

Despite this small victory, by mid-October the company's position changed dramatically. No longer did it enjoy the support of widespread public opinion. No longer were the strikers isolated, without sufficient financial support to continue their struggle. Although it successfully began operations in Mills No. 2, 3 and 4, no appreciable defections took place from the strikers' ranks, and few new employees signed on. Orders piled up unfilled, and A. D. Juilliard found itself in the position of losing tens of thousands of dollars in potential income during the lucrative fall buying season, which in 1916 was made all the more profitable by the increase in fabric orders spurred by World War I. On Sunday night, October 15, at a meeting in Bagg's Hotel in Utica, the first break in the company's position came with an offer of a two percent increase in wages.[78]

By now, the strikers were gaining the upper hand, and they knew it. Further, the rough tactics employed by A. D. Juilliard's detectives, the eviction of families from their homes in the now inclement October weather, and the other attempts by the company to break the union and force an end to the strike fostered a great sense of bitterness among the strikers. Many of them harbored a tremendous sense of personal anger toward Andrew Young, the man they held responsible for their treatment. "I remember the name distinctly," Stella Furgal, then only eight years old, recalled over half a century later, "because it was a household word — this Young. Everyone criticized him and everyone was bitter and angry against him." The offer of a few cents, probably sufficient to end the strike a month ago, was no longer acceptable. The strikers refused. On the following day the company increased the offer to five percent, but the strikers once again refused. Now, for the first time, Local 753 also spoke openly of the removal of Young as a condition for ending the strike.[79]

The sixteenth annual convention of the United Textile Workers of America met at the Broadway Central Hotel in New York City from October 16 through 21. Minszewski, of course, attended the meeting, with Local 753 being represented by Jan Kwieciński.[80] In his annual report to the convention, international first vice president Jesse Walker, claiming more credit for his own effectiveness than he deserved, stated:

"I went to New York Mills on several occasions,
where a demand for increases in wages and changes in
working conditions was in progress. I held conferences
with the agent and the other officials of the company on
many occasions. I was able to secure about all the concessions asked for, with the exception of the increase in
wages, the former claiming that they had granted two
wage increases this year.

I also took up the wage increase asked for while there
in the Campbell Spring [sic] Company. They took the
same stand as the New York Mills. The strike is still on
there and is being bitterly contested. Organizer Minszewski deserves much credit for the able way he has
conducted this affair."[81]

When called upon for his report, Minszewski gave prominent
treatment to the strike in New York Mills. After reviewing the
circumstances of the strike, he noted that:

"As the company refused to grant the increase in
wages, the strike was still in progress, the company using
all the rough and inhumane methods to break the strike,
hiring thugs and gunmen to act as deputy sheriffs. The
strikers were evicted from their homes by the company,
and these co-called deputy sheriffs did everything within
their power to make matters uncomfortable for our
strikers. Also the Justice of the Peace there was influenced by the company, and strikers who were arrested were
convicted without any justice."[82]

Minszewski continued on to praise the Utica Trades Assembly for
its efforts to assist the strikers, and for its willingness to send members
to stand with the picketers. "Each night and morning," Minszewski
said, "they are found on the picket line, and their presence alone has
been sufficient to curb the clubs of the thugs and gunmen who have
been appointed as deputy sheriffs to guard the property of the mill
company."[83] He continued on to describe the evictions and the subsequent death of Chrzan, evicted while ill with tuberculosis. "This
strike is still on," he concluded, "and anyone looking at the grim,
determined faces of the strikers will know that it is a fight to a finish.
This is the kind of strikers and the kind of people who do not know the
meaning of the word 'quit'."[84]

Due in large part to Minszewski's impassioned description of the strike in New York Mills, the U.T.W.A. convention drafted Resolution No. 44 which read:

> "Whereas, 2,700 Textile Workers have been on strike for over four months for an increase in wages in New York Mills, N.Y.; and,
>
> Whereas, The most brutal methods ever practiced upon strikers have been put in operation by the officials of the New York Mills Corporation in order to defeat the strikers who have been evicted from the company houses wholesale; and,
>
> Whereas, The thugs and gunmen employed by the Mill Corporation have beaten up many of the strikers along with our Polish Organizer; and,
>
> Whereas, Those 2,700 people are only demanding a living wage for the labor they perform; ... therefore, be it
>
> Resolved, That this Convention go on record as tendering their moral and financial support to the striking Textile Workers in ... New York Mills, N.Y.; and, be it further
>
> Resolved, That the International Officers be instructed to immediately send out an appeal to our Local Unions and to others, who in their judgment they feel they can appeal to, to give their financial aid to the Textile Workers now on strike in the above named cities; and, be it further
>
> Resolved, That in the appeal we urge the members of all our Local Unions to give as generously as their financial conditions will allow and give immediately."[85]

"You have heard the resolution," president John Golden intoned from the podium. "What is your pleasure?"

Several representatives rose to speak in favor of the resolution, including Minszewski who again provided a "graphic" account of the conditions in New York Mills. When the question was finally called, the resolution passed unanimously.[86]

As soon as the U.T.W.A. convention concluded on October 21 Minszewski and Kwieciński departed for New York Mills to rejoin the fight.[87]

On the same day, with Minszewski and Kwieciński still enroute back from New York City, there was another meeting between representatives of the company, Local 753, and the Utica Trades Assembly. Once again the company offered a five percent wage increase. Once again it was rejected. The representatives of Local 753 informed the company that they wanted a twelve and one-half percent increase, but would be willing to settle the strike for ten percent. They would accept no less.[88]

Upon Minszewski's return, another conference was held on the evening of October 24 in the office of Mill No. 1. Minszewski represented the strikers, Madison G. Roberts and Edward T. Martin attended from the Utica Trades Assembly, and John Leiper and Alexander Hobbs represented the owners of the New York Mills Corporation and the Oneida Bleachery respectively. It is significant that Andrew Young, who the strikers now viewed with disdain as a major part of the problem between them and the New York Mills Corporation, did not attend. Without his presence, the parties agreed in principle to a final settlement to be committed to writing and explained to the workers at a meeting in Union Hall on the following day.[89]

The strike was one of the longest ever staged in Oneida County. It lasted fourteen weeks and one day, with an estimated loss in wages of some $140,000. During the course of the strike ninety-six families were evicted from company-owned housing.[90] In the official report of the New York State Industrial Commission, Third Deputy Commissioner Frank Bret Thorn, responsible for the Bureau of Mediation and Arbitration, wrote that of the twenty-two textile strikes in New York State that took place in the year between July 1, 1916 and June 30, 1917, "The most serious strike in this industry occurred at New York Mills on July 18, 1916, and involved 874 carders, spinners and others directly and 511 other persons indirectly." In all, the strike included some 1,375 employees in the factories operated by the New York Mills Corporation and the Oneida Bleachery, and another 245 in the Walcott & Campbell spinning operations. Thus, of the 4,721 persons effected by the twenty-two strikes, 1,620 people, or 34.3% of the total, were accounted for in the New York Mills strike. Thorn further noted that of the total of 144,464 working days lost in the twenty-two strikes, 82,614 days, or 57.2%, were due to the strike in New York Mills.[91]

According to the terms of the final agreement, manufacturing operations in all departments resumed immediately with all of the strikers being reinstated within two weeks. The employees received the requested ten percent wage increase; all those evicted from company owned housing who desired to return were moved back to their previous homes at the company's expense without having to pay rent for the weeks between July 18 and October 21 when they were on strike; all of the strikers were reinstated in their former positions, or equivalent positions, without discrimination; the company agreed to recognize the union as a representative of the employees; the card system was abolished; the company agreed to eliminate discrimination against any employees; the company agreed to drop its $25,000 legal action against the union leaders; and, the company agreed to pay the legal costs and attorney's fees associated with the appeal of the evictions.[92] The union gave up its demand for a reduction in the number of looms to be operated, a demand the U.T.W.A. and many of the weavers in the mills themselves felt was not justified to begin with, but it achieved not only all of the other demands it enumerated at the beginning of the strike, but several others added after the confrontations and evictions during the strike. By any definition, it was a stunning victory for the strikers.

Yet, more was to come. During the long fourteen weeks they were idle, the strikers developed a bitter hatred for Andrew Young, the general manager in charge of all the New York Mills Corporation activities in the village. So upset were they at his stubborn refusal to negotiate, his demeaning attitude toward the strikers, his broken promises and his repressive methods of dealing with the union, that in the latter stages of negotiations Local 753 demanded his removal as a condition of settling the strike. This demand does not appear in the formal agreements ending the strike, but union officials maintained later that they secured an unwritten understanding that Young would be removed.

On October 27 Andrew M. Young announced his resignation as director, treasurer and general manager of the New York Mills Corporation, and director of the Oneida Bleachery. The *Utica Daily Press*, which led the reader to believe that the resignation was a voluntary one contemplated for some time, lauded Young and his contributions to both the company and the surrounding community, concluding that "He retires with the good will of all with whom he has been so long connected."[93] The *Utica Saturday Globe* reviewed Young's career in an article titled "From Mule Boy to Manager" in its October 28 edition. In it the paper maintained that "The corporation which he served received the best that was in him; the employees found in him the qualities of justice and humaneness; the community received his active assistance in every movement directed toward civic betterment. He retires from the service of the corporation with the good will of all."[94] According to the *Utica Observer*, which also commended his services, "Mr. Young has no immediate plans for the future, but he is considering a number of business propositions and will take his time before entering a new position."[95] Such reactions could not to be found in the Polish community. "They fired him!" insisted Józef Piszcz emphatically. "They demanded that he be fired. That was a workers demand. ... The newspapers won't tell you anything. They cover everything up."[96]

In any case, the strike was over and the *Utica Herald-Dispatch* could report in earnest that "The public will be glad that the strike is over.

The resumption of work will send many thousands of dollars into circulation weekly and better feeling will prevail."[97]

Yes, the strike was over. People could now return to the normal routine of daily life. And for the people of New York Mills, whether employer or employee, whether English, Welsh, French, Italian, Syrian, or Polish, there was no doubt about the outcome of *this* strike. "After a struggle of more than four months," *The Textile Worker* reported to U.T.W.A. members, "striking Textile Workers of New York Mills, New York, have won a splendid victory. Evicted from the company houses and brutally treated by the hired thugs and gunmen, this band of Textile Workers still continued to fight on, with the result that the splendid courage and determination displayed finally resulted in a victory for these strikers."[98]

At the next annual convention of the United Textile Workers of America, Joseph Minszewski could report with pride, "The strike at New York Mills, which was carried over from last year, was a decided victory for our Polish members. I do not need to tell you again of the sufferings endured by these noble people for several months, most of it in the depths of a severe Winter. However, victory crowned our efforts and peace reigns in New York Mills." The strike of Local 753 was one of only two major strikes specifically mentioned as victories during that year.[99] So complete was it that John Golden, president of the U.T.W.A., deemed it to be "one of the greatest victories ever secured."[100]

Yet it remained for *Słowo Polskie*, the voice of the Polish community in the Utica area, to pronounce the last word on the significance of the 1916 strike over a decade later when it concluded, with knowledge gained from the perspective of time, that the strike "ended with complete victory, and from that time on the capitalists paid attention to the workers and avoided conflicts with them."[101]

Chapter 9

Epilogue

The victory of Local 753 in the 1916 strike resulted in many far-reaching consequences. In addition to the immediate gains acquired through the negotiated settlement, the successful strike also served as a stimulus to further cohesive action within the Polish community and proved to be the beginning of a long process that eventually resulted in a single community replacing the ethnic divisions that existed at the beginning of the century.

In the aftermath of the strike the Polish workers in New York Mills continued to support Local 753 as their collective representative to management. Union organizers handled several minor grievances, but in general the company exhibited a new respect for the strength of the union and any outstanding complaints were quickly resolved to the satisfaction of all parties.[1] Indeed, some substantial gains were negotiated. In 1925, when declining profits in the textile industry resulted in a nationwide wage reduction of 10%, Local 753 was strong enough to prevent the reduction in New York Mills. As prices rose somewhat in the latter years of the 1920s, it negotiated wage increases. Later, even in the depths of the Depression, with unemployment greatly reducing its ranks, Local 753 continued to support the U.T.W.A. by successfully joining in the nationwide textile strike in September, 1934, closing down the A. D. Juilliard operations until the conclusion of a national settlement.[2]

Despite the often tumultuous nature of the national labor scene during the years between the two world wars, labor relations in New York Mills were generally amicable, with the activities of Local 753 focusing primarily on internal affairs rather than employer-employee relations. Throughout the two interwar decades members of Local 753 played an important part in the national affairs of the U.T.W.A., with several performing valuable service on national committees. The most important of these activities took place in 1926 when Józef Piszcz, then president of Local 753, became the first person from the Utica district, and the first Polish American elected to the Executive Board of the U.T.W.A. As a member of the national board he frequently spoke to labor groups throughout the northeast, and was involved as a representative of the U.T.W.A. in the historic Passaic strike, speaking on that occasion to an audience of over 6,000 strikers.[3]

Although active on the national level, the leaders of Local 753 did not neglect their primary duty to their members. By 1945, a new contract negotiated with A. D. Juilliard proved to be exceptionally beneficial to labor. In fact, *The Textile Challenger*, the newspaper of the U.T.W.A., carried a feature article announcing that "The finest contract ever signed for workers in the cotton textile industry was won for the 2,000 workers of A. D. Juilliard, New York Mills Division.... This contract should be a model, in many respects, for the other locals of the U.T.W.A."[4] Indeed, the contract so impressed Benjamin Haskell, Director of the U.T.W.A.'s Research and Publicity Department, that he wrote to Local 753 president William Silcox to ask: "Would you kindly see to it that we receive a few copies of your excellent agreement with the New York Mills? We have had a few requests for our best contract and yours is probably the best one at present. I would appreciate receiving this at your earliest convenience."[5]

With the conclusion of World War II the prohibition on labor strikes ended and national labor leaders became anxious to test their new strength. Consequently, in November, 1945, the United Auto Workers initiated the first large-scale post-war walkout by striking General Motors. In January, 1946, the United Steel Workers walked out and in April they were followed by the United Mine Workers. Before 1946 was over, it became the worst strike year in history with more than 4,750,000 workers on strike at some time during the year, and an estimated loss of 116,000,000 work days.

In this atmosphere of labor pressure, representatives of A. D. Juilliard met with union leaders to discuss new contract terms once their earlier agreement expired. The negotiations were generally friendly, resulting in a new contract that included liberal vacation benefits, special provisions for apprenticeship for loomfixers, and an employee insurance program, the entire cost of which was borne by the company. The insurance included a $500 death benefit; $1,000 for accidental death; a percentage of $500 for loss of a limb, eye, etc.; hospitalization and surgical benefits up to $150; sick benefits of $12 per week for 13 weeks. Benefits did not apply for any accident or death compensable under the New York State compensation law. In his thorough study of unionism in the Utica area textile industries, Norman Bourke noted that as a result of the 1946 contract "The New York Mills plant has a more liberal vacation plan in granting a week and a half vacation period in addition to the usual one and two week periods. This extra vacation is the exception for this industry and also for the Utica area." Bourke maintains that there was no particular reason for the vacation clause other than that the union asked for the benefit and the company granted it. He speculates that it may have been granted because the union existed for a long time and had "very good relations with management."[6]

This new contract was also looked upon very favorably by the national union. As soon as it was signed Haskell wrote to Silcox to ask for a copy: "We are very much in need of a copy of the wage scale at New York Mills inasmuch as it is one of the best cotton wage schedules in the north. Would you please see to it that we receive a copy just as soon as it is possible for you to send it to us? We would appreciate your cooperation in this matter very much."[7]

In fact, the contracts signed by Locals 753 and 1442 at the conclusion of World War II were so favorable it proved difficult to justify requests for further concessions. In March, 1946, when the loomfixers requested information on wage scales from the national U.T.W.A. headquarters to support their negotiations with management, Haskell replied to Edward Robellard, secretary of Loomfixers Local 1442: "I regret to say that from our information on wage rates in the area, the Union has won for the workers in your plant just about as much as can be obtained at the present time. You are at the top of the wage ladder."[8]

In 1947 the U.T.W.A. recognized Local 753's success in its negotiations with A. D. Juilliard by nominating the local for study in a national project. In July of that year Haskell wrote to Silcox to inform him that "The National Planning Association which consists of representatives of industry, labor, economists, government administrators, etc., is undertaking a study on 'The Causes of Industrial Peace under Collective Bargaining.' We have been asked to nominate various plants under contract with the United Textile Workers of America to be considered for inclusion in that study, and we have included, among others, the A. D. Juilliard Co., New York Mills, New York."[9]

The confidence of the U.T.W.A. in Local 753 was again rewarded in 1948 when a contract renewal negotiated with A. D. Juilliard and the Oneida Bleachery provided for wage increases totaling some $500,000 per year. The contract included raises ranging from $.10 to $.19 per hour, with six paid holidays. In reporting the new contract, *The Textile Challenger* noted that "The average hourly wage rate at New York Mills plants, thus hitting a new high of $1.245, is the highest average hourly wage rate paid for any northern cotton textile mill." At the same time, the "Loomfixers' hourly wages are advanced to $1.62, which is the highest hourly wage rate for plain cotton loomfixers in the country."[10]

The fact that labor relations were relatively calm in New York Mills during the thirty-three years between 1917 and 1950 was a direct result of the victory gained by Local 753 in 1916. Similarly, there were a number of other activities in which union leaders played leading roles that led to the further development and strengthening of the Polish community. Chief among these was the formation of Lodge 2066 of the *Związek Narodowy Polski* [Polish National Alliance], a national fraternal organization providing insurance benefits while also promoting educational and cultural causes. Under its first president, former union activist Michał Tuman, the lodge established a respectable library and sponsored special Polish language classes for children, theatrical performances, social banquets to commemorate important events in Polish history, historical assemblies and lectures. By 1922 the Alliance was large enough to purchase land and raise funds for a permanent building to house the rapidly expanding organization.[11]

As the Polish community continued to develop, the village itself underwent another important change in the evolutionary process from company town to civic municipality when, on March 29, 1922, the State of New York issued a Certificate of Incorporation for the Village of New York Mills.[12] The political consequences of this event were immediately grasped. In fact, the Poles in New York Mills were long aware of the political implications of their situation. They recognized that the influence of the owners and the Anglo-Saxon community extended to the political and law enforcement establishments and realized that if they were to gain true equality and mastery over their own collective destiny they must gain an entry into political power. Their experiences in the strikes of 1912 and 1916 provided them with a remarkable awareness and understanding of the workings of the American political and judicial systems. They realized that collective action was necessary, and that this action *must* come within the context of the established American political system. Thus, since those in political power dominated the Republican Party, closing its doors to them, they chose allegiance with the Democratic Party as a means of obtaining political influence.

In 1918 the *Klub Krakówski* [Kraków Club] changed its name and incorporated itself as the *Klub Polsko-Amerykańsko-Obywatelski* [Polish American Citizens Club]. Originally founded by union activists Jan Sroka, Michał Tuman, Józef Smoła, Jerzy Kozakiewicz and others, during the years between the strikes and the granting of the Certificate of Incorporation to the village, this organization sponsored concerted efforts to obtain citizenship for as many people as possible. Józef Piszcz, himself an active leader in this movement, later recalled how "Kazimierz Dziedzic and Jan Mucha went house to house to encourage people to gain citizenship and vote. They each spoke Polish, English and German." By the time the Certificate of Incorporation was issued, many of the village's immigrant residents had either become citizens or begun the necessary naturalization process.[13]

The efforts of Piszcz, Dziedzic, and Mucha, actively supported by Father Fijałkowski and others, eventually bore fruit. The Polish American Citizens Club soon became the New York Mills Polish Democratic Club. "The Polish Democratic Club was very active in politics," recalled Peter Kogut. "They knew they had to get into politics to be recognized and be part of the community — to be represented."[14]

The Poles adroitly allied themselves with Dennis Shannon, Democratic Party leader for the Town of Whitestown. "Denny Shannon was the guy who helped an awful lot," Peter Kogut recalled. "He was, you might say, smart enough to know that some day these people are going to vote and that they are going to vote for the people who actually helped them.... [Shannon] encouraged the people to become citizens. He helped them to find ways to get into village government.... He saw possibilities in the Polish people. He realized that the Polish people are known to be solid citizens."[15] Using this new combined political clout, the Democrats were able to wrest control of the Town of Whitestown from the traditional Republican majority.

From these beginnings the political strength of the Polish community continued to grow. By 1923 the organization became powerful enough to elect Antoni Zamiarski as the first Polish American village trustee. Later, Józef Piszcz and Walenty Mądry gained election as Democratic Committeemen for the Town of Whitestown, and in 1927 Jan Sliski was elected to the New York Mills Village Board. Two years later, in 1929, Jan Kiełbasa became the first Polish American named by the Village Board to the important position of police chief, while in 1930 Stanley Federowski joined Sliski on the Village Board, thus giving the Poles half of the four Village Board positions for the first time. During the decade of the 1930s the Poles continued to make inroads into the village's political structure and began to share in the patronage appointments derived from this new status: Stanley Mikulski was named village electrician, Dr. F. F. Chaya became the village health officer, Józef Piszcz served five years as Town of Whitestown assessor, and in 1933, during the depths of the Depression, the Village Board passed a resolution proposed by Antoni Zamiarski that "the work of the village be divided between the Polish and American workmen as near equal as possible." The Poles were major players in the village's political arena.[16]

In 1935 the political complexion of village life permanently changed when villagers elected Jan Rogowski, Stanley Federowski and Jan Furgał village Trustees, filling three of the four available positions. The results of this majority were immediately felt with the appointment of Michał Tuman as village road commissioner, Stanley Walewski as

Village Clerk, Stanley Sleczkowski as village Tax Collector, and Jan Rogowski as Deputy Mayor. But the Polish community won more than the right to political patronage, it won the right and the ability to shape its own collective destiny. What began as a workers' movement for better wages and treatment ended as a political movement for control of the decisions effecting the living conditions and the very lives of the people. In a sense, it culminated in the election of Antoni Zamiarski as mayor in 1939, an event that inaugurated a half-century of Polish control of the Village Board and the mayor's office, a control that still exists at this writing. Thus, in time, the minority group became the dominant group.[17]

In the short-term this active participation in village governance proved valuable in guaranteeing equality of treatment for the village's Polish population. In the long-term, it was important not only because it gave the Poles a voice in the democratic process, but because it also helped to break down some of the cultural misunderstandings that polarized the village after the arrival of the Poles. As early as the 1920s Polish names such as Kazimierz Dziedzic, Józef Łachut, Jan Greczkowski, Józef Tobiasz and Jan Puła began to surface in the elite and hitherto Anglo-Saxon dominated ranks of the loomfixers. By the end of the 1930s, Stanley Zima was elected as the first Polish president of Loomfixers Local 1442, while in another example of the ongoing integration of the communities, William Silcox became the first non-Polish president of Local 753.[18] Community picnics sponsored by A. D. Juilliard, athletic contests at a community park donated by the company, and the integration of children into a consolidated community high school also sped the processes of community integration. World War II accelerated it even more, bringing community members together in war bond drives, public events and in the armed services.

Yet, despite growing integration of the community, the successful contract negotiations with A. D. Juilliard, the glowing rhetoric of U.T.W.A. officials, and the prominent roles played by representatives of Local 753 in national union affairs, the labor situation in New York Mills was, by 1950, beginning to deteriorate. Throughout the twentieth century, the cotton textile industry stood on uncertain ground. At the beginning of the century competition increased from new synthetic products such as nylon and dacron, which increasingly made inroads into the market share enjoyed by cotton fabrics. The older cotton-based textile manufacturers, such as the A.D. Juilliard holdings, could not compete effectively without expensive new machinery, research and advertising campaigns. Another intrusive factor that traced its roots to near the turn of the century was the gradual relocation of the textile industry to the Southern states where lower wage scales, coupled with cheaper land, favorable local tax incentives, and state laws inhibiting the development of labor unions, made textile production less expensive for the manufacturers. The advantages of transportation and power enjoyed by the North in the nineteenth century became a thing of the past with the development of a nationwide rail network and the construction of the massive power facilities of the Tennessee Valley Authority and other New Deal programs.[19]

A. D. Juilliard's New York Mills Division was the recognized name in corduroy beginning in the 1930s, but the company never reinvested in its machinery and physical plant, both of which became obsolete, resulting in declining profits. "The machinery was made in 1900," Józef Piszcz recalled. "Everything they had here was behind the times.... They couldn't compete."[20] This proved symptomatic of all the Juilliard holdings as those in control amassed personal fortunes while the businesses became outmoded and uncompetitive. "Juilliard was here for a long time," Richard Rosiński explained some thirty-five years later, "and probably did an awful lot of good in terms of the local community and what it had to offer in terms of jobs, ... because most of our parents knew nothing more than going to work, coming home, raising a family and going to church. This was a solid community. The tragedy that unfolded was that they never put money back into the business. So that after the war, when you had all these eager young guys investing in new businesses, and buying new equipment in textiles, here you had a company that was twenty years behind the times. They were using old weaving machines that were back, hell, thirty or forty years old."[21]

Further, the advent of new and very expensive machinery often required certain physical configurations such as long buildings for the assembly line, not the rectangular multi-storied brick structures in New York Mills. As a result, both buildings and equipment were obsolete. "One big thing," William Silcox explained, "was straight line production. They put these long buildings, one story, you would bring your bale of cotton [in one end] and you would take the finished product out [the other end]. We had to go up and down and up and down stories here. Also, we had leather belts and old-fashioned machinery here and they had ball bearing machinery where if you went into a spinning room there wouldn't be an end down. Over here they were constantly putting up ends. The mill was worn out."[22]

Given the large costs attending an extensive renovation of both factories and machinery, Juilliard officials felt it was cheaper in the long run to relocate where the cost advantages were greater and where abundant suburban land could be found for new factories, large parking lots, and greater access to rail and highway transportation. Indeed, A.D. Juilliard had already taken advantage of these conditions when it opened its Aragon Mills in Mississippi.[23]

An ambitious modernization plan for the New York Mills Division
was developed in 1950, but never materialized. In 1951 A. D. Juilliard
closed its large No. 2 mill, citing obsolescence "as one of the reasons
for the closing."[24] Company officials explained that the closing was a
result of several factors including: (1) obsolescence, (2) high production costs in the North, (3) cost of transporting raw materials, and (4)
increased competition from Southern mills.[25] All of the reasons dealt
with the costs of continued operation, making it obvious that Juilliard
favored a relocation of its factories to more profitable areas. With the
closing of No. 2, the mills which had at one time employed as many as
2,500 operatives saw their work force decline to 1,400, and then 1,200
people.[26]

In the end, A. D. Juilliard closed its New York Mills Division
permanently in 1953 when it sold its physical plant and arranged to sell
some 124 company-owned houses, mostly two-family, with those who
resided in them at that time having the first opportunity to buy.
"Juilliard made it possible for the people to buy these houses by keeping the price right," Stephen Zurek recalled. "They didn't turn it over
to a real estate broker who would inflate the prices. ... They went
through the process at that time of bringing the surveyors in and stak-
ing out all the lots, Juilliard went through that, so when the people
bought these homes they were ready to be bought. You didn't have to
go through the expense of hiring a surveyor, there were no closing
costs, there was none of that stuff that you experience today ... every
family who worked for this company and occupied these homes got a
great deal. No question about it." Many people took advantage of this
opportunity to purchase the houses they lived in for so long, and the
company was said to have received about $700,000 from the sales. In
the case of the two-family houses, sometimes one family moved out
and the building was purchased by the remaining family, while in other
cases both families opted to purchase their respective halves, which
sometimes led to strange situations where, as Stanley Zima laughed,
"people who owned half of the house would paint or put a roof on their
half and the other half would not."[27]

With the closing of the mills, Local 753 also ceased to exist. Yet,
one more victory remained to be won. In a final irony, the national
headquarters of the U.T.W.A. laid claim to the deed to Union Hall in
New York Mills, arguing that as the property of Local 753 it was
rightly now the property of the U.T.W.A. A bitter court battle ensued,
with the judge finally handing down a ruling that since the property was
originally deeded to the Polish Workingmen's Hall Association, Inc.,
the building belonged to the local people and not the national organization.[28]

When the mills began closing people in the village became very discouraged, fearing for what the future might bring. "Everybody said that New York Mills would die and that the people would die of starvation," said Stella Furgal. "They never did. They are better today than they ever were. And a lot of those people who were working in the mills would have died in the mills."[29]

With the passing of the textile era, the fabric that held the community together weakened. Local patterns of employment underwent a forced change, with former textile operatives finding jobs in the businesses and industries of nearby localities such as Utica and Rome, while some commuted up to twenty-six miles to work in the Oneida Limited Silversmiths in Sherrill. As children matured, they no longer stayed with their parents, but increasingly took jobs outside the village, often moving away to be near their new places of employment. Rather than a self-contained economic unit, New York Mills became a satellite, suburban residential community. Although the new diversity of employment created a more stable economy than the old single-employer company town enjoyed, and provided more opportunity for civic involvement, the lack of a single major indigenous employer also led to the weakening of community bonds. Because people no longer worked for the same employers, in the same industries in their own home town, they no longer shared the bonds of economic commonality that united them into a vibrant ethnic community. The new employment patterns led to a new sense of assimilation following World War II, eliminating most of the barriers that previously divided the village into two separate communities. Men and women who no longer worked in the village began to join organizations such as the Lions Club, Rotary, the Chamber of Commerce, and mainstream social and cultural organizations. Workers who once found common ground in Locals 753 now belonged to various unions throughout many industries located in a number of communities. And with this new diversity of opportunity, and the attending assimilation, their children began to join the Boy or Girl Scouts, public school clubs, and to participate in Little League baseball. With the end of the mill era, the vibrant, self-sustaining Polish American community also declined.[30]

Yet, the Polish community in New York Mills did not forget its origins; rather, studies by trained historians, sociologists and anthropologists found that even some thirty-five years after the closing of the mills, the community retained a strong identification with both its ethnic and industrial heritage. "Because the original Polish immigrant population linked land ownership to economic prosperity," one study concluded, "a strong identification with the local urban environment has resulted. While the textile company's control was instrumental in physically shaping the townscape during the nineteenth and early twentieth centuries, it has been during the post-company era, when Polish-American residents could buy property, that they have truly made the environment their own. They have chosen to emphasize civic improvement and the village's appearance as a sign of their success in terms of American standards. Yet the means of achieving this community image has had its roots in some basic ethnic values: a desire for group cohesion, concern for the care of land and property, and the belief in civic participation as a personal duty. All these values are recognizable in New York Mills, in its landscape, and in the mental image its residents have formed of it."[31]

The textile economy disappeared, taking with it not only the union but the village's longstanding insular lifestyle. The barriers of employer domination and ethnicity no longer existed. As a result, the need for a close-knit, cohesive Polish American community gradually disappeared along with all but the more symbolic of the traditions the village's early residents brought with them from the Old Country. The village became a single community where people were free to seek employment of their own choosing, to associate with whom they pleased, and to take part in whatever organizations and social activities they wished. The first generation of Polish immigrants who arrived in New York Mills at the beginning of the twentieth century sought a better life for themselves and their children in a new land promising economic opportunity and freedom. The struggle may have been longer and more difficult than they first imagined, but in the end the very assimilation of their descendants stood as an indication of their success in achieving the new life they sought.

Chapter 10

Summary and Conclusion

Soon after the conclusion of American independence the beginnings of a commercial textile industry were laid with the erection of a mill along Sauquoit Creek, some two miles southeast of the small city of Utica, New York. During the nineteenth century, this business grew to become one of the largest producers of cotton textiles outside New England, and to enjoy a reputation for the extraordinary quality of its products. In the process of building their company, the owners, the Walcott and Campbell families, proved to be equally paternalistic about the village which slowly grew up around their mills. They took a great interest in the lives of their workers, both on the job and off, building company housing, providing company stores, and enforcing company rules throughout the village. Thus, by the beginning of the twentieth century, the Walcott and Campbell holding developed into not only a successful business concern, but a very rigidly controlled society in which curfews were enforced, church attendance was required and the consumption of alcoholic beverages was cause for the termination of employment.

By the turn of the century, the growth of the business caused the Walcotts and Campbells to begin a serious effort to recruit European labor, leading to an influx of Polish immigrants. The coming of the Poles led to a serious polarization within the community. Speaking a different language, the Poles were Catholics amid a sea of Protestants, Slavs amidst an Anglo-Saxon community, people whose east European heritage and traditions were alien and often unfathomable to the earlier settlers from the British Isles and French Canada. Immediately suspect as competitors for jobs and housing, the Poles also ran afoul of the rigid proprietary control of the village which viewed with shocked concern their use of alcoholic beverages, their Sunday afternoon picnics, and the many other cultural differences that proved virtually impenetrable in setting them apart from the earlier settlers, promoting distrust and suspicion that often led to open discrimination.

Moving into the community, these new arrivals sought shelter in company housing where extended families often numbering a dozen people or more lived in two and three room homes and many families were forced to take in boarders to pay for rent and food. The homes were old and barren, they lacked plumbing, water had to be carried from a single well that served a whole street and repairs were often neglected by company officials. The diet was meager, consisting mainly of bread, potatoes and fatback supplemented when possible by the produce of small gardens.

Relegated by the barriers of language and culture to the lowest, unskilled positions in the mills, the Poles worked long hours in carding rooms where lint and dust ruined their lungs, in weave shops where noise impaired their hearing, and in a bleachery where open chemical vats exposed them to carcinogenic materials. Health and safety standards were largely non-existent, while bosses frequently subjected them to abuse and ill-treatment.

In order to protect themselves and better their lot, the Poles first turned to the religious and community traditions they brought with them from the Old Country. They founded a parish and supporting religious organizations to care for their spiritual needs, while at the same time establishing ethnic fraternals to provide insurance and other sorely needed secular support. This ethnic infrastructure served to provide a sense of community and collective security against the outside world, a support system essential to their survival.

Soon, the poor wages, working conditions and treatment they found in the textile mills caused them to discuss the formation of a union to lobby for "more pay and better treatment." But, when these efforts became known, the company took steps to crush the infant movement: their leaders were fired, evicted from company housing and "blacklisted" to prevent future employment. Faced with this concerted effort to deny them representation, the Polish leaders made a fateful decision to cast their lot with the United Textile Workers of America. In doing this, they moved outside the confines of the ethnic community into the mainstream of American labor activity, and ultimately into contact with political and labor leaders from other communities and other ethnic groups.

When the company refused to consider their grievances, the members of the new union voted to strike. During the cold spring of 1912 these poor workers walked picket lines, solicited support in neighboring communities and withstood all of the pressures that the influential company could bring to bear. Company officials were sworn in as deputy sheriffs, under which authority they provoked confrontations with pickets. The company hired outside strike-breakers, martial law was declared, the state militia was called in to protect company property, and company officials systematically lied to the press and the state government about conditions in the mills and their attitude toward their employees. Yet, despite the cold, the privations and the company's duplicitous actions, the union held out for a negotiated settlement in which it won a wage increase, public posting of piece rates, improvements to company housing, the rehiring of all strikers, and promises of better treatment.

The 1912 strike was important not only because of the concessions won from the company, or the renewed sense of confidence in the Polish community, but because it provided an opportunity for the Poles to reach beyond the confines of their ethnic community to join a national American organization, the United Textile Workers of America. Similarly, for the first time the Poles were successful in soliciting support from other non-Polish groups such as the Utica Trades Assembly. This interaction with other groups began to break down the isolation of the Polish community, while at the same time providing evidence that success could be achieved by working through the existing American economic and political structures.

When conditions again deteriorated in the mills in the years following the 1912 strike, another work stoppage took place in 1916 to renew the earlier demands for equal pay and decent treatment. On this occasion the strikers once again faced a serious and determined effort by the company to crush the union. Company officials were once again hired as deputy sheriffs, while private detectives were employed to infiltrate the union and to secure evidence and testimony that could be used in legal actions against union leaders. Efforts were made to divide the Poles from the Italian, Syrian, French-Canadian and English workers, and large numbers of Italian strikebreakers were hired in an attempt to further inflame ethnic passions. The company was unsuccessful in efforts to bribe the parish priest to use his influence to end the strike, while similar pressure was brought to bear on the press to obtain favorable coverage for the company's position. During the height of an epidemic of infantile paralysis, families were evicted from company housing and hundreds of people were forced to live in tents or with relatives during the cold nights of September and October. The company disseminated false information and filed legal actions for damages against union leaders. In the end, it even attempted to use its "deputies" to provoke violence that could be blamed on the strikers. Despite all of this, the strikers maintained a remarkable discipline that allowed them to continue their peaceful protest in the face of seemingly overwhelming odds.

The immediate result of this second strike was an overwhelming victory for the workers who gained wage increases, an end to the restrictive "card system," recognition of the union as a collective bargaining agent, the rehiring of all strikers, the firing of the mill superintendent, and several other concessions. Yet the long-term results were even more important as the strike once again brought the Poles into contact with non-Polish labor organizations, political leaders and community groups who were won over to support of the strikers' cause. These contacts served to decrease the social and cultural walls that separated the Poles from the other ethnic groups in the area, beginning a long but steady process of integration. Further, the fact that the Poles were once again successful in working through the American labor and political systems not only assured them that this would bring favorable results, but gave them valuable experience in developing an understanding of how American institutions worked. Their experience in dealing with the U.T.W.A. and the other organizations brought them into the mainstream of American economic and political life, an extremely important development if successful integration was to occur.

The development of organized labor in New York Mills represented a melding of Polish political and cultural values with those of the United States. The Old World traditions of the Polish workers could clearly be seen in their efforts to organize along the communal lines of Polish rural culture. As the traditional guardians of family and culture, Polish women were greatly in evidence among the picketers and among those who cared for the evicted and the destitute. Similarly, the rhetoric reported by the Polish press was clearly European in context, with the police being referred to as "Cossacks," the owners as "Czars," and so on. These and other factors provide clear evidence of a Polish perspective or world view in transition.

Yet, it was equally obvious that a significant transition was indeed taking place. The strikers wrapped themselves in the symbolism of the American flag. While invoking images from their Old World past amongst themselves, the Poles very adeptly alluded to the Constitutional guarantees of freedom and equality, to the images of the "Founding Fathers," and to the value of liberty in presenting their case to the American public. This awareness of the American milieu in which they resided was crucial not only to the success of the strikes, but to the future integration of the Polish community.

The strikes of 1912 and 1916 provided the Polish community with much more than the immediate gains outlined in the negotiated settlements. The strikes conveyed to the workers not only a sense of their collective organization, but a sense of *power* in collective action and a sense of how to channel that power to their own advantage *through* the mainstream American economic and political institutions. With this awareness, they successfully developed a political presence that eventually propelled them from minority to dominant status within the village. Much as they worked within the structure of the United Textile Workers of America to win concessions from management, they soon became successful in working within the Democratic Party to take permanent control of their own collective destiny. Unlike the stereotypical views of Polish American communities, the Poles in New York Mills developed a vibrant social and cultural ethnic community *and* were successful in organizing to control their own lives.

Why were they so successful? Initially, the Poles in New York Mills developed along the lines of other Polish communities. Although they had a single parish in the village, they developed a number of religious and secular organizations that were ethnic in nature. While these assisted them in meeting the spiritual and worldly necessities of life, they provided neither a single unified organization encompassing the bulk of the population nor an entry into or a means of controlling their position vis-à-vis the dominant community about them. Rather, these ethnic associations were insular organizations which, though they performed very valuable social, cultural and religious functions, did not provide unity or influence within the dominant community. The union was the key ingredient. Given the nature of New York Mills as a small village where the vast majority of the workers were employed by a single industry, the union could transcend the divisions that existed in the Polish community, uniting the people through their common interest in the one factor that had a direct effected on all of their lives. Further, once this unity was achieved, the union provided them with an outlet for collective action *within* the context of the American mainstream. They were working through the system, rather than remaining within the confines of a restrictive ethnic ghetto. The final step was to turn that collective action to politics.

Clearly, the success of the strikes was crucial to both the short-term welfare of the Polish immigrants in New York Mills, and the long-term well-being of their sons and daughters in succeeding generations. Yet the strikes were also important in other ways as well. They had a direct impact on the surrounding communities, and also carry an important message for scholars interested in the study of immigrant community and labor development.

While the consequences of the strikes were most keenly felt in the village where they occurred, their influence also spread to surrounding communities. News of the strikes and their progress was carried not only in the English language press throughout central New York, but also in the ethnic press including such influential Polish-language national and regional newspapers as *Dziennik Ludowy*, *Telegram Codzienny* and *Trybuna Robotnicza*. All of these papers followed the strikes in New York Mills, reporting on their success to readers hungry to improve their own lives.[1] Then too, the influence of the strikes was not limited to Poles, the benefits reached workers of all nationalities causing, for example, the Italian newspaper *La Luce* to comment favorably on the struggle of the Poles and urge Utica's Italian population to emulate their example.

The success of the Poles in New York Mills stirred worker hopes in other areas, and also provided tangible assistance to workers in the surrounding area. Even as the strikes progressed, for example, textile mills throughout the Utica area announced increases in wages in an effort to prevent the strikes from spreading to their establishments. With the success of the strikes, the A. D. Juilliard Company was eliminated as a leader of the hard-line policies it espoused before the strikes, thus making it easier for unions in other companies to negotiate favorable settlements. Further, the success of the strikes brought new prestige in the central New York area to the Utica Trades Assembly and the U.T.W.A., the two organizations most active in supporting Local 753, thus increasing their influence among workers and the rate of unionization among Utica-area industries.

In the broader perspective, the role that Polish workers played in the New York Mills textile strikes of 1912 and 1916 provides substantial evidence for historians, sociologists and economists studying the immigrant experience in America. From the earliest arrival of southern and eastern Europeans in the United States in large numbers in the 1870s, various stereotypical views developed to explain their differing customs, traditions, and work experiences. Gradually, these views began to find their way into both personal and public life so that by the first decade of the twentieth century commonly-held beliefs on these so-called "new" immigrants included characterizing them as the illiterate, docile pawns of corporate owners, as people who lived in disorganized masses lacking any social cohesion, and as politically ignorant of America's democratic institutions. These attitudes can be seen in popular writings that emphasized the natural superiority of the Anglo-Saxon race, in the founding of the Immigration Restriction League, and in the stand of organized labor in favor immigration restriction. We have already seen how Samuel Gompers and the American Federation of Labor argued against the continued influx of immigrant labor, emphasizing that "Cheap labor, ignorant labor, takes our jobs and cuts our wages." These arguments were not confined to organized labor. As early as 1883 the American Economic Association offered a $150 prize for the best essay on "The Evil Effects of Unrestricted Immigration," while in 1891 Henry Cabot Lodge introduced a bill into Congress to enact a literacy test for admittance into the United States as a means of keeping out southern and eastern Europeans.[2]

These stereotypical attitudes were also supported by early scholarship in both community studies and labor history. In the former, for example, the first systematic academic study of the Polish community undertaken by William I. Thomas and Florian Znaniecki, *The Polish Peasant in Europe and America*, portrayed Polish American settlements as suffering from divisiveness and disorganization that seriously limited their ability to deal with the outside world or to provide socioeconomic mobility for their members.[3] This portrait, along with the social disorganization theory that it spawned, was generalized to other immigrant groups from southern and eastern Europe and dominated scholarly thought for two generations beginning around 1920. Indeed, its theme was central to the very influential writings of such eminent recent historians as Oscar Handlin who, in his popular work *The Uprooted*, argued that the Atlantic voyage robbed the immigrants of the fundamental social institutions of their European heritage including church, family, neighbors and traditions.[4] What was not lost, he maintained, was rendered insignificant by the new environment that the immigrants faced. Worse still, Handlin, among others, argued that the rural, non-industrial perspectives that Poles and others brought with them actually retarded their ability to integrate into the capitalist system and enjoy any amount of socioeconomic mobility.

One of the first to disagree with this concept was John Bodnar who maintained in *The Transplanted* that the immigrants were not as helpless and "uprooted" as Handlin and his predecessors maintained.[5] Bodnar argues that the immigrants where not ignorant of the world around them; rather, they had at least a general knowledge of European industrialization, they were quite knowledgeable about opportunities that existed in the New World, and they arrived in America with a real sense of what they wanted and how they were going to achieve it. In short, Bodnar believes that immigrant workers were very much cognizant of their new surroundings and developed reasonable means of gaining control both of their individual lives and their collective destiny.

Richard J. Oestreicher, in a study of Detroit, provided an excellent analysis of the divisiveness in the immigrant community, but concluded that while such factors as nationality, occupation level, religion and competing cultures were responsible for substantial divisions, the common concerns of wages, work environment and authoritarian ownership were sufficient to bind immigrants together into a united labor force.[6] In the same manner, Tamara Hareves, in a recent examination of the textile industry in Manchester, New Hampshire, concluded that the immigrant workers were not the passive victims portrayed in earlier studies, but were actually people with well-developed identities who worked to influence their own lives.[7]

The experience of the Poles in New York Mills supports the interpretations of Bodnar, Oestreicher and Hareves. From the available sources, it appears that most of them had a rather detailed idea of what was available in America and what they hoped to attain, both in terms of job opportunities and freedoms. The Polish language newspapers that they read carried news from Europe, local interest items, and a very heavy dose of labor news and rhetoric. Rather than being uninformed, they were actually quite aware of not only their circumstances, but various options that were available to them to influence the course of their lives. Similarly, they were neither the psychologically uprooted portrayed by Handlin nor the disorganized mass described by Thomas and Znaniecki. Rather, they brought with them significant elements from their European heritage including extended family groups, neighborhood loyalties, ethnic traditions, and most importantly a deep religious faith, and adapted them to their new environment in such a manner that they made rational sense and assisted in maintaining a rather cohesive ethnic support group. Similarly, despite the divisive factors of the work environment, residence and province of origin, the Poles in New York Mills, from an early date, were successful in organizing to meet the needs of everyday life. Their organizations provided opportunities for social outlets and status acquisition through group leadership, they provided economic support through insurance programs and cooperative stores, they established formal religious institutions to provide moral and psychological support, and they founded civic organizations for recreation, village improvement, the promotion of citizenship, and other diverse causes. Within a relatively brief few years, the success they enjoyed through this collective action was turned from the internal affairs of the ethnic community to a successful use of "American" labor unions and political parties to gain both economic and political control of their lives and their community.

Just as the early community studies pictured Poles and other immigrant groups as disorganized, confused masses, early labor historians developed similar views. The pioneering labor historian John R. Commons, for example, portrayed immigrant labor as at once both too passive and too radical for organized labor.[8] Much as American Federation of Labor president Samuel Gompers and United Mine Workers president John Mitchell, Commons described the immigrants as a generally docile lot, not particularly enthusiastic about the cause of organized labor. At the same time, however, echoing the concerns of corporate owners, and even President Theodore Roosevelt, Commons also noted that when immigrant workers were aroused they became too radical and uncontrollable for organized labor in America.

One of the first to disagree with these views was David Brody who, in *The Steelworker in America: The Non-Union Era* (1960), argued that contrary to this early view, as early as 1909 Poles and others frequently engaged in organized union activity.[9] Indeed, by the time of the steel strike in 1919 Slavic workers emerged as a vital and cohesive element in labor organization. Brody's work is supported by that of Victor Greene and John J. Bukowczyk who present examples of very well-organized and cohesive Polish presence in the anthracite strikes in Pennsylvania and Bayonne refinery strikes of 1915 respectively.[10]

The role of Poles in the New York Mills textile strikes of 1912 and 1916 support the views of Brody, Greene and Bukowczyk. In this instance, Poles not only participated in an organized strike, they were the primary stimulus to forming the union and the two strikes were initiated locally, not by the parent United Textile Workers of America. In each instance the Poles received assistance from the national union, but both of the strikes were initiated locally, that latter apparently against the wishes of the national union and without its financial backing until the latter stages of the walkout. In both instances the Poles remained remarkable united, were generally successful in negotiating support from other unions and ethnic groups, and maintained a disciplined, peaceful, but stern position until substantial concessions were gained.

Despite the interest of historians in the labor movement, there have been relatively few studies of the textile industry. In a study of a southern textile community, David L. Carlton found that the businessmen who owned the mills operated them under a profit motivation, which conflicted with the values of the rural, white, Anglo-Saxons who served as operatives.[11] A similar situation was uncovered by Jonathan Prude in his study of textile factories in rural Massachusetts, while Cynthia J. Shelton found friction between immigrant workers and corporate owners in Philadelphia.[12] In each of these cases, however, the results were quite different. In Carlton's study the workers were suspicious and distrustful of both union reformers and local government, with the result that they cast their lot with the election of a reactionary, racist conservative named Cole Blease. In Prude's study the rural Massachusetts workers were also conservative in their approach to unionism and strikes, although they never reached the reactionary extreme of their southern counterparts. In contrast to these rural cases, Shelton's study of Philadelphia concluded that the urban immigrants, possibly because they were more directly exposed to urban overcrowding and political diversity, gravitated more toward radicalism as a solution to their problems. In New York Mills, the immigrant workers eschewed both the radical and reactionary extremes to ally themselves with the moderate United Textile Workers of America and later with the established Democratic Party to gain political control.

Thus, although the above is certainly not an exhaustive list, it is apparent that the Polish experience in New York Mills does provide support for many of the more recent theories in community studies and labor history which picture immigrants and their communities as well-organized, cohesive, and capable of collective action toward the attainment of commonly-held goals. The story is indeed one with a meaning. Yet, in the end, the most tangible effects of the role of Polish immigrants in the New York Mills textile strikes of 1912 and 1916 rests with the dramatic increase in status, socioeconomic mobility and political control enjoyed by the one-time minority group as it moved successfully toward assimilation into American society.

Appendix A

Union Organizers Local 753, United Textile Workers of America

The following lists were pieced together from information contained in a number of newspapers and other publications including those of the United Textile Workers of America. The authors have made every effort to be as complete and accurate as possible, however, some names remain unknown, while others appear in differing forms from one publication to another. Thus, complete accuracy cannot be assured.

Founding Officers

Michał Tuman, President
Michał Wolak, Vice President
Jan Czyżycki, Recording Secretary
Ludwik Krupa, Financial Secretary
Tomasz Osika, Treasurer
Jan Solnica, Marshal
Michał Smoła, Trustee
Stanisław Pluta, Collector
Wojciech Ryczek, Collector
Jan Wolak, Collector

Officers During 1912 Strike

Rudolf Ząbek, President
Tomasz Mótyka, Vice President
[Balanced Unknown]

1912 Strike Committee

Tomasz Mótyka, Chair
Piotr Karpiński
Antoni Sokal
Jan Solnica
Michał Smoła
[Balance Unknown]

Officers Elected January 1914

Antoni Knutelski, President
Michał Chrabąszcz, Vice President
Zofia Kowal, Recording Secretary
Stanisław Puła, Financial Secretary
Jan Solnica, Treasurer
Piotr Brykala, Conductor
Antoni Sokal, Warden

Officers Elected February 1915

Tomasz Osika, President
Antoni Knutelski, Vice President
W. Herchell, Recording Secretary
F. Matusiak, Financial Secretary
Wojciech Nowak, Treasurer
Walenty Mądry, Conductor
Antoni Sokal, Warden
Jerzy Kozakiewicz, Trustee
Stefan Zamoryłło, Trustee

Officers During 1916 Strike

Jan Sroka, President
Stefan Zamoryłło, Vice President
Antoni Knutelski, Recording Secretary
Kazimierz Dziedzic, Treasurer
[Balance Unknown]

1916 Strike Committee

Antoni Knutelski, Chair
Stanisław Noga, Co-chiar for Fundraising
Kazimierz Wróblewski, Co-chair for Fundraising
Jan P. Baran, Translator
Jan Kwieciński
Piotr Maziarz
Wojciech Nowak
F. Śliski
Józef Sypek
[Balance Unknown]

Appendix B

List of Those Evicted
in 1916

The following list is a composite drawn from several sources including the surviving Rent Rolls of the New York Mills Corporation and newspaper accounts of the strike. The names are those specifically mentioned as being evicted. Where possible, these have been checked against census records and membership lists of St. Mary's Church for correct identification. Inevitably, these people were only the heads of households, or the person officially listed as the rentor of the property. Given the extended families of that era and the tendency of people to rent out rooms to boarders, the actual number evicted was considerably larger than the ninety-six families that union records claim were evicted. This list is very incomplete, including only sixty-four families. The names have been alphabetized as if the Polish letters were English to facilitate use.

Walenty Bobrek	Jan Kantor
P. Bachara	J. Karuzo
F. Borys	Andrzej Kiljan [Killian]
P. Borys	Piotr Knych
Józef Burysz	Ludwik Korzec
Jan Chrabąszcz	Stanisław Kowal
Józef Chrabąszcz	J. Kukułka
Stanisław Chrabąszcz	Józef Kułaga
Jan Chrzan	Józef Kulpa
Wacław Czerniak	Stanisław Kumerek
Józef Dubiel	J. Kupiec
Jan Fila	Jan Łabuz
Michał Gadziała	Jan Lopata
Mikołaj Gil	G. Markowski
Józef Głód	Michał Miga
S. Goodyear	Andrzej Miodunka
Marek Hałat	Jan Misterka
J. Houle	Stanisław Misterka

Grzegorsz Młynarski
Wacław Nogaś
A. Pędrak [Pendrak]
Jan Piekielniak
Marcin Pietryka
Stanisław Prymas
M. Samboni
J. Sambor
Józef Satera
S. Sheppard
J. Shortear
Jan Soja
J. Sułkowski
Jan Swierat

A. Szczepański
Władysław Szczerba
Jan Szymański
J. Topór
Stanisław Trzepacz
J. Wiatr [Waiter]
F. Warchałowski
Jan Wąż [Wasz]
Piotr Wójcik
Roman Wójcik
J. Zalewski
Józef Ziemien
Józef Zientara
J. Zytowski

The following names were compiled from census reports, company housing records and newspaper articles. They represent family members, relatives and boarders known to have resided with thirty-six of the sixty-four families listed above prior to the 1916 strike. These are the only families it has been possible to identify and trace. Our assumption is that when a family was evicted, all of those in the residence were likewise forced to leave, as appears to be the case from company records which indicate in many instances that other families were assigned to the residences whose inhabitants were evicted. The list is extremely tentative and incomplete, but it is included here in the belief that an incomplete listing is better than none at all.

Assyngier [Asynger], Jan
Assyngier, Katarzyna
Assyngier, Stanisław
Bachara, Anna
Bachara, Antoni
Bachara, Sadie
Bachara, Wilhelmina
Banaś, Jan
Banaś, Wojciech
Bawol, Józef
Bilenska, Agnieszka

Bis, Franciszek
Bobowiec, Józefa
Bobowiec, Kaspar
Bobrek, Jan
Bobrek, Marya
Bochniewicz, Marya
Bożędowski, Władysław
Bukowski, Józef
Bukowski, Teresa
Buris, Emelia
Buris, William

Buris, Władysław
Buris, Zina
Burysz, Józef
Butchery [?], Helen
Butchery [?], Mary
Caforek, Emelia
Caforek, Józefa
Caforek, Roman
Chrabąszcz, Anna
Chrabąszcz, Ignacy
Chrabąszcz, Michał
Chrabąszcz, Wawrzeniec
Ciećko, Stanisław
Czech, Antoni
Czech, Antoni, Jr.
Czech, Ludwika
Czerniak, Wacław
Czerwiecki, Kazimierz
Czerwiecki, Tekla
Czymajna [Cysmyna ?], Piotr
Czymajna [Cysmyna ?], Szymon
Dlostowa, Julja
Dlostowa, Stansiław
Dubiel, Agatha
Dubiel, Anna [2]
Dubiel, Jan
Dubiel, Julja
Dubiel, Marya
Dubiel, Mateusz
Dubiel, Michał
Dubiel, Paweł
Dubiel, Stanisław
Dubiel, Stefan
Dudek, Andrzej
Dudek, Anna
Dudek, Jan
Dudek, Tomasz
Dychorobiec, Marya
Dynar, Paweł
Dyrdek, Benedikta
Dziedzic, Andrzej

Dziedzic, Jan
Dziedzic, Johanna
Dziedzic, Józef
Dziedzic, Walter
Dziekan, Bertha
Dziekan, Katarzyna
Dziekan, Szymon
Furgał, Katarzyna
Furgał, Marcin
Furgał, Marya
Furgał, Stanisław
Furgał, Wojciech
Furgał, Zofia
Gadziała, Agnieszka
Gadziała, Bertha
Gadziała, Jan (2)
Gadziała, Józef
Gadziała, Rozalia
Gadziała, Wojciech
Galary, Agnieszka
Galary, Leo
Garish, John
Gil, Elżbieta
Gil, Jan
Gil, Marya
Glica, Karolina
Golombek, Adam
Golombek, Marcin
Golombek, Wojciech
Gondek, Jan
Gondek, Rozalia
Gondek, Stefan
Gondek, Zuzanna
Gorecki, Maryanna
Gorecki, Piotr
Gorecki, Walerya
Gorecki, Wanda
Gromny, Kajetan
Hałat, Rozalia
Hałat, Zofia
Hameliczek, Aniela

Hameliczek, Elżbieta
Hameliczek, Stanisław
Hameliczek, Walerya
Hamelik, Franciszek
Hamelik, Helena
Hamelik, Jan
Hamelik, Marya
Heratyk, Katrina
Hodek, Marya
Jarosz, Jan
Jasiak, Agnieszka
Kantor, Edward
Kantor, Jan
Kantor, Józef
Kantor, Karolina
Kantor, Michał
Kantor, Mieczysław
Kantor, Paweł
Kantor, Piotr
Kantor, Sattie
Kantor, William E.
Kapałka, Aniela
Kapałka, Genevieve
Kapałka, Wojciech
Karasz, Zofia
Kasprzyk, Franciszek
Kiljan, Bertha
Kiljan [Killian], Jan
Kiljan [Killian], Julja
Kiljan [Killian], Marcin
Kiljan [Killian], Marya
Kiljan [Killian], Michał
Kiljan [Killian], Stanisław
Klimczak, Bronisława
Klimczak, Marya
Knych, Michał
Kobielski, Andrzej
Kobielski, Anna
Kobielski, Helena
Kobielski, Zygmunt
Kolano, Jan

Kolano, Marya
Kolano, Stanisław
Kolodziej, Julja
Kolodziej, Michał
Kopyto, Walenty
Korczewski, Sylwester
Korzec, Władysław
Kosman, Franciszek
Kowal, Agatha
Kowal, Anna
Kowal, Bertha
Kowal, Jan
Kowal, Józef
Kowal, Marya
Kowal, Michał
Kowal, Zofia
Kozicki, Tomasz
Krawczyk, Julja
Kułaga, Anna
Kułaga, Michał
Kulasz, Sobestyjan
Kumerek, Rozalia
Kupiec, Emelia
Kupiec, Józef
Kupiec, Stanisław
Kurdziołek, Katarzyna
Kurdziołek, Stanisław
Łabus, Stanisław
Łachut, Agnieszka
Łachut, Jan
Lasek, Adam
Lazarek, Jan
Lazarek, Katrina
Lazarek, Stanisław
Lazarek, Wojciech
Lepa, Jan
Lepa, Katrina
Lepa, Stanisław
Lichwała, Jan
Lichwała, Józef
Lichwała, Marya

Leśniak, Anna
Lubaś, Adam
Lupa, Apolonia
Luranc, Józef
Luranc, Marya
Luranc, Stanisław
Lurzac, Andrzej
Lurzac, Jan
Lurzac, Stanisław
Łuszczyk, Antoni
Łuszczyk, Jan
Łuszczyk, Marya
Mądry [Mandry], Antonina
Mądry [Mandry], Walenty
Majka, Sadie
Majka, Mieczysław
Markut, Walenty
Maziarz, Piotr
Miga, Emelia
Miga, Julja
Miga, Lottie
Miga, Marya
Miga, Michał
Miga, Stanisław
Milanowicz, Petronella
Miodunka, Antonina
Miodunka, Julja
Misiaszek, Józef
Moryl, Jan
Mótyka, Tomasz
Mowroch, Michał
Mydlasz, Karolina
Niejadlik, Jan
Niejadlik, Marya
Niziołek, Józef
Nowak, Antoni
Nut, Jan
Ogrodnik, Antoni
Ogrodnik, Wojciech
Ogurek, Jan
Paciorek, Józef

Pawelac, Marcella
Pędrak [Pendrak], Jan
Pędrak [Pendrak], Paweł
Pędrak [Pendrak], Tekla
Pędrak [Pendrak], Teresa
Pędrak, [Pendrak], William
Pędrak [Pendrak], Władysław
Piekielniak, Agatha
Piekielniak, Anna
Piekielniak, Emelia
Pietryka, Anna
Pietryka, Jan
Pietryka, Marya
Pietryka, William
Pilut, Geriak
Pobiegło, Michał
Popadansic, Maggie
Popadansic, Mary
Popadansic, Roch
Prymas, Mateusz
Puła, Jan
Puła, Katarzyna
Raczka, Agnieszka
Raczka, Aniela
Raczka, Antoni
Raczka, Genowefa
Raczka, Hannah
Raczka, Katarzyna
Raczka, Marya
Rizok, Jan
Rogowski, Wincenty
Rygielski, Jan
Rymanowski, Ignacy
Ryś, Margaret
Ryś, Michał
Ryś, Szczepan
Sajur, Julja
Sambor, Aniela
Sambor, Józef
Sambor, Władysław
Samój, Anna

Samój, Jan
Sidlonka, Ludwika
Sikora, Michał
Skowron, Kaspar
Skrzek, Adam
Skrzek, Józef
Skrzek, Ludwika
Skrzek, Marja
Skrzek, Władysław
Skutnik, Antonina
Smolik, Andrzej
Smolik, Katrina
Sobieraj, Stanisław
Soja, Anna
Soja, Berta
Soja, Leo
Soja, Zofia
Stachura, Adam
Stachura, Jan
Starsiak, Antoni
Starsiak, Marya
Starsiak, Maryanna
Starsiak, Zofia
Stelmach, Władysław
Strynk, Józef
Świątek, Katrina
Swiech, Fransiczek
Swiech, Zofia
Swierat, Franciszek
Swierat, Katarzyna
Swierat, Margaret
Swierszek, Feliks
Swierszek, Stanisław
Szczelezk, Marya
Szczepanek, Aniela
Szczepański, Sadie
Szczepański, Weronika
Szczepański, Wojciech
Szczerba, Bessie [Barbara ?]
Szydło, Bartłomiej
Szymański, Apolonia

Szymański, Edward
Szymański, Józef
Tadir, Helen
Thelk, Katrina
Tobijasz, Józef
Tobijasz, Marya
Topór, Bertha
Topór, Bolesław
Topór, Jakób
Topór, Józef
Topór, Marya
Tracz, Józefa
Tracz, Marya
Tracz, Zofia
Trzepacz, Dorothy
Trzepacz, Helena
Trzepacz, Jan
Trzepacz, Karolina
Trzepacz, Katrina
Trzepacz, Marya
Trzepacz, Michał
Trzepacz, Sadie
Trzepacz, Wanda
Trzepacz, Zofia
Tuman, Józef
Urszulak, Aniela
Urszulak, Józef
Urszulak, Karolina
Urszulak, Teresa
Urszulak, Walenty
Urszulak, Władysław
Urszulak, Wojciech
Uszczak, Zofia
Viszułak, Michał
Wiatr, Magdelena
Wiatr, Walenty
Władasz, Balbina
Wójcik, Tomasz
Wolanin, Jan
Wolanin, Karolina
Wolanin, Stanisław

Woźniak, Katarzyna
Woźniak, Marya
Zak, Karol
Zek, Katarzyna
Ziemba, Feliks
Ziemien, Helena
Ziemien, Marya
Ziemien, Rozalia

Ziemien, Władysław
Ziombro, Paweł
Złotnicki, Jan
Żola, Aniela
Zomera, Marya
Żurek, Karolina
Żurek, Tomasz
Zygo, Maryanna

References

Introduction

¹Quoted in Robin W. Winks, ed., *The Historian as Detective: Essays on Evidence* (New York: Harper & Row, Publishers, 1969), p. 17

Chapter 1: Rise of a Company Town

¹Interview of Mary Jones by Winifred S. Pula, ca. 1975 [hereafter cited as Jones interview].

²Daniel E. Wager, ed., *Our County and its People. A Descriptive Work on Oneida County, New York* (The Boston History Company, 1896), p. 622; Ernest J. Savoie, "The New York Mills Company 1807-1914, A Study of Managerial Attitudes and Practices in Industrial Relations," M.S. Thesis, Cornell University, 1955, pp. 11-12.

³Wager, p. 628; Henry J. Cookinham, *History of Oneida County, New York, From 1700 to the Present Time*, Vol. I (Chicago: S. J. Clarke Publishing Company, 1912), p. 434; Jeff Toczydlowski and Jim Pawlak, "The History of New York Mills," unpublished paper dated May 16, 1975, in possession of the authors; Barbara C. Fisler, "The Textile Industry in New York Mills: Development and Decay," unpublished paper dated July 1968 in possession of the authors; Linnie H. Thuma, "Image and Imagination: How an Ethnic Community Sees Itself," *New York Folklore*, Vol. 4, No. 1-4 (Summer-Winter 1978), p. 8; *Utica Saturday Globe*, March 30, 1912, p. 11; Stephen B. Jareckie, "An Architectural Survey of New York Mills From 1808 to 1908," M.A. Thesis, Syracuse University, June, 1961, p. 4; Savoie, pp. 13-14.

⁴Wager, p. 628; Toczydlowski and Pawlak, pp. 2-3; Cookinham, p. 434; Fisler, pp. 4-5; Thuma, p. 8; Jareckie, pp. 1, 5-6; quotes from W. W. Canfield and J. E. Clark, *Things Worth Knowing About Oneida County* (Utica: Thomas J. Griffiths, 1909), p. 107; Savoie, p. 15-17.

⁵Fisler, p. 13; Cookinham, p. 434; Wager, p. 628; *Utica Saturday Globe*, March 30, 1912, p. 11; Toczydlowski and Pawlak, p. 4; Jareckie, p. 8; Savoie, pp. 18-20.

⁶Cookinham, p. 434; quotes from Canfield and Clark, pp. 108-109; *Utica Saturday Globe*, March 30, 1912, p. 11; Toczydlowski and Pawlak, p. 6; Jareckie, pp. 10-11, 13; Savoie, pp. 25, 32.

⁷Canfield and Clark, p. 109; Cookinham, p. 435; Fisler, p. 5; *Utica Saturday Globe*, March 30, 1912, p. 11; Jareckie, pp. 16, 18-20; Savoie, p. 39.

[8]Wallace Lamb, *Lamb's Sectional Histories of New York State* (Phoenix, NY: Frank E, Richards, Publisher, n.d.), p. 15.

[9]Alexander C. Flick, ed., *History of the State of New York* (New York: Columbia University Press, 1934), Vol VI, p. 196.

[10]Joseph Kelly, "Company Houses Reminder of Old," *Utica Observer-Dispatch*, January 18, 1976, p. 4B; Toczydlowski and Pawlak, p. 10; Jareckie, p. 22; *History of Oneida County* (Philadelphia: Everts & Fariss, 1878), pp. 615, 617.

[11]Dwight H. Bruce, ed., *The Empire State in Three Centuries*, Vol. III (New York: The Century History Company, n.d.), p. 22.

[12]Thuma, pp. 8-9.

[13]*Whitestown 1784-1984: Official Commemorative Book for the 200th Anniversary of the Settlement of Whitestown, New York* (n.p., n.d.), p. 42; Jareckie, pp. 11, 14, 24, 36; Fisler, p. 10; Toczydlowski and Pawlak, p. 11; Wager, p. 629; quote from Pomroy Jones, *Annals and Recollections of Oneida County* (Rome, NY: privately published, 1851), p. 826.

[14]Bruce, p. 20; quote from Fisler, p. 5.

[15]Cookinham, p. 435.

[16]Bruce, pp. 20-22; Wager, p. 629; Jareckie, p. 26; quote from Cookinham, p. 435.

[17]Bruce, pp. 23-25.

[18]Pomroy Jones, p. 828.

[19]*History of Oneida County*, p. 624; Bruce, p. 23; Cookinham, p. 521.

[20]Fisler, p. 7; Jareckie, p. 41; quote from *History of Oneida County*, p. 624. Eventually, Mill No. 3 was dismantled. Over the passage of time, No. 4, which stood next to No. 3, became known as No. 3 in the absence of the earlier structure. Thus, by the time interviews were conducted for this book, most village residents identified the large four-story mill as "No. 3," when in actuality it was originally No. 4.

[21]*History of Oneida County*, p. 627.

[22]Toczydlowski and Pawlak, p. 12, state that this took place on February 12, 1884, while Wager, p. 630, cites the date as January 22, 1884. See also Jareckie, p. 37; Savoie, p. 61.

[23]Fisler, p. 7, indicates that this information come from Mrs. Joseph Finnegan.

[24]Jareckie, pp. 44-45.

[25]Kelly, p. 4B, who quotes Evelyn Morgan Evans.

[26]David Dudajek, "For Whom the Bell Tolls," *County Courier-News* [Clinton, NY], December 17, 1975, n.p., attributes this to a quote from Mrs. Joseph Finnegan; see also Savoie, p. 46-48; "New York Mills History," an original manuscript in the possession of the authors which was apparently prepared by an employee of the New York Mills Corporation as a brief company history (undated).

[27]Fisler, p. 6; Dudajek, n.p., attributes the quotation to Mrs. Chaplo.

[28]*Utica Saturday Globe*, July 10, 1915, p. 5.

Chapter 2: New People, New Perspectives

¹Eugene Dziedzic, "Ten Fingers," an unpublished manuscript in the possession of the authors, p. 3; Interview of Stanley Zima by the authors, November 19, 1988 [hereafter cited as Zima interview].

²Eugene Dziedzic, "Ten Fingers," an unpublished manuscript in the possession of the authors, p. 3; Interview of Zenon Chrabas by the authors, July 13, 1988 [hereafter cited as Z. Chrabas interview]

³Z. Chrabas interview.

⁴John J. Walsh, *Vignettes of Old Utica* (Utica: Utica Public Library, 1982), p. 319; T. Wood Clarke, *Utica For a Century and a Half* (Utica: Widtman Press, 1952), p. 66; *Utica Saturday Globe*, June 9, 1906, p. 9; New York Mills Corporation Payroll Book, 1898-1901, MSS.2, NYM.3, PBO.14. This and all other records of the New York Mills Corporation cited in this work, unless otherwise specified, are in the possession of the Oneida County Historical Society, Utica, N.Y. The names of individuals, particularly those of Polish origin, which appear in the records of the New York Mills Company, the press and other contemporary records often suffer from poor or nearly incomprehensible spelling. The authors have compared company records, newspaper accounts, and other printed sources to the names that appear on the parish records of St. Mary's Church in an effort to render names as accurately as possible. Undoubtedly, some errors have occurred because of incomplete records or because names which appear in printed sources may themselves be incomplete or so poorly spelled as to render them indecipherable.

⁵New York Mills Corporation Payroll Book, February-July, 1904, MSS.2, NYM.3, PBO.16.

⁶Walsh, p. 320; *Utica Saturday Globe*, June 9, 1906, p. 9.

⁷*Congressional Record*, March 16, 1896.

⁸James S. Pula, "American Immigration Policy and the Dillingham Commission," *Polish American Studies*, Vol. XXXVII, No. 1 (Spring 1980), pp. 5-31, *passim*.

⁹*Utica Herald-Dispatch*, July 5, 1907, p. 3

¹⁰*Utica Saturday Globe*, July 6, 1907, p. 28. In this article and in other newspaper accounts of the period the word "employees" is consistently spelled "employes," without the final double e. For consistency, and to avoid the frequent use of the designation "[sic]", the authors have rendered this word in the more contemporary double e form throughout. With this exception, all quotations appear as they did in the original source from which they were taken.

¹¹*Utica Daily Press*, July 5, 1907, p. 4.

¹²Jones interview; quote from *Utica Herald-Dispatch*, July 5, 1907, p. 3.

¹³Interview of Bertha Nowicki Kozak by the authors, June 13, 1987 [hereafter cited as Kozak interview]. The word "Polak" is a Polish word meaning "Polish" or "a Pole." It was used in various Anglicized spellings by Anglo-Saxons as a term of disparagement. It is spelled here

in the original Polish, except where direct quotations are taken from documents which spell it as "Pollock" or some other incorrect variation.

[14]Interview of Stella Furgal by the authors, September 13, 1987 [hereafter cited as Furgal interview].

[15]Interview of Stephanie Nowicki [Stefania Nowicka] by the authors, October 31, 1987 [hereafter cited as Nowicki interview].

[16]Kozak interview.

[17]Kozak interview.

[18]Interview of Stanley Krawiec by the authors, October 11, 1987 [hereafter cited as Krawiec interview].

[19]Interview of Cecilia Powroźnik Chrabas by the authors, July 13, 1988 [hereafter cited as C. Chrabas interview].

[20]Z. Chrabas interview.

[21]Kozak interview; interview of Peter Kogut by the authors, July 1, 1988 [hereafter cited as Kogut interview]; quotation from Indenture for Lot 13, Woodhull Tract, Oneida County, State of New York, in the possession of Eugene Dziedzic.

[22]Susan G. Davis, "Women's Roles in a Company Town: New York Mills, 1900-1951," *New York Folklore*, Vol. 4, No. 1-4 (Summer-Winter 1978), p. 40; Furgal interview; quotes from Zima interview and Kozak interview.

[23]Thirteenth Census of the United States: 1910 - Population, Town of Whitestown, Oneida County, New York, Supervisor's District No. 11, Enumeration District No. 180, Sheets No. 11B and 14A.

[24]Kozak interview; Krawiec interview; Z. Chrabas interview; interview of Michael Dziedzic by the authors, January 16, 1988 [hereafter cited as Dziedzic interview].

[25]Kozak interview; Krawiec interview; C. Chrabas interview; quote from Furgal interview.

[26]Davis, "Women's Roles," p. 41.

[27]Davis, p. 41; Elizabeth Goldstein and Gail Green, "Pierogi- and Babka-Making at St. Mary's," *New York Folklore*, Vol. 4, No. 1-4 (Summer-Winter 1978), *passim*; Kozak interview; Krawiec interview; C. Chrabas interview; Dziedzic interview; Nowicki interview.

[28]Kogut interview.

[29]Z. Chrabas interview; C. Chrabas interview; Davis, "Women's Roles," p. 41.

[30]C. Chrabas interview.

[31]C. Chrabas interview.

[32]C. Chrabas interview.

[33]Susan G. Davis, "Old-Fashioned Polish Weddings in Utica, New York," *New York Folklore*, Vol. 4, No. 1-4 (Summer-Winter 1978), pp. 91-92; Kozak interview; Peter Hartman and Marc Tull, "Photographic Documentation of a Polish-American Community," *New York Folklore*, Vol. 4, No. 1-4 (Summer-Winter 1978), *passim*.

[34]Davis, "Weddings," p. 99.

[35]Davis, "Weddings," pp. 99-100.

250   *United We Stand*

[36]Walsh, pp. 320-321; Cookinham, p. 347; Eugene Dziedzic, "A Brief Account of the Polish Community in Utica," in *Uniquely ... Utica* (Utica, NY: City of Utica, 1982), pp. 49; *Diamond Jubilee, 1896-1971, Holy Trinity Church, Utica, N.Y.* (Utica, NY: Holy Trinity Parish, 1971), pp. 19-23; *Złota Księga czyli pięć lat pracy dla Polski w Utica, N.Y.* (Utica, NY: Published by the Polish Community, 1919), pp. 6-10.

[37]C. Chrabas interview; Z. Chrabas interview; interview of Stanley Zima by authors, November 19, 1988 [hereafter cited as Zima interview].

[38]Anna Chrypinski, ed., *Polish Customs* (Detroit: Friends of Polish Art, 1973), pp. 9-27 *passim*; Eugene Dziedzic, "A 'Happy Easter' in the Best Traditions of Their Religion," *Utica Observer-Dispatch*, March 26, 1978; Mieczysław Giergielewicz and Ludwik Krzyżanowski, eds., *Polish Civilization: Essays and Studies* (New York: New York University Press, 1979), pp. 14-17.

[39]Chrypinski, pp. 9-27 *passim*; Eugene Dziedzic, "Christmas Customs Part of a Beautiful Legacy," *Utica Observer-Dispatch*, December 24, 1978; Giergielewicz, pp. 2-9; Dziedzic interview..

[40]*Diamond Jubilee, 1910-1985, St. Mary of Our Lady of Częstochowa Church, New York Mills, New York* (published by the parish, 1985), n.p.[hereafter cited as *Diamond Jubilee*]; *Pamiętnik z okazyi Poświęcenia Kościoła oraz Wykaz Ofiar Imiennych z lat 1912-1918 włącznie w Parafii M. B. Częstochowskiej w New York Mills, N. Y.* (Utica: Drukiem Słowa Polskiego, 1919), n.p.[hereafter cited as *Pamiętnik z okazyi*]; *Pamiętnik Złotego Jubileuszu Towarzystwa Krakusów Polskich Pod Op. Kazimierza, Kr. przy Parafji M. B. Częstochowskiej* (New York Mills, NY: St. Casimir's Society, 1961), n.p. [hereafter cited as *Pamiętnik Złotego*]; *Pamiętnik Srebrnego Jubileuszu Parafji Rzymsko Katolickiej Matki Boskiej Częstochowskiej w New York Mills, N. Y.* (New York Mills, NY: St. Mary's Parish, 1935), n.p. [hereafter cited as *Pamiętnik Srebrnego*]; *Golden Anniversary, St. Mary's Parish, 1910-1960* (New York Mills. NY: St. Mary's Parish, 1960), n.p. [hereafter cited as *Golden Anniversary*]; "Historical Information," a manuscript in the St. Mary's Parish Archives [hereafter cited as "Historical Information"].

[41]*Diamond Jubilee*, n.p.; "Historical Information."

[42]*Diamond Jubilee*, n.p.; Dziedzic interview; Zofia Rozanow and Ewa Smulikowska, *The Cultural Heritage of Jasna Góra* (Warsaw: Interpress, 1979), pp 6-7.

[43]*Pamiętnik z okazyi*, n.p.; Wacław Kruszka, *Historya Polska w Ameryce* (Milwaukee: Drukiem Spółki Wydawniczej Kuryera, 1905-1908), Vol. III, pp. 142-144; *Pamiętnik Złotego Jubileuszu Tow. Najśw. Rodziny Nr. 459 Zjednoczenie P. R. K. w Ameryce* (New York Mills, N.Y.: Group 459, Z.P.R.K., 1959), n.p.; "Historical Information"; *Słowo Polskie*, November 18, 1927, pp. 20-21.

[44]*Diamond Jubilee*, n.p.; Krawiec interview; quote from M. Dziedzic interview. See also two letters from Chester A. Braman, a major stockholder and member of the Board of Directors of the A. D.Juilliard Com-

pany, to W. Pierrepont White, then President of the New York Mills
Corporation, dated June 15, 1910 and June 20, 1910. In the former,
Braman commented that "we have always felt that they [the Poles] were
good cotton mill employees and the building of this church will be of
assistance to the New York Mills. In regard to a contribution toward the
building of the new church, how would it be to give them the land which
was offered to them for a building site instead of a check, and they can
then realize all that is possible by its sale for this purpose." The letters
are found in the William Pierrepont White Papers [hereafter cited as the
White Papers], Olin Library, Cornell University, Group #399, Box dated
1910-1913. A letter from White to Rev. Stefan Płaza detailing the exact
location of the property is in the St. Mary's Parish Archives in New
York Mills, N.Y.

[45]*Pamiętnik z okazyi*, n.p., *passim*; quote from *Diamond Jubilee*,
n.p.; "Historical Information."

[46]*Słowo Polskie*, November 23, 1911, p. 4.

[47]*Pamiętnik z okazyi*, n.p.; Kruszka, Vol. IV, pp. 53-56; *Pamiętnik
Złotego*, n.p.; *Słowo Polskie*, February 29, 1912, p. 8, March 18, 1927,
p. 2, and November 18, 1927, p. 20-21.

Chapter 3: Seeds of Dissension

[1]Jarecki, p. 52; Toczydlowski and Pawlak, p. 12; Fisler, p. 15;
Cookinham, p. 435; Savoie, pp. 67-68.

[2]Quotation from Krawiec interview. For information on the
length of the work week and the age and gender of the work force, see
John Williams, Commissioner, "Eighth Annual Report of the Commissioner of Labor," New York State Assembly Document No. 30A,
January 18, 1909.

[3]Davis, "Women's Roles," p. 37.

[4]Davis, "Women's Roles," p. 37, provides this quotation from an
unidentified worker.

[5]Interview of Richard Rosinski by the authors, September 12,
1987 [hereafter cited as Rosinski interview].

[6]Nowicki interview.

[7]Davis, "Women's Roles," p. 38; Rosinski interview; Nowicki
interview; Krawiec interview; Furgal interview; Z. Chrabas interview;
quote from Zima interview.

[8]*Annual Report of the Bureau of Statistics of Labor, 1884*
(Albany: New York State Bureau of Labor), pp. 108-112; Savoie, p.
71.

[9]Davis, "Women's Roles," p. 38; *Towpaths, Turnpikes and Towns*
(New Hartford, NY: Oneida County Board of Cooperative Educational
Services, 1986), pp. 57-58; Rosinski interview; Nowicki interview;
Krawiec interview; quotes from *Preliminary Report of the Factory In-
vestigating Commission, 1912, Vol. I* (Albany: The Argus Company,
Printers, 1912), p. 289 (New York State Senate Document No. 30).

For additional information on the conditions and dangers involved in the dyeing calico see John Williams, Commissioner, "Ninth Annual Report of the Commissioner of Labor," New York State Assembly Document No. 30A, January 24, 1910, pp. 80-86.

[10]Rosinski interview.

[11]Krawiec interview; Rosinski interview; Davis, "Women's Roles," p. 39; Dziedzic interview; Interview of Stephen Zurek by the authors, May 25, 1989 [hereafter cited as Zurek interview]; quote from Robert W. Dunn and Jack Hardy, *Labor and Textiles: A Study of Cotton and Wool Manufacturing* (New York: International Publishers), p. 144.

[12]Rosinski interview; Zima interview; Zurek interview; *Towpaths, Turnpikes and Towns*, p. 65; quote from Dunn and Hardy, p. 151; *Dangers in Manufacture of Paris Green and Scheele's Green* (Albany: The Industrial Commission, July, 1917), Special Bulletin No. 83 of the New York State Department of Labor, pp. 3, 16-17.

[13]Nowicki interview.

[14]Furgal interview.

[15]Quotation from Kozak interview.

[16]Z. Chrabas interview; Nowicki interview.

[17]Savoie, p. 72.

[18]Fisler, p. 15; Savoie, pp. 4, 68, 84.

[19]*Utica Saturday Globe*, March 30, 1912, p. 3.

[20]Quotation from, Letter, Chester A. Braman to W. Pierrepont White, January 24, 1911, White Papers, Box D-5-C-4-B. See also letters, Chester A. Braman to W. Pierrepont White, November 11, 1910 and November 12, 1910, White Papers, Group #399, Box dated 1910-1913; Bernard Yabroff and Ann J. Herlihy, "History of Work Stoppages in Textile Industries," *Monthly Labor Review* (April 1953), p. 368; Savoie, p. 78.

[21]Quote from letter, Chester A. Braman to Timothy Mooney, agent, January 11, 1911, White Papers, Box D-5-C-4-B. See also Yabroff and Herlihy, p. 368; Savoie, p. 78; letters, Chester A. Braman to Timothy Mooney, agent, January 24, 1911, and Chester A. Braman to E. M. Coughlin, assistant treasurer, January 24, 1911, White Papers, Box D-5-C-4-B.

[22]Kozak interview; Kogut interview.

[23]Kozak interview.

[24]Seymour E. Harris, *American Economic History* (New York: McGraw-Hill Book Company, Inc., 1961), *passim* especially chapter 13.

[25]Melvyn Dubofsky, "Organized Labor and the Immigrant in New York City, 1900-1918," *Labor History*, Vol. II (1961), p. 185.

[26]Harris, chapter 13; quote from A. A. Graham, "The Un-Americanization of America," *American Federationist*, Vol. XVII, No. 4 (April 1910), pp. 302-304, quote from 304.

[27]See Samuel Gompers, "Reasons for Immigration Restriction," *American Federationist*, Vol. XXIII, No. 4 (April 1916), pp. 253-256;

Samuel Gompers, "Immigration Legislation Effected," *American Federationist*, Vol. XXIV, No. 3 (March 1917), pp. 189-195.

[28]Harris, chapter 13.

[29]"Membership of the A.F. of L. 1881-1911," *American Federationist*, Vol. XIX, No. 1 (January 1912), pp. 54-55; *The Story of Industrial and Labor Relations* (Albany: New York State Joint Legislative Committee on Industrial and Labor Conditions, 1943), p. 53.

[30]Dziedzic interview; Nowicki interview; Rosinski interview; Davis, "Women's Roles," pp. 37-38.

[31]Quotations from, letter, Chester A. Braman to W, Pierrepont White, January 27, 1911, and Braman to White, February 6, 1911, White Papers, Box D-5-C-4-B.

[32]Quotation from letter, Chester A. Braman to W. Pierrepont White, March 23, 1911, White Papers, Box D-5-C-4-B. See also Savoie, p. 86.

[33]Quotation from letters, Chester Braman to W. Pierrepont White, February 21, 1911, February 18, 1911, March 23, 1911, and May 8, 1911, White Papers, Box D-5-C-4-B.

[34]Kozak Review; E. Dziedzic, "Ten Fingers"; Dziedzic interview; Krawiec interview; *Whitestown 1784-1984*, p. 45; Interview of Józef Piszcz by Eugene and Michael Dziedzic, August 17, 1981 [hereafter cited as Piszcz]; *Słowo Polskie*, November 18, 1927, p. 20; *Utica Daily Press*, October 21, 1938, p. 5; *Proceedings of the Eleventh Annual Convention of the United Textile Workers of America* (Published by the U.T.W.A., 1911), p. 42. Some sources list the financial secretary as Ludwik Krzypa, but most agree on the surname as Krupa. Additionally, there is no record of a Krzypa in St. Mary's Parish, while there was a Ludwik Krupa.

[35]Yabroff and Herlihy, p. 367; Harold S. Roberts, *Roberts' Dictionary of Industrial Relations* (Washington, DC: BNA Inc., 1966), p. 419; Florence Peterson, *Handbook of Labor Unions* (Washington, DC: American Council on Public Affairs, 1944), pp. 378-380; Gary M. Fink, ed., *Labor Unions* (Westport, CT: Greenwood Press, 1977), pp. 380-383.

[36]*Utica Observer*, April 14, 1911.

[37]Letter, Chester Braman to W. Pierrepont White, April 11, 1911, White Papers, Box D-5-C-4-B.

[38]Letter, Chester Braman to W. Pierrepont White, April 17, 1911, White Papers, Box D-5-C-4-B.

[39]Quote from letter, Chester A. Braman to W. Pierrepont White, April 19, 1911, White Papers, Box D-5-C-4-B.

[40]Quote from letter, Chester A. Braman to W. Pierrepont White, March 16, 1911, White Papers, Box D-5-C-4-B. It appears that some union leaders were at first fired, then rehired, only to be fired once more before the beginning of the 1912 strike. This explains, for example, why Michał Tuman is fired on at least two separate occasions. Some of the fired union activists opened businesses, thus beginning a prosperous middle-class business group within the Polish

community. Tuman and Walenty Mądry, for example, opened meat and grocery stores.

⁴¹Quote from letter, Chester A. Braman to W. Pierrepont White, May 2, 1911, White Papers, Box D-5-C-4-B.

⁴²Letter, Chester A. Braman to W. Pierrepont White, March 10, 1911, White Papers, Group #399, Box dates 1910-1913.

⁴³*Słowo Polskie*, September 25, 1911, p. 1 and November 18, 1927, p. 20; Piszcz interview. For publication information on the newspaper see Jan Wepsiec, *Polish American Serial Publications, 1842-1966, An Annotated Bibliography* (Chicago, IL: 1968), p. 146.

⁴⁴*Słowo Polskie*, October 12, 1911, p. 5.

⁴⁵*Proceedings of the Eleventh Annual Convention of the United Textile Workers of America*, pp. 43, 45; Piszcz interview.

⁴⁶Letter, John Golden to W. Pierrepont White, May 3, 1911, White Papers, Box D-5-C-4-B.

⁴⁷Letter, Chester Braman to W. Pierrepont White, May 8, 1911, White Papers, Box D-5-C-4-B.

⁴⁸*Słowo Polskie*, November 18, 1927, p. 20; quote from Piszcz interview; *Proceedings of the Eleventh Annual Convention of the United Textile Workers of America*, pp. 43, 45; Letter, Chester Braman to W. Pierrepont White, March 23, 1911, White Papers.

⁴⁹Robert E. Snyder, "Women, Wobblies, and Workers' Rights: The 1912 Textile Strike in Little Falls, New York," *New York History* (January 1979), pp. 30-31.

⁵⁰Snyder, p. 30.

⁵¹Letter, Chester Braman to W. Pierrepont White, February 10, 1911, White Papers; Savoie, p. 4.

⁵²Chester A. Braman to W. Pierrepont White, December 23, 1909, White Papers, Group #399, Box dated 1910-1913.

⁵³Chester A. Braman to W. Pierrepont White, February 3, 1910, White Papers, Group #399, Box dated 1910-1913.

⁵⁴Chester A. Braman to W. Pierrepont White, April 22, 1910, White Papers, Group #399, Box dated 1910-1913.

⁵⁵Kenneth Fones-Wolf, "Revivalism and Craft Unionism in the Progressive Era: The Syracuse and Auburn Labor Forward Movements of 1913," *New York History* (October 1982), pp. 390-391, 401, 405, quote from 401.

⁵⁶Al Priddy, "Controlling the Passions of Men -- In Lawrence," *The Outlook*, October 19, 1912, p. 343; Yabroff and Herlihy, pp. 367, 369. For coverage in *Słowo Polskie*, see February 1, 1912, and succeeding issues throughout February and March.

⁵⁷Letter, Chester Braman to W. Pierrepont White, February 17, 1912, White Papers.

⁵⁸*Utica Observer*, March 28, 1912, p. 1; *Utica Daily Press*, March 29, 1912, p. 5; *Utica Daily Press*, March 30, 1912, p. 3.

⁵⁹*Utica Observer*, March 28, 1912, p. 8; *Utica Observer*, March 29, 1912, p. 8; *Utica Saturday Globe*, March 30, 1912, p. 3; *Utica Daily Press*, April 13, 1912, p. 5.

[60]Letter, Albert Hibbert to William Pierrepont White, February 29, 1912, White Papers, Box D-5-C-4-B.

[61]Letter, Chester A. Braman to John P. Campbell, March 1, 1912, White Papers, Box D-5-C-4-B.

[62]Letter, Chester Braman to W. Pierrepont White, March 4, 1912, White Papers, Box D-5-C-4-B.

[63]*Utica Observer*, March 3, 1912, includes quote; *Utica Daily Press*, April 13, 1912, p. 5.

[64]*Twenty-sixth Convention and Concert, Polish Singers Alliance of America, District 6* (Utica: n.p., 1958), n.p.; Kogut interview; *Utica Daily Press*, April 9, 1958, p. 4A; *Pamiętnik Srebrnego*, n.p.; Transcript from the Public Register of Deaths in the Village of New York Mills for Father Fijałkowski is in the St. Mary's Parish Archives; "Historical Information."

[65]*Utica Observer*, March 29, 1912, p. 8.

[66]*Utica Observer*, March 1, 1912, p. 1; *Utica Observer*, March 2, 1912, p. 1; *Utica Observer*, March 4, 1912, p. 1; *Utica Observer*, March 23, 1912, p. 1; *Utica Observer*, March 26, 1912, p. 1.

[67]*Utica Observer*, March 28, 1912, p. 1.

[68]*Utica Observer*, March 28, 1912, p. 1.

Chapter 4: Strajk!

[1]*Utica Daily Press*, March 30, 1912, p. 3; *Utica Saturday Globe*, March 30, 1912, p. 3; *Utica Observer*, March 29, 1912, p. 8.

[2]*Utica Saturday Globe*, March 30, 1912, p. 3; *Utica Sunday Tribune*, March 31, 1912, p. 2; *Utica Observer*, March 28, 1912, p. 8; *Słowo Polskie*, March 28, 1912, p. 8; Savoie, p. 100; *Utica Herald-Dispatch*, April 6, 1912.

[3]Quotation from *Utica Daily Press*, April 1, 1912, p. 6. See also *Utica Sunday Tribune*, March 31, 1912, p. 2; *Utica Observer*, March 28, 1912, p. 8; *Bulletin* No. 66, State of New York, Department of Labor, Bureau of Mediation and Arbitration, Series on Industrial Relations No. 1 (1913), p. 32.

[4]Słowo Polskie, March 28, 1912, p. 8.

[5]*Utica Observer*, March 28, 1912, p. 8; *Utica Daily Press*, April 1, 1912, p. 6.

[6]Quotation from *Utica Observer*, March 28, 1912, p. 8. See also *Utica Sunday Tribune*, March 31, 1912, p. 2; *Utica Daily Press*, March 29, 1912, p. 5.

[7]*Utica Observer*, March 28, 1912, p. 8).

[8]*Annual Report of the Bureau of Labor Statistics* (Albany: Department of Labor, 1912), Vol. III, Pt. II, pp. 161-162, 486.

[9]*Annual Report of the Bureau of Labor Statistics* (Albany: Department of Labor, 1913), Senate Doc #48C, pp. 159, 40, 42-43.

[10]*Utica Observer*, March 28, 1912, p. 8, including quotations.

256   *United We Stand*

[11]Quotations from *Utica Observer*, March 28, 1912, p. 8 and letter, Chester A. Braman to W. Pierrepont White, April 3, 1912, White Papers, Box D-5-C-4-B. See also *Utica Daily Press*, March 29, 1912, p. 5; *Utica Daily Press*, March 30, 1912, p. 3; *Utica Observer*, March 29, 1912, p. 8.

[12]Quotations from *Utica Daily Press*, March 30, 1912, p. 3. See also *Utica Observer*, March 28, 1912, p. 8; *Utica Saturday Globe*, March 30, 1912, p. 3; *Utica Daily Press*, March 29, 1912, p. 5.

[13]*Utica Observer*, March 28, 1912, p. 8; *Utica Saturday Globe*, March 30, 1912, p. 3; *Utica Daily Press*, March 29, 1912, p. 5.

[14]Quotation from *Utica Observer*, March 29, 1912, p. 8. See also *Utica Daily Press*, March 30, 1912, p. 3.

[15]*Utica Sunday Tribune*, March 31, 1912, p. 2; *Utica Daily Press*, March 30, 1912, p. 3; Letter, Raymond Motyka to Eugene Dziedzic, January 28, 1989.

[16]Quotation from *Utica Observer*, March 29, 1912, p. 8. See also *Utica Sunday Tribune*, March 31, 1912, p. 2; *Utica Daily Press*, March 30, 1912, p. 3.

[17]Quotation from *Utica Daily Press*, March 30, 1912, p. 3. See also *Utica Saturday Globe*, March 31, 1912, p. 3; *Utica Sunday Tribune*, March 31, 1912, p. 3.

[18]*Utica Sunday Tribune*, March 31, 1912, p. 2.

[19]*Utica Observer*, March 29, 1912, p. 8. Also contained in *Utica Daily Press*, March 30, 1912, p. 3.

[20]*Utica Saturday Globe*, March 30, 1912, p. 3.

[21]*Utica Observer*, March 28, 1912, p. 8.

[22]*Utica Daily Press*, March 30, 1912, p. 3.

[23]*Utica Observer*, March 30, 1912, p. 8.

[24]*Utica Daily Press*, March 30, 1912, p. 3; *Utica Observer*, March 29, 1912, p. 8.

[25]Letter, Chester A. Braman to W. Pierrepont White, March 30, 1912, White Papers, Box D-5-C-4-B.

[26]*Utica Observer*, March 30, 1912, p. 8; *Utica Sunday Tribune*, March 31, 1912, p. 2. Some Utica newspapers place this meeting on Saturday, March 30, but it is clear from the context of their stories and the report of the Bureau of Mediation and Arbitration that it took place late Friday afternoon, March 29.

[27]*Utica Observer*, March 30, 1912, p. 8.

[28]*Utica Sunday Tribune*, March 31, 1912, p. 2; *Utica Observer*, March 30, 1912, p. 8; "Report of the Bureau of Mediation and Arbitration," *New York Labor Bulletin*, Vol. XIV, No. 1 (June, 1912), p. 126.

[29]Letter, Chester Braman to W. Pierrepont White, April 3, 1912, White Papers, Box D-5-C-4-B.

[30]"Report," *New York Labor Bulletin*, Vol. XIV, No. 1 (June, 1912), p. 126.

[31]Letters, Chester Braman to W. Pierrepont White, March 29, 1912, White Papers, Box D-4-C-4-B and Chester Braman to The New York Mills, March 29, 1912, White Papers, Box D-5-C-4-B.

[32]Quotation from *Utica Saturday Globe*, March 30, 1912, p. 3. See also, *Utica Sunday Tribune*, March 31, 1912, p. 2.

[33]*Utica Observer*, March 30, 1912, p. 8.

[34]Quotation from *Utica Observer*, March 30, 1912, p. 8. See also, *Utica Sunday Tribune*, March 31, 1912, p. 2; *Utica Daily Press*, April 1, 1912, p. 6.

[35]*Utica Observer*, March 30, 1912, p. 8.

[36]*Utica Observer*, March 30, 1912, p. 8.

[37]*Utica Daily Press*, April 1, 1912, p. 6.

[38]*Utica Observer*, March 30, 1912, p. 8.

[39]*Utica Observer*, March 30, 1912, p. 8.

[40]*Utica Sunday Tribune*, March 31, 1912, p. 2.

[41]*Utica Sunday Tribune*, March 31, 1912, p. 2; *Utica Daily Press*, March 30, 1912, p. 3, and April 1, 1912, p. 6.

[42]*Utica Observer*, March 29, 1912, p. 8.

[43]*Utica Sunday Tribune*, March 31, 1912, p. 2.

[44]*Utica Daily Press*, April 1, 1912, p. 6.

[45]*Utica Observer*, April 1, 1912, p. 8.

[46]Quotations from *Utica Observer*, April 1, 1912, p. 8. See also *Utica Observer*, March 30, 1912, p. 8; *Utica Daily Press*, April 1, 1912, p. 6.

[47]*Utica Daily Press*, April 1, 1912, p. 6; Kozak interview.

[48]Newspaper quotation from *Utica Daily Press*, April 1, 1912, p. 6; reminiscence quotation from Kozak interview.

[49]*Utica Observer*, April 1, 1912, p. 8.

[50]Quotation from *Utica Observer*, April 1, 1912, p. 8. See also, *Utica Daily Press*, April 2, 1912, p. 3.

[51]"Report," *New York Labor Bulletin*, Vol. XIV, No. 1 (June, 1912), p. 126.

[52]Letters, Chester Braman to W. Pierrepont White, April 6 and 8, 1912, White Papers.

[53]*Utica Observer*, April 2, 1912, p. 8; *Utica Observer*, April 3, 1912, p. 8.

[54]*Utica Observer*, April 3, 1912, p. 8.

[55]*Utica Observer*, April 3, 1912, p. 8.

[56]Walsh, pp. 297-299; Cookinham, p. 348; Clarke, pp. 65-66; *Utica Observer*, March 18, 1912, p. 3; John W. Briggs, *An Italian Passage: Immigrants to Three American Cities, 1890-1930* (New Haven: Yale University Press, 1978), pp. 113, 141, 149, 173-175, 177-178; *La Luce*, February 17, 1912, p. 1, June 8, 1912, p. 1, and June 29, 1912, p. 1.

[57]*Utica Deutsche Zeitung*, April 5, 1912, p. 5. Despite the obvious attempts by the A. D. Juilliard Company to hire strikebreakers and resume operations at its various mills, W. Pierrepont White still steadfastly maintained, when queried by a reporter on the evening of April 3 about the company hiring strikebreakers, that: "I give you my word we shall not import any people for that purpose" (*Utica Herald-Dispatch*, April 4, 1912, p. 3).

[58]*Utica Observer*, April 3, 1912, p. 8; *Utica Daily Press*, April 4, 1912, p. 3.

[59]*Utica Observer*, April 3, 1912, p. 8.

[60]*Utica Observer*, April 3, 1912, p. 8.

[61]Quotation from *Utica Observer*, April 3, 1912, p. 8. See also *Utica Deutsche Zeitung*, April 5, 1912, p. 5.

[62]Quotations from *Utica Observer*, April 3, 1912, p. 8. See also *Utica Daily Press*, April 4, 1912, p. 3.

[63]*Utica Observer*, April 3, 1912, p. 8.

[64]*Utica Observer*, April 4, 1912, p. 8; *Utica Deutsche Zeitung*, April 5, 1912, p. 5.

[65]*Utica Daily Press*, April 4, 1912, p. 3.

[66]*Utica Observer*, April 4, 1912, p. 8.

[67]*Utica Daily Press*, April 4, 1912, p. 3.

[68]*Utica Observer*, April 4, 1912, p. 8.

[69]*Utica Observer*, April 4, 1912, p. 8; *Utica Daily Press*, April 5, 1912, p. 3.

[70]Quotation from *Utica Observer*, April 4, 1912, p. 8. See also *Utica Saturday Globe*, April 6, 1912, p. 9.

[71]*Utica Observer*, April 5, 1912, p. 8. Some of the Polish names in this newspaper article are hopelessly mangled. Mary Kawa may actually be Maryanna Kowal; Josephine Dziziel may in fact be surnamed Dzięgiel or Dziadzio; while Helen Doronogo, Mary Rouczka and Kate Bieva cannot be identified at this time.

[72]Both quotations from *Utica Observer*, April 4, 1912, p. 8.

[73]*Utica Daily Press*, April 5, 1912, p. 3.

[74]*Utica Observer*, April 4, 1912, p. 8; *Utica Daily Press*, April 5, 1912, p. 3.

Chapter 5: Martial Law

[1]*Utica Observer*, April 4, 1912, p. 8; *Utica Deutsche Zeitung*, April 5, 1912, p. 5; *Annual Report of the Adjutant General of the State of New York for the Year 1912* (Albany: J. B. Lyon Company, Printers, 1913), pp. 46, 235-237.

[2]*Utica Observer*, April 4, 1912, p. 8; *Utica Deutsche Zeitung*, April 5, 1912, p. 5; *Utica Herald-Dispatch*, April 4, 1912, p. 8.

[3]*Utica Observer*, April 4, 1912, p. 8.

[4]*Utica Observer*, April 4, 1912, p. 8.

[5]*Utica Daily Press*, April 4, 1912, p. 3, and April 13, 1912, p. 4; *Utica Observer*, April 4, 1912, p. 8; *Utica Sunday Tribune*, April 14, 1912.

[6]Quotation from *Utica Observer*, April 18, 1912, p. 13; see also *Utica Observer*, April 5, 1912, pp. 8, 12; *Utica Daily Press*, April 5, 1912, p. 10.

[7]*Utica Observer*, April 5, 1912, p. 8.

[8]*Utica Observer*, April 5, 1912, p. 8.

[9]*Utica Saturday Globe*, April 6, 1912, p. 9; *Utica Daily Press*, April 5, 1912, p. 10; *Utica Observer*, April 5, 1912, p. 8.

[10]*Utica Daily Press*, April 5, 1912, p. 10.

[11]*Utica Observer*, April 5, 1912, p. 8.

[12]*Utica Observer*, April 5, 1912, p. 8.

[13]*Utica Daily Press*, April 5, 1912, p. 3. The Polish press also noted that the militia "has behaved flawlessly. There have been no incidents of harassment as there were with the local policemen" (*Slowo Polskie*, April 11, 1912, p. 8).

[14]*Utica Sunday Tribune*, April 7, 1912, p. 2.

[15]*Utica Daily Press*, April 8, 1912, p. 4; Krawiec interview.

[16]*Utica Observer*, April 8, 1912, p. 8.

[17]Quotations from *Utica Daily Press*, April 13, 1912, p. 5; see also *Utica Daily Press*, April 8, 19 12, p. 4.

[18]*Utica Daily Press*, April 9, 1912, p. 6.

[19]*Utica Observer*, April 8, 1912, p. 8.

[20]*Utica Observer*, April 8, 1912, p. 8.

[21]*Utica Daily Press*, April 9, 1912, p. 6.

[22]*Utica Observer*, April 8, 1912, p. 8.

[23]*Utica Advocate*, April 13, 1912, p. 1; *Utica Daily Press*, April 10, 1912, p.3.

[24]*Utica Daily Press*, April 10, 1912, p. 3; *Utica Advocate*, April 13, 1912, p. 1.

[25]Letter, Chester A. Braman to W. Pierrepont White, April 6, 1912, White Papers, Box D-5-C-4-B.

[26]Quotation from *Utica Daily Press*, April 10, 1912, p. 3. See also *Utica Observer*, April 10, 1912, p. 8, and April 11, 1912, p. 8.

[27]*Utica Saturday Globe*, April 6, 1912, p. 9.

[28]*Utica Observer*, April 11, 1912, p. 8.

[29]*Utica Observer*, April 11, 1912, p. 8; *Utica Daily Press*, April 11, 1912, p. 4, and April 13, 1912, p. 5.

[30]*Utica Daily Press*, April 11, 1912, p. 12.

[31]"Report of the Bureau of Mediation and Arbitration for 1912," *New York Labor Bulletin*, Vol. XIV, No. 1, pp. 126-127, including quotations.

[32]"Report of the Bureau of Mediation and Arbitration for 1912," *New York Labor Bulletin*, Vol. XIV, No. 1, pp. 126-127.

[33]Letter, Chester A. Braman to W. Pierrepont White, April 9, 1912, White Papers, Box. D-5-C-4-B.

[34]Quotations from letter, Chester Braman to W. Pierrepont White, April 8, 1912, White Papers, Box D-5-C-4-B. See also Braman to White, April 10, 1912, White Papers, Box D-5-C-4-B.

[35]Letter, Chester Braman to W. Pierrepont White, April 8, 1912, White Papers, Box D-5-C-4-B.

[36]Chester A. Braman, draft statement, attached to letter, Chester A. Braman to W. Pierrepont White, April 8, 1912, White Papers, Box D-5-C-4-B.

[37]Letter, W. Pierrepont White to Chester A. Braman, April 9, 1912, White Papers, Group #399, Letter Book 34.

[38]Quotation from *Utica Daily Press*, April 12, 1912, p. 7. For the company's tactics in this instance, see also Savoie, p. 105.

[39]*Utica Observer*, April 12, 1912, p. 12.

[40]*Utica Daily Press*, April 15, 1912, p. 10.

[41]*Utica Daily Press*, April 15, 1912, p. 10.

[42]*Utica Daily Press*, April 15, 1912, p. 10.

[43]*Utica Saturday Globe*, April 13, 1912, p. 12.

[44]*Utica Saturday Globe*, April 13, 1912, p. 12.

[45]*Utica Observer*, April 5, 1912, p. 8.

[46]*Utica Daily Press*, April 17, 1912, p. 3; *Utica Observer*, April 16, 1912, p. 8.

[47]*Utica Daily Press*, April 15, 1912, p. 10, and April 16, 1912, p. 5; *Utica Observer*, April 15, 1912, p. 8; *Utica Deutsche Zeitung*, April 19, 1912, p. 5.

[48]*Utica Observer*, April 15, 1912, p. 8; *Utica Deutsche Zeitung*, April 19, 1912, p. 5.

[49]*Utica Observer*, April 15, 1912, p. 8.

[50]Quotation from *Utica Observer*, April 16, 1912, p, 8. See also *Utica Observer*, April 15, 1912, p. 8; *Utica Daily Press*, April 16, 1912, p. 5.

[51]*Utica Daily Press*, April 17, 1912, p. 3.

[52]*Utica Observer*, April 16, 1912, p. 8.

[53]*Utica Daily Press*, April 16, 1912, p. 5 and April 17, 1912, p. 3; *Utica Observer*, April 16, 1912, p. 8.

[54]*Utica Observer*, April 17, 1912, p. 8.

[55]*Utica Observer*, April 18, 1912, p. 8; *Utica Daily Press*, April 18, 1912, p. 5 and April 19, 1912, p. 5.

[56]*Utica Daily Press*, April 18, 1912, p. 5.

[57]"Report of the Bureau of Mediation and Arbitration for 1912," *New York Labor Bulletin*, XIV, No. 1, pp. 126-127, including quotations from p. 127.

[58]*Utica Observer*, April 18, 1912, p. 8; *Utica Daily Press*, April 18, 1912, p. 5; *Utica Saturday Globe*, April 20, 1912, p. 9. Savoie, p. 107, maintains that at this point "the company had already broken the strike." This conclusion is certainly difficult to sustain in view of the continuing financial support that the strikers were receiving, their stubborn refusal to return to work, and the fact that the company had been able to employ only enough strike-breakers to resume minimal operations with skeleton crews.

[59]*Utica Daily Press*, April 18, 1912, p. 5.

[60]*Utica Observer*, April 18, 1912, p. 8.

[61]*Utica Daily Press*, April 19, 1912, p. 5.

[62]*Utica Daily Press*, April 19, 1912, p. 5.

[63]*Utica Daily Press*, April 20, 1912, p. 3.

[64]*Utica Daily Press*, April 20, 1912, p. 3.

[65]*Utica Observer*, April 20, 1912, p. 8.

[66]Quotation from *Utica Sunday Tribune*, April 21, 1912, p. 2. See also *Utica Observer*, April 20, 1912, p. 8; *Utica Daily Press*, April 22, 1912, p. 6. Superintendent Braman was the son of Chester A. Braman the New York City stockholder and member of the A. D. Juilliard Company Board of Directors (*Utica Herald-Dispatch*, April 6, 1912, p. 3).

[67]Quotation from *Utica Daily Press*, April 23, 1912, p. 6. See also *Utica Observer*, April 22, 1912, p. 8.

[68]*Utica Daily Press*, April 23, 1912, p. 6.

[69]*Utica Daily Press*, April 24, 1912, p. 3.

[70]*Utica Observer*, April 24, 1912, p. 4.

[71]Quotations from *Utica Daily Press*, April 25, 1912, p. 4. For evidence of Juilliard's manipulation of the press see letter, W. Pierrepont White to Chester A. Braman, April 25, 1912, White Papers, Group #399, Letter Book 34.

[72]Letter, Chester Braman to W. Pierrepont White, April 26, 1912, White Papers.

[73]Utica Sunday Tribune, April 28, 1912, p. 14.

[74]*Utica Advocate*, April 27, 1912, p. 1.

[75]*Proceedings of the Twelfth Annual Convention of the United Textile Workers of America* (U.T.W.A., 1912), p. 22.

[76]Report of Charles A. Miles, *Proceedings of the Twelfth Annual Convention of the United Textile Workers of America* (U.T.W.A., 1912), pp. 35-36.

[77]*Proceedings*, 12th UTWA, p. 35; "Report ... 1912," *New York Labor Bulletin*, p. 128; *Strikes and Lockouts in 1912 and 1913*, New York State Department of Labor Bulletin No. 66, Bureau of Mediation and Arbitration, 1913, p. 33; *Twelfth Annual Report of the Commissioner of Labor for the Twelve Months Ended September 30, 1912* (Albany, NY: New York State Department of Labor, 1913), p. 109.

[78]*Strikes and Lockouts in 1912 and 1913*, Bulletin No. 66, p. 33; *The Textile Worker*, Vol. I, No. 1 (June 1912), p. 6.

[79]"Report ... 1912," *New York Labor Bulletin*, p. 128; *Proceedings*, 12th UTWA, p. 35.

[80]"Report ... 1912," *New York Labor Bulletin*, p. 128; *Proceedings*, 12th UTWA, p. 35.

[81]Savoie's study of the New York Mills Corporation concludes that "Management, possessing advantages of able leadership, tactical position, and ample economic resources, carried the day. The union of one year found itself unable to muster sufficient staying power to withstand the employers' counter-attack" (p. 4). This position is difficult to support given the actual settlement agreement. That both sides claimed victory is fact, that both really felt they won is equally as certain. It was, no doubt, a good compromise settlement that each side felt comfortable with.

[82]Quotation from *Utica Saturday Globe*, April 27, 1912, p. 12, See also *Strikes and Lockouts in 1912 and 1913*, Bulletin No. 66, pp. 5, 6, 32-33; *Proceedings*, 12th UTWA, p. 22; *Utica Daily Press*, April 24,

1912, p. 3 and April 27, 1912, p. 3; *Utica Observer*, April 26, 1912, p. 3; *The Textile Worker*, Vol. I, No. 1 (June 1912), p. 6.

Chapter 6: *Bóg i Ojczyzna*

[1] *American Federationist*, Vol. XIX, No. 11 (November 1912), p. 938.

[2] John Williams, Commissioner, "Annual Report of the Bureau of Labor Statistics," (Albany: New York State Assembly Document No. 48C, March 17, 1913), pp. 73, 159, 289, 391, 534.

[3] *Proceedings*, 12th UTWA, pp. 5, 35.

[4] "Ten Fingers," pp. 10, 14; *Stowo Polskie*, June 27, 1912, p. 8; Dziedzic interview; *Utica Daily Press*, August 4, 1968, p. 7D; Piszcz interview; quotation from *Pamiętnik Srebrnego*.

[5] *Stowo Polskie*, March 13, 1913, p. 8.

[6] *Stowo Polskie*, February 6, 1913, p. 8.

[7] Quotation from *Stowo Polskie*, May 8, 1913, p. 8. See also Wepsiec, p. 85 (for publication information on *Mtotek Duchowny*); *Stowo Polskie*, April 17, 1913, p. 8. Many of the leaders of the union movement in New York Mills employed socialist rhetoric and at least one, F. Sliski, was a member of the Polish Section of the Socialist Party of America. The fact that many flirted with socialist ideology does not at all mean that they were radical socialists of "communists." Rather, while they accepted the idea that workers deserved better wages, better treatment, better conditions, and a voice in determining their collective future, they rejected the radicalism which later came to characterize some of the more widely publicized activities of prominent American socialists. Evidence of this is their rejection of overtures from the more radical International Workers of the World and their allegiance to the relatively conservative United Textile Workers of America.

[8] *Stowo Polskie*, May 8, 1913, p. 8.

[9] *Stowo Polskie*, May 5, 1913, p. 8.

[10] *Stowo Polskie*, May 8, 1913, p. 8.

[11] *Stowo Polskie*, May 29, 1913, p. 5.

[12] *Stowo Polskie*, June 26, 1913, p. 5.

[13] *Stowo Polskie*, June 26, 1913, p. 5.

[14] *Pamiętnik z Okazyi*, n.p.

[15] "Ten Fingers," n.p.; *Diamond Jubilee*, n.p.

[16] *Stowo Polskie*, November 18, 1927, p. 20.

[17] *Stowo Polskie*, July 24, 1913, p. 7.

[18] Mortgage of the Polish Workingmen's Hall Association of New York Mills, Inc., to Thomas Szlosek, Anthony Knutelski, John Solnica, Peter Kozak and Albert Nowak, July 17, 1914, courtesy of Bertha Solnica; Piszcz interview; "Ten Fingers," p. 10; *Stowo Polskie*, July 31, 1913, p. 8 and November 18, 1927, p. 20 and May 4, 1962.

[19]Quotations from *Konstytucya Pol. Hali Robotniczej Inkorporowanej w New York Mills, N. Y.* (New York Mills, NY: Drukiem J. Łabuz, 1913), n.p., courtesy of Bertha Solnica and Joseph Kielbasa. See also Piszcz interview; "Ten Fingers," p. 10; *Słowo Polskie*, May 4, 1962.

[20]Cecilia interview; Rosinski interview; *Whitestown 1784-1984*, p. 44; Davis, "Women's Roles," pp. 39-40.

[21]Susan G. Davis, "Utica's Polka Music Tradition," *New York Folklore*, Vol. 4, No. 1-4 (Summer-Winter 1978), pp. 110-111.

[22]Quotation from Davis, "Utica's Polka," p. 111, see also p. 103.

[23]M. Dziedzic interview; *Góralu, Czy Ci Nie Żal* was written by the Polish writer and playwrite Michał Bałucki. This translation was prepared by Helen Dziedzic.

[24]"Changes in Union Wages and Hours in 1913," New York State Department of Labor Bulletin No. 64, Series on Wages and Hours No. 1, prepared by the Bureau of Statistics and Information, published in August, 1914, pp. 60-61; *The Textile Worker*, Vol. III, No. 8 (January 1915), p. 11.

[25]"Union Rates of Wages and Hours in 1913," State of New York Department of Labor Bulletin No. 65, Series on Wages and Hours No. 2, published in September, 1914, prepared by the Bureau of Statistics and Information, p. 60; quotation from *Słowo Polskie*, July 25, 1912, p. 8.

[26]Quotation from W. Pierrepont White to John W. Wood, August 5, 1912, White Papers, Group #399, letter book 35. See also White to Charles A. Graves, January 9, 1913, White Papers, Group #399, letter book 36.

[27]Quotation from W. Pierrepont White to Chester A. Braman, January 21, 1913, White Papers, Group #399, letter book 36.

[28]Quotation from W. Pierrepont White to Mrs. John B. Ethridge, January 31, 1913, White Papers, Group #399, letter book 36. See also White to Chester A. Braman, January 28, 1913, White Papers, Group #399, letter book 36.

[29]Quotation from W. Pierrepont White to Mrs. Augusta M. Wilcox, White Papers, Group #399, letter book 36.

[30]Quotation from W. Pierrepont White to Chester A. Braman, June 29, 1912, White Papers, Group #399, letter book 34. See also White to Braman, June 25, 1912, *ibid.* See also White to Braman, November 12, 1912, WHite Papers, Group #399, letter book 35.

[31]Letter, Chester A. Braman to W. Pierrepont White, July 1, 1912, White Papers, Box D-5-C-4-B.

[32]Letters, W. Pierrepont White to William W. Farley, Commissioner, New York State Department of Excise, July 19, 1912, White Papers, Group #399, letter book 35; White to Braman, July 22, 1912, *ibid.*; Braman to White, July 20, 1912, Box D-5-C-4-B.

[33]Quotation from letter, W. Pierrepont White to Chester A. Braman, January 17, 1912, White Papers, Group #399, letter book 36. See also White to Braman, February 20, 1913 and White to Braman, February 26, 1913, White Papers, Group #399, letter book 36.

[34]Quotation from Chester A. Braman to "The New York Mills," February 21, 1913, White Papers, Box D-5-C-4-B.

[35]*Słowo Polskie*, August 15, 1912, p. 8.

[36]*Słowo Polskie*, July 17, 1913, p. 4.

[37]*Proceedings*, 13th UTWA, p. 45.

[38]Quotation from *Słowo Polskie*, July 17, 1913, p. 4. See also, *Słowo Polskie*, June 26, 1913, p. 8.

[39]*Słowo Polskie*, July 10, 1913, p. 8.

[40]*Słowo Polskie*, the quotations regarding Pezdek are from July 31, 1913, p. 8, the remaining quotations are from July 17, 1913, p. 4.

[41]*Słowo Polskie*, July 24, 1913, p. 5.

[42]*Słowo Polskie*, July 17, 1913, p. 4.

[43]*Proceedings*, 13th UTWA, pp. 45, 47-48. The Polish organizer's surname is variously spelled as Minszewski or Mniszewski. The former appears in the U.T.W.A. records, while the latter appears in the Town of New Hartford Court records. The newspapers used both, but favored the former, which is adopted here throughout for the sake of consistency.

[44]*Słowo Polskie*, August 28, 1913, p. 5.

[45]*Słowo Polskie*, July 24, 1913, p. 5.

[46]*Słowo Polskie*, July 24, 1913, p. 7.

[47]Quotation from *Słowo Polskie*, September 18, 1913, p. 4; see also *Słowo Polskie*, September 10, 1926, p. 1..

[48]"Statistics of Trade Unions in 1913," Bureau of Statistics and Information, State of New York, Department of Labor Bulletin No. 60, pp. 57, 114; "Statistics of Trade Unions in 1914," Bureau of Statistics and Information, State of New York, Department of Labor Bulletin No. 74, pp. 67, 120; *Słowo Polskie*, November 18, 1927, p. 20.

[49]Quotations from *Proceedings*, 14th UTWA, p. 106. See also, "Directory of Trade Unions 1914," Bureau of Statistics and Information, State of New York Department of Labor Bulletin No. 63, p. 72.

[50]Quotation from *Słowo Polskie*, November 27, 1913, p. 8; see also *Słowo Polskie*, August 14, 1913, p. 6.

[51]*Słowo Polskie*, August 7, 1913, p. 4.

[52]*Słowo Polskie*, quotations from August 14, 1913, p. 6; see also August 21, 1913, p. 6 and August 28, 1913, p. 5.

[53]*The American Story of Industrial and Labor Relations*, pp. 82, 84.

[54]*Słowo Polskie*, August 14, 1913, p. 6.

[55]*Słowo Polskie*, July 30, 1914, p. 4.

[56]*Utica Daily Press*, July 19, 1916, p. 4.

[57]*Utica Herald-Dispatch*, July 19, 1916, p. 2. Fish resigned because, in the words of W. Pierrepont White, "when we had a strike some time ago, he, apparently, did not like some action that was taken, and resigned." See letter, White to "Gentlemen," August 7, 1912, White Papers, Group #399, letter book 35.

[58]*Utica Herald-Dispatch*, July 18, 1916, p. 2; *Utica Daily Press*, July 19, 1916, p. 4; *Utica Advocate*, June 17, 1916, p. 1.

[59]Letter, Chester A. Braman to John P. Campbell, January 7, 1916, in the Piszcz Papers in the possession of Alfred Piszcz.

[60]*Słowo Polskie*, November 28, 1912, p. 8.

[61]*Utica Herald-Dispatch*, July 18, 1916, p. 2; *Utica Daily Press*, July 19, 1916, p. 4.

[62]*Utica Herald-Dispatch*, July 18, 1916, p. 2; *Utica Daily Press*, July 19, 1916, p. 4.

Chapter 7: "United We Stand"

[1]*Utica Herald-Dispatch*, July 18, 1916, p. 2; *Utica Daily Press*, July 19, 1916, p. 4 and July 22, 1916, p. 5; *Utica Saturday Globe*, July 22, 1916, p. 6; *Utica Deutsche Zeitung*, July 21, 1916, p. 4; *Utica Observer*, July 18, 1916.

[2]*Utica Herald-Dispatch*, July 18, 1916, p. 2; *Utica Daily Press*, July 19, 1916, p. 4 and July 22, 1916, p. 5; *Utica Saturday Globe*, July 22, 1916, p. 6; *Utica Deutsche Zeitung*, July 21, 1916, p. 4; *Utica Observer*, July 18, 1916.

[3]Quotation from *Utica Observer*, July 18, 1916. See also *Utica Herald-Dispatch*, July 18, 1916, p. 2; *Złota Księga*, p. 48.

[4]*Utica Herald-Dispatch*, July 18, 1916, p. 2 and July 19, 1916, p. 2; *Utica Daily Press*, July 19, 1916, p. 4.

[5]*Utica Herald-Dispatch*, July 18, 1916, p. 2; *Utica Saturday Globe*, July 22, 1916, p. 8.

[6]*Utica Herald-Dispatch*, July 18, 1916, p. 2; *Utica Saturday Globe*, July 22, 1916, p. 8.

[7]Quotations from *Utica Herald-Dispatch*, July 18, 1916, p. 2. See also *Utica Saturday Globe*, July 22, 1916, p. 8.

[8]*Utica Herald-Dispatch*, July 18, 1916, p. 2; *Utica Daily Press*, July 19, 1916, p. 4; *Utica Observer*, July 18, 1916; *Utica Saturday Globe*, July 22, 1916, p. 8.

[9]*Utica Herald-Dispatch*, July 18, 1916, p. 2.

[10]*Utica Herald-Dispatch*, July 19, 1916, p. 2.

[11]*Utica Herald-Dispatch*, July 19, 1916, p. 2.

[12]Quotations from *Utica Daily Press*, July 20, 1916, p. 6. See also *Utica Herald-Dispatch*, July 19, 1916, p. 2.

[13]Quotations from *Utica Daily Press*, July 20, 1916, p. 6. See also *Utica Herald-Dispatch*, July 19, 1916, p. 2.

[14]*Utica Observer*, July 19, 1916.

[15]*Utica Daily Press*, July 21, 1916, p. 4; *Utica Observer*, July 20, 1916.

[16]*Utica Daily Press*, July 21, 1916, p. 4; *Utica Observer*, July 20, 1916.

[17]*Utica Daily Press*, July 21, 1916, p. 4.

[18]*Utica Herald-Dispatch*, July 21, 1916, p. 3.

[19]*Utica Herald-Dispatch*, July 21, 1916, p. 3; *Utica Daily Press*, July 22, 1916, p. 5.

[20]*Utica Daily Press,* July 20, 1916, p. 6.

[21]*Utica Observer,* July 20, 1916.

[22]*Utica Observer,* July 20, 1916.

[23]Quotation from Kozak interview. Also, Krawiec interview; C. Chrabas interview.

[24]Kozak interview; Krawiec interview; C. Chrabas interview.

[25]*Utica Herald-Dispatch,* July 20, 1916, p. 3; *Utica Daily Press,* July 21, 1916, p. 4.

[26]Quotation from *Utica Herald-Dispatch,* July 20, 1916, p. 3. It also appeared in *Utica Daily Press,* July 21, 1916, p. 4. Shiro later told reporters that he was misquoted and that he had said such action should only be taken when the discharged employee had been unfairly dismissed without just cause. This assertion can be found in *Utica Herald-Dispatch,* July 21, 1916, p. 3. See also *Utica Daily Press,* July 22, 1916, p. 5.

[27]*Utica Herald-Dispatch,* July 21, 1916, p. 3; *Utica Daily Press,* July 21, 1916, p. 4 and July 22, 1916, p. 5.

[28]*Utica Herald-Dispatch,* July 20, 1916, p. 3.

[29]Quotations from *Utica Herald-Dispatch,* July 21, 1916, p. 3. See also *Utica Daily Press,* July 21, 1916, p. 4 and July 22, 1916, p. 5.

[30]*Utica Daily Press,* July 21, 1916, p. 5.

[31]*Utica Herald-Dispatch,* July 22, 1916, p. 3.

[32]*Utica Herald-Dispatch,* July 22, 1916, p. 3; *Utica Sunday Tribune,* July 23, 1916, p. 5.

[33]*Utica Herald-Dispatch,* July 22, 1916, p. 3; *Utica Sunday Tribune,* July 23, 1916, p. 5.

[34]*Utica Observer,* July 22, 1916, p. 10; *Utica Herald-Dispatch,* July 22, 1916, p. 3; *Utica Saturday Globe,* July 22, 1916, p. 6.

[35]*Utica Observer,* July 22, 1916, p. 10.

[36]*Utica Saturday Globe,* July 22, 1916, p. 8.

[37]*Utica Daily Press,* July 25, 1916, p. 7. The newspaper calls him Rizek, but his correct name was undoubtedly Ryczek.

[38]*Utica Daily Press,* July 24, 1916.

[39]Quotation from *Utica Herald-Dispatch,* July 24, 1916, p. 2. See also *Utica Daily Press,* July 25, 1916, p. 7; *Utica Observer,* July 24, 1916, p. 10.

[40]*Utica Observer,* July 24, 1916, p. 10.

[41]Quotation from *Utica Herald-Dispatch,* July 25, 1916, p. 2; *Utica Observer,* July 25, 1916.

[42]*Utica Herald-Dispatch,* July 25, 1916, pp. 2, 7.

[43]*Utica Herald-Dispatch,* July 26, 1916, p. 2; *Utica Observer,* July 26, 1916, p. 10.

[44]Quotation from *Utica Herald-Dispatch,* July 26, 1916, p. 2; *Utica Daily Press,* July 27, 1916, p. 3; *Utica Observer,* July 26, 1916, p. 10.

[45]John G. Moses, *From Mt. Lebanon to the Mohawk Valley: The Story of Syro-Lebanese Americans in the Utica Area* (Utica, NY: Privately Printed, 1981), pp. 3, 4, 7, 11, 14, 19-20.

[46]*Utica Herald-Dispatch*, July 26, 1916, p. 2; *Utica Herald-Dispatch*, July 26, 1916, p. 2; *Utica Daily Press*, July 27, 1916, p. 3; *Utica Observer*, July 26, 1916, p. 10.

[47]*Utica Herald-Dispatch*, July 27, 1916, p. 2 and July 31, 1916, p. 2.

[48]*Utica Herald-Dispatch*, July 27, 1916, p. 2.

[49]*Utica Herald-Dispatch*, July 28, 1916, p. 8; *Utica Saturday Globe*, July 29, 1916, p. 8; *Utica Daily Press*, July 28, 1916.

[50]*Utica Herald-Dispatch*, July 27, 1916, p. 2; *Utica Saturday Globe*, July 29, 1916, p. 8.

[51]*Utica Daily Press*, July 27, 1916, p. 3.

[52]*Utica Daily Press*, July 27, 1916, p. 3; *Utica Herald-Dispatch*, July 27, 1916, p. 2; *Utica Observer*, July 27, 1916, p. 8; *Utica Deutsche Zeitung*, July 28, 1916, p. 5.

[53]Quotation from *Utica Daily Press*, July 27, 1916, p. 3. See also *Utica Herald-Dispatch*, July 27, 1916, p. 2; *Utica Observer*, July 27, 1916, p. 8; *Utica Deutsche Zeitung*, July 28, 1916, p. 5.

[54]Quotation from *Utica Daily Press*, July 27, 1916, p. 3. See also *Utica Herald-Dispatch*, July 27, 1916, p. 2; *Utica Deutsche Zeitung*, July 28, 1916, p. 5.

[55]*The Bulletin*, Vol. 3, No. 3 (December, 1917), p. 87. This is a publication of the New York State Industrial Commission, Albany, N.Y.

[56]*Utica Herald-Dispatch*, July 27, 1916, p. 2; *Utica Daily Press*, July 27, 1916, p. 3.

[57]*Utica Herald-Dispatch*, July 27, 1916, p. 2.

[58]*Utica Observer*, July 26, 1916, p. 10 and July 27, 1916, p. 8; *Utica Herald-Dispatch*, July 27, 1916, p. 2.

[59]*Utica Observer*, July 28, 1916.

[60]*Utica Herald-Dispatch*, July 29, 1916, p. 2.

[61]*Utica Observer*, July 28, 1916.

[62]*Utica Daily Press*, July 29, 1916; *Utica Herald-Dispatch*, July 28, 1916 and July 31, 1916, p. 2; *Utica Observer*, July 31, 1916, p. 10.

[63]*Utica Herald-Dispatch*, July 31, 1916, p. 2 and August 1, 1916, p. 2.

[64]*Utica Observer*, July 31, 1916, p. 10.

[65]*Utica Herald-Dispatch*, July 31, 1916, p. 2.

[66]*Utica Observer*, August 1, 1916. One indication of dissent within the strikers' ranks might be seen in a notice that Louis Eurpola was elected to replace Sroka as president of Local 753. This appeared in the July 29, 1916, issue of the *Utica Herald-Dispatch*, p. 2. It proved to be false, but it may have indicated either dissent, or possibly a mistake in identifying a leader of the Italian faction as a leader of the union local itself.

[67]*Utica Herald-Dispatch*, August 2, 1916, p. 2.

[68]*Utica Observer*, August 1, 1916.

[69]*Utica Daily Press*, August 1, 1916, p. 9 and August 2, 1916, p. 7.

[70]*Utica Herald-Dispatch*, August 1, 1916, p. 2.

[71]*Utica Herald-Dispatch*, August 2, 1916, p. 2; *Utica Deutsche Zeitung*, August 4, 1916, p. 4.

[72]*Utica Herald-Dispatch*, August 2, 1916, p. 2; *Utica Deutsche Zeitung*, August 4, 1916, p. 4; *Utica Saturday Globe*, August 5, 1916, p. 3; *Utica Daily Press*, August 3, 1916, p. 3; *Utica Observer*, August 2, 1916, p. 10.

[73]*Utica Herald-Dispatch*, August 2, 1916, p. 2.

[74]*Utica Herald-Dispatch*, August 2, 1916, p. 2.

[75]*Utica Observer*, August 2, 1916, p. 10; *Utica Saturday Globe*, August 5, 1916, .p. 3; *Utica Herald-Dispatch*, August 2, 1916, p. 2; *Utica Daily Press*, August 3, 1916, p. 3.

[76]*Utica Observer*, August 2, 1916, p. 10; *Utica Saturday Globe*, August 5, 1916, p. 3; *Utica Herald-Dispatch*, August 2, 1916, p. 2; Kogut interview.

[77]*Utica Observer*, August 2, 1916, p. 10; *Utica Herald-Dispatch*, August 2, 1916, p. 2; *Utica Daily Press*, August 3, 1916, p. 3.

[78]*Utica Observer*, August 2, 1916, p. 10.

[79]*Utica Herald-Dispatch*, August 2, 1916, p. 2.

[80]*Utica Herald-Dispatch*, August 2, 1916, p. 2.

[81]*Utica Observer*, August 2, 1916, p. 10; *Utica Herald-Dispatch*, August 2, 1916, p. 2.

[82]*Utica Daily Press*, August 3, 1916, p. 3.

[83]Quotations from *Utica Herald-Dispatch*, August 3, 1916, p. 2. See also *Utica Observer*, August 3, 1916.

[84]*Utica Daily Press*, August 4, 1916, p. 5.

[85]*Utica Saturday Globe*, August 5, 1916, p. 3.

[86]*Utica Observer*, August 4, 1916, p. 10.

[87]*Utica Herald-Dispatch*, August 4, 1916, p. 3.

[88]*Utica Daily Press*, August 5, 1916, p. 3; *Utica Herald-Dispatch*, August 4, 1916, p. 3.

[89]*Utica Herald-Dispatch*, August 4, 1916, p. 3.

[90]*Utica Observer*, August 4, 1916, p. 10.

[91]Quotation from *Utica Daily Press*, August 5, 1916, p. 3. See also *Utica Saturday Globe*, August 5, 1916, p. 3.

[92]Quotation from *Utica Observer*, August 5, 1916. See also *Utica Herald-Dispatch*, August 5, 1916, p. 2.

[93]*Utica Herald-Dispatch*, August 5, 1916, p. 2.

[94]*Utica Herald-Dispatch*, August 5, 1916, p. 2.

[95]*Utica Herald-Dispatch*, August 5, 1916, p. 2.

[96]*Utica Herald-Dispatch*, August 5, 1916, p. 2.

[97]*Utica Saturday Globe*, August 5, 1916, p. 5; *Utica Sunday Tribune*, August 6, 1916, p. 2.

[98]*Utica Sunday Tribune*, August 6, 1916, p. 2.

[99]*Utica Observer*, July 20, 1916.

[100]Kozak interview; Furgal interview; Dziedzic interview.

[101]Kozak interview; Dziedzic interview; Furgal interview.

[102]*Utica Herald-Dispatch*, August 8, 1916, p. 14.

[103]*Utica Herald-Dispatch*, August 7, 1916, p. 2.

[104]*Utica Herald-Dispatch*, August 7, 1916, p. 2.

[105]*Utica Herald-Dispatch*, August 7, 1916, p. 2.

[106]*Utica Herald-Dispatch*, August 7, 1916, p. 2.

[107]*Utica Daily Press*, August 8, 1916, p. 9.

[108]*Utica Herald-Dispatch*, August 8, 1916, p. 14 and August 9, 1916, p. 2; *Utica Daily Press*, August 8, 1916, p. 9; *Utica Observer*, August 8, 1916.

[109]*Utica Observer*, August 9, 1916, p. 10.

[110]Quotation from *Utica Observer*, August 9, 1916, p. 10. See also *Utica Herald-Dispatch*, August 9, 1916, p. 2.

[111]*Utica Herald-Dispatch*, August 9, 1916, p. 2.

[112]Quotation from *Utica Herald-Dispatch*, August 10, 1916, p. 3. See also *Utica Observer*, August 10, 1916, which indicates that the deputies were under Tobin.

[113]*Utica Herald-Disaptch*, August 10, 1916, p. 3; *Utica Daily Press*, August 11, 1916, p. 5; *Utica Saturday Globe*, August 12, 1916, p. 4.

[114]*Utica Herald-Dispatch*, August 10, 1916, p. 3.

[115]*Utica Daily Press*, August 11, 1916, p. 5; *Utica Observer*, August 10, 1916; *Utica Deutsche Zeitung*, August 11, 1916, p. 4.

[116]*Utica Observer*, August 10, 1916.

[117]*Utica Daily Press*, August 11, 1916, p. 5; *Utica Herald-Dispatch*, August 11, 1916, p. 3.

[118]*Utica Herald-Dispatch*, August 11, 1916, p. 3.

[119]*Utica Herald-Dispatch*, August 11, 1916, p. 3.

[120]*Utica Herald-Dispatch*, August 11, 1916.

[121]*Utica Herald-Dispatch*, August 14, 1916, p. 3; *Utica Daily Press*, August 15, 1916, p. 6.

[122]*Utica Herald-Dispatch*, August 12, 1916, p. 2 and August 14, 1916, p. 3; *Utica Sunday Tribune*, August 13, 1916, p. 3.

[123]*Utica Herald-Dispatch*, August 14, 1916, p. 3.

[124]*Utica Daily Press*, August 15, 1916, p. 6.

[125]*Utica Daily Press*, August 15, 1916, p. 6.

[126]*Utica Daily Press*, August 16, 1916, p. 3; *Utica Observer*, August 14, 1916, p. 8.

[127]*Utica Observer*, August 14, 1916, p. 8.

[128]Giergielewicz and Krzyżanowski, p. 20.

[129]*Utica Observer*, August 15, 1916, p. 8; *Utica Herald-Dispatch*, August 15, 1916.

[130]*Utica Observer*, August 15, 1916, p. 8; *Utica Herald-Dispatch*, August 15, 1916.

[131]*Utica Observer*, August 17, 1916, p. 10.

[132]*Utica Herald-Dispatch*, August 16, 1916, p. 3.

[133]*Utica Observer*, August 17, 1916, p. 10; *Utica Herald-Dispatch*, August 17, 1916; *Utica Daily Press*, August 18, 1916.

[134]*Utica Herald-Dispatch*, August 18, 1916, p. 2.

[135]*Utica Observer*, August 17, 1916, p. 10.

[136]*Utica Observer*, August 19, 1916, p. 12; *Utica Herald-Dispatch*, August 18, 1916, p. 2.

[137]*Utica Daily Press*, August 19, 1916, p. 3.

[138]*Utica Observer*, August 19, 1916.

270 *United We Stand*

139*Utica Sunday Tribune*, August 20, 1916, p. 3.

Chapter 8: A Fight to the Finish

¹*Utica Observer*, August 23, 1916, p. 8; *Utica Herald-Dispatch*, August 21, 1916, p. 2. Ironically, the building at 315 Nichols street would later become the Polonia Community Home in East Utica.

²Quotation from *Utica Observer*, August 23, 1916, p. 8. See also *Utica Herald-Dispatch*, August 23, 1916, p. 2.

³*Utica Herald-Dispatch*, August 23, 1916, p. 2, August 25, 1916, p. 2 and August 26, 1916, p. 8.

⁴*Utica Observer*, August 23, 1916, p. 8.

⁵*Utica Observer*, August 26, 1916, p. 10.

⁶*Utica Observer*, August 26, 1916, p. 10; *Utica Herald-Dispatch*, August 25, 1916, p. 2.

⁷*Utica Herald-Dispatch*, August 28, 1916, p. 3.

⁸Quotation from *Utica Herald-Dispatch*, August 28, 1916, p. 3. See also *Utica Daily Press*, August 30, 1916, p. 12; *Utica Observer*, August 28, 1916, p. 8.

⁹*Utica Herald-Dispatch*, August 28, 1916, p. 12. Also printed in *Utica Observer*, August 28, 1916, p. 8.

¹⁰*Utica Herald-Dispatch*, July 28, 1916, p. 16.

¹¹*Utica Observer*, August 29, 1916, p. 2; *Utica Herald-Dispatch*, August 30, 1916, p. 5.

¹²Quotation from *Utica Observer*, August 29, 1916, p. 8. See also *Utica Observer*, August 29, 1916, p. 2; *Utica Herald-Dispatch*, August 30, 1916, p. 5.

¹³*Utica Observer*, August 30, 1916.

¹⁴*Utica Observer*, August 29, 1916, p. 8 and August 30, 1916; Rent Roll Book, 1916-1920, New York Mills Corporation, MSS.2/NYM4/ RRO.4.

¹⁵*Utica Daily Press*, August 30, 1916, p. 12; *Utica Herald-Dispatch*, August 30, 1916, p. 5 and September 6, 1916, p. 2; *Utica Observer*, August 31, 1916, p. 8.

¹⁶*Utica Observer*, August 30, 1916.

¹⁷*Utica Observer*, August 30, 1916.

¹⁸*Utica Daily Press*, August 30, 1916, p. 12; *Utica Herald-Dispatch*, August 30, 1916, p. 2 and September 6, 1916, p. 2; *Utica Observer*, August 31, 1916, p. 8.

¹⁹*Utica Observer*, August 29, 1916, p. 8 and August 31, 1916, p. 8; *Utica Daily Press*, August 30, 1916, p. 12; *Utica Herald-Dispatch*, August 30, 1916, p. 5 and September 6, 1916, p. 2.

²⁰Quotation from *Utica Herald-Dispatch*, August 31, 1916, p. 4, See also *Utica Daily Press*, August 31, 1916, p. 10; *Utica Observer*, August 31, 1916, p. 8.

²¹*Utica Herald-Dispatch*, August 31, 1916, p. 4; *Utica Daily Press*, August 31, 1916, p. 10.

[22]*Utica Herald-Dispatch*, August 31, 1916, p. 4; *Utica Daily Press*, August 31, 1916, p. 10.

[23]*Utica Daily Press*, August 30, 1916, p. 12; *Utica Herald-Dispatch*, August 30, 1916, p. 5.

[24]*Utica Herald-Dispatch*, August 31, 1916, p. 4; *Utica Daily Press*, August 31, 1916, p. 10.

[25]*Utica Herald-Dispatch*, August 31, 1916, p. 4; *Utica Daily Press*, August 31, 1916, p. 10.

[26]*Utica Daily Press*, September 1, 1916, p. 6 and September 2, 1916, p. 8; *Utica Herald-Dispatch*, September 1, 1916, p. 2.

[27]*Utica Daily Press*, September 1, 1916, p. 6; *Utica Herald-Dispatch*, September 1, 1916, p. 2.

[28]*Utica Daily Press*, September 1, 1916, p. 6.

[29]Quotation from *Utica Daily Press*, September 1, 1916, p. 6; *Utica Herald-Dispatch*, September 1 ,1916, p. 2.

[30]*Utica Herald-Dispatch*, September 1, 1916, p. 2. The charge was violation of Section 2090 of the Penal Code. Bradley Fuller represented the people. See Justice's Criminal Docket, Hon. W. E. Nelson, in the Town of New Hartford court records, p. 296.

[31]*Utica Observer*, September 1, 1916, p. 10.

[32]*Utica Herald-Dispatch*, September 1, 1916, p. 2; *Utica Daily Press*, September 2, 1916, p. 8; *Utica Observer*, September 1, 1916, p. 10; Justice's Criminal Docket, Hon. W. E. Nelson, Town of New Hartford, p. 296.

[33]*Utica Daily Press*, September 1, 1916, p. 6.

[34]Quotation from *Utica Daily Press*, September 2, 1916, p. 6. It was also carried in *Utica Herald-Dispatch*, September 2, 1916, p. 3.

[35]*Utica Daily Press*, September 2, 1916, p. 6.

[36]*Utica Daily Press*, September 2, 1916, p. 6.

[37]*Utica Daily Press*, September 2, 1916, p. 6.

[38]*Utica Daily Press*, September 2, 1916, p. 6; *Utica Herald-Dispatch*, September 2, 1916, p. 3.

[39]*Utica Daily Press*, September 2, 19 16, p. 8.

[40]*Utica Daily Press*, September 2, 1916, p. 8.

[41]Quotations from *Utica Daily Press*, September 2, 1916, p. 8; *Utica Herald-Dispatch*, September 2, 1916, p. 2; *Utica Observer*, September 2, 1916, p. 10.

[42]*Utica Herald-Dispatch*, September 2, 1916, p. 2.

[43]*Utica Daily Press*, September 2, 1916, p. 8; *Utica Observer*, September 2, 1916, p. 10; *Utica Herald-Dispatch*, September 2, 1916, p. 2.

[44]*Utica Daily Press*, September 2, 1916, p. 8; *Utica Observer*, September 2, 1916, p. 10.

[45]*Utica Daily Press*, September 2, 1916, p. 8.

[46]*Utica Observer*, September 2, 1916, p. 10.

[47]*Utica Daily Press*, September 4, 1916, p. 6.

[48]*Utica Daily Press*, September 4, 1916, p. 6 *Utica Herald-Dispatch*, September 4, 1916, p. 11.

272   *United We Stand*

⁴⁹*Utica Daily Press*, September 4, 1916, p. 6. It also appeared in *Utica Herald-Dispatch*, September 4, 1916, p. 11.

⁵⁰*Utica Herald-Dispatch*, September 6, 1916, p. 2; *Utica Daily Press*, September 6, 1916; Furgal interview.

⁵¹*Utica Daily Press*, September 4, 1916, p. 6; *Utica Herald-Dispatch*, September 5, 1916, p. 4.

⁵²*Utica Herald-Dispatch*, September 5, 1916, p. 4.

⁵³*Utica Daily Press*, September 6, 1916.

⁵⁴*Utica Herald-Dispatch*, September 7, 1916, p. 5.

⁵⁵*Utica Herald-Dispatch*, September 7, 1916, p. 5.

⁵⁶*Utica Herald-Dispatch*, September 8, 1916, p. 2; Furgal interview; Dziedzic interview; Rosinski interview; Kupiec interview; Rent Roll Book, 1916-1920, New York Mills Corporation Papers, MSS.2/NYM.4/RRO.4; Justice's Criminal Docket, Hon. Seymour Bentley, Town of New Hartford, September 7, 1916. According to the justice's docket, Borek was charged with a misdemeanor violation of Section 43, but was deemed not guilty and discharged.

⁵⁷Giergielewicz and Krzyżanowski, p. 21.

⁵⁸*Utica Herald-Dispatch*, September 8, 1916, p. 2.

⁵⁹*Utica Advocate*, September 16, 1916, p. 1.

⁶⁰*Utica Herald-Dispatch*, September 15, 1916, p. 8.

⁶¹Rent Roll Book, 1916-1920, New York Mills Corporation Papers, MSS.2/NYM.4/RRO.4.

⁶²Kozak interview; Krawiec interview; Dziedzic interview.

⁶³Kozak interview.

⁶⁴Dziedzic interview.

⁶⁵Furgal interview; Records of the New York Mills Corporation, MSS.2/NYM.4/RRO.4 - Rent Roll, 1916-1920.

⁶⁶Interview of Sadie Nassif by Stella Furgal, November 23, 1987 [hereafter cited as Nassif interview]. Ferris George was an Anglicized name; they original name was probably Farash Nassif.

⁶⁷Records of the New York Mills Corporation, MSS.2/NYM.4/RRO.4 - Rent Roll, 1916-1920.

⁶⁸Dziedzic interview.

⁶⁹*Utica Herald-Dispatch*, September 20, 1916, p. 2; *Utica Daily Press*, September 21, 1916, p. 5.

⁷⁰*Utica Herald-Dispatch*, September 20, 1916, p. 2; *Utica Daily Press*, September 21, 1916, p. 5).

⁷¹*Utica Advocate*, September 23, 1916, p. 1 and September 30, 1916, p. 1; *Utica Herald-Dispatch*, September 21, 1916, p. 4.

⁷²*Utica Daily Press*, September 22, 1916, p. 16.

⁷³Rent Roll Book, 1916-1920, New York Mills Corporation Papers, MSS.2/NYM.4/RRO.4.

⁷⁴*Utica Herald-Dispatch*, October 4, 1916, p. 12.

⁷⁵*Utica Sunday Tribune*, October 15, 1916, p. 3; *Utica Herald-Dispatch*, September 8, 1916, p. 2.

⁷⁶*Utica Sunday Tribune*, October 15, 1916, p. 3.

[77]*Utica Sunday Tribune*, October 15, 1916, p. 3; *Utica Sunday Tribune*, October 15, 1916, p. 3.

[78]*Utica Herald-Dispatch*, October 21, 1916, p. 8.

[79]Quotation from Furgal interview. See also *Utica Herald-Dispatch*, October 21, 1916, p. 8.

[80]*Proceedings of the Sixteenth Annual Convention of the United Textile Workers of America* (New York: Freytag Printing Co., 1916), p. 4.

[81]*Proceedings*, 16th UTWA, p. 27.

[82]*Proceedings*, 16th UTWA, p. 38.

[83]*Proceedings*, 16th UTWA, p. 39.

[84]*Proceedings*, 16th UTWA, p. 39.

[85]*Proceedings*, 16th UTWA, pp. 157-158.

[86]*Proceedings*, 16th UTWA, pp. 158-160.

[87]*Proceedings of the Seventeenth Annual Convention of the United Textile Workers of America* (New York: Freytag Printing Co., 1917), p. 54.

[88]*Utica Herald-Dispatch*, October 21, 1916, p. 8; *Utica Sunday Tribune*, October 22, 1916, p. 3.

[89]*Utica Herald-Dispatch*, October 25, 1916, p. 3.

[90]*Utica Herald-Dispatch*, October 25, 1916, p. 3.

[91]*Annual Report of the Industrial Commission for the Twelve Months Ended June 30, 1917* (Albany: New York State Department of Labor, 1918), pp. 168, 174-175, quotes from p. 168; *The Bulletin*, a publication of the New York State Industrial Commission, Vol. 3, No. 5 (February, 1918), p. 126; *Proceedings*, 17th UTWA, p. 54. The latter source gives 96 as the number of families evicted, while the *Utica Herald-Dispatch* (October 25, 1916, p. 3) says 73. The difference may result from counting only the New York Mills Corporation houses, while overlooking those in boarding houses, or those in houses owned by the Walcott & Campbell Spinning Company.

[92]*Proceedings*, 17th UTWA, p. 54; *Utica Advocate*, November 18, 1916.

[93]*Utica Daily Press*, October 28, 1916, p. 3.

[94]*Utica Saturday Globe*, October 28, 1916, p. 6.

[95]*Utica Observer*, October 28, 1916, p. 8.

[96]Piszcz interview.

[97]*Utica Herald-Dispatch*, October 25, 1916, p. 3.

[98]*The Textile Worker*, Vol. V, Nos. 5-6 (October-November 1916), p. 4.

[99]*Proceedings*, 17th UTWA, p. 34. The comment about "the depths of a severe Winter" is certainly an overstatement, although the weather in late September and October was indeed cold and inclement, especially for those in the tent encampment.

[100]*Utica Advocate*, November 18, 1916.

[101]*Słowo Polskie*, November 18, 1927, p. 20.

274   *United We Stand*

Chapter 9: Epilogue

[1]*Proceedings of the Nineteenth Annual Convention of the United Textile Workers of America* (New York: Freytag Printing Co., 1919), p. 99.

[2]*Słowo Polskie*, November 18, 1927, p. 20; *Third Biennial and Twenty-Seventh Annual Convention of the United Textile Workers of America* (New York: UTWA, 1928), p. 44; Bourke, p. 27.

[3]*Proceedings*, 13th UTWA, p. 13; *Utica Observer-Dispatch*, October, 1944, p. 8B; Piszcz interview; *Słowo Polskie*, November 18, 1927, p. 20.

[4]*The Textile Challenger*, June 1945, p. 1.

[5]Quotation from letter, Benjamin Haskell, Director, Research & Publicity Department, UTWA, to William Silcox, President, Local 753, May 18, 1945, Southern Labor Archives, Georgia State University, Papers of Local 753 [hereafter cited as SLA/GSU, 753]. See also *The Textile Challenger*, June 1945, p. 1.

[6]Quotation from Bourke, p. 104. See also Bourke, pp. 91, 101-103; *The Textile Challenger*, December 1946, p. 3.

[7]Letter from Benjamin Haskell to William Silcox, January 22, 1946, SLA/GSU, 753.

[8]Letter Benjamin Haskell to Edward Robellard, Recording Secretary of Local 1442, March 5, 1946, Southern Labor Archives, Georgia State University, Papers of Local 1442 [hereafter cited as SLA/GSU, 1442].

[9]Letter, Benjamin Haskell to William Silcox, July 8, 1947, SLA/GSU, 753.

[10]*The Textile Challenger*, March 1948, p. 6.

[11]*Pamiętnik Srebrnego*; Dziedzic interview; Kozak interview; *Słowo Polskie*, November 18, 1927, pp. 20-21.

[12]Toczydlowski and Pawlak, p. 15; New York Mills Village Records, Vol. 1, p. 23, Village Board minutes from April 17, 1922.

[13]Quotation from Piszcz Interview. See also Furgal interview; Kozak interview; *Pamiętnik Srebrnego*.

[14]Quotation from Kogut interview. See also Piszcz interview; Furgal interview; Kozak interview.

[15]Quotation from Kogut interview.

[16]Piszcz interview; Kozak interview; Furgal interview; New York Mills Village Records, Vol. 1, Village Board minutes for March 26, 1923 and April 4, 1927; Vol. 2, Village Board Minutes for April 1, 1929, April 7, 1930, quotation from April 3, 1933 and May 15, 1934; Vol. 3, Village Board Minutes for April 1, 1935.

[17]New York Mills Village Board Minutes, Vol. 3, April 1, 1935 and September 13, 1939.

[18]Zima interview; Piszcz interview.

[19]Fisler, pp. 17-19; "New York Mills History"; Rosinski interview; Furgal interview; Dziedzic interview; Piszcz interview.

[20]Quotation from Piszcz interview. See also Fisler, pp. 17-19.

[21]Quotation from Rosinski interview. See also Fisler, pp. 17-19.

²²Quotation from Silcox interview. See also Fisler, pp. 17-19.
²³Fisler, pp. 17-19.
²⁴Fisler, p. 19.
²⁵Fisler, pp. 19-20.
²⁶Fisler, p. 20; Kelly, p. 4B.
²⁷First quotation from Zurek interview; second quotation from Zima interview. See also Rosinski interview; Kelly, p. 4B.
²⁸Dziedzic, "Ten Fingers."
²⁹Quotation from Furgal interview. See also Kogut interview.
³⁰Thuma, pp. 7, 13-14.
³¹Thuma, pp. 13-14.

Chapter 10: Summary and Conclusion

[1]See, for example, *Dziennik Ludowy* of July 25, 1916; *Telegram Codzienny* for July 20, July 25, September 24, and October 28 and 29, 1916; and *Trybuna Robotnicza* of January 30, 1926. See also Walaszek, *Polscy Robotnicy*, pp. 168-169.

[2]Pula, "Dillingham Commission," p. 6-7.

[3]William I. Thomas and Florian Znaniecki, *The Polish Peasant in Europe and America* (Boston: 1918-1920, 5 vols.).

[4]Oscar Handlin, *The Uprooted* (Boston: 1951).

[5]John Bodnar, *The Transplanted: A History of Immigrants in Urban America* (Bloomington: 1985). See also Bodnar, *Immigration and Industrialization: Ethnicity in an American Mill Town, 1870-1940* (Pittsburgh: 1977).

[6]Richard J. Oestreicher, *Solidarity and Fragmentation: Working People and Class Consciousness in Detroit, 1875-1900* (Urbana: 1986).

[7]Tamara K. Hareves, *Amoskeag: Life and Work in an American Factory-City* (New York: 1978), and *Family Time and Industrial Time: The Relationship between the Family and Work in a New England Industrial Community* (Cambridge, Eng.: 1982)..

[8]John R. Commons, *History of Labour in the United States* (New York: 1918-1935, 4 vols.)

[9]David Brody, *The Steelworker in America: The Non-Union Era* (Cambridge, MA: 1960).

[10]Victor Greene, *The Slavic Community on Strike* (Notre Dame, 1968).

[11]David L. Carlton, *Society and Town in South Carolina, 1880-1920* (Baton Rouge: 1982).

[12]Jonathan Prude, *The Coming of Industrial Order: Town and Factory Life in Rural Massachusetts, 1810-1860* (Cambridge, Eng.: 1983) and Cynthia J. Shelton, *The Mills of Manayunk: Industrialization and Social Conflict in the Philadelphia Region, 1787-1837* (Baltimore: 1986).

Bibliography

Manuscript Collections

American Federation of Labor Papers, State Historical Society of Wisconsin.

Court Records, Town of New Hartford, New Hartford, New York.

Court Records, Town of Whitestown, Whitesboro, New York.

New York Mills Company Records, Oneida County Historical Society, Utica, NY. This valuable collection includes some 188 volumes of rent books, account ledgers, journal and day books, sales books, cash books, laboratory test records, and other topics relating the the operation and management of the New York Mills Corporation, 1809 through the 1920s.

New York Mills Library, local history collection, New York Mills, New York.

New York Mills Village Archives, New York Mills, New York.

St. Mary, Our Lady of Częstochowa, Parish Archives, New York Mills, New York.

Thirteenth Census of the United States: 1910 - Population, Town of Whitestown , Oneida County, New York, Supervisor's District No. 11, Enumeration District No. 180, Sheets No. 11B and 14A.

United Textile Workers of America Records, Southern Labor Archives, Georgia State University. This collection includes correspondence between the years 1940 and 1951 for Local 753 (Box 417, Folder 883) and Local 1442 (Box 418, Folder 910).

William Pierrepont White Papers, Department of Regional History, Olin Library, Cornell University. This collection of over 10,000 items arranged in 113 boxes includes some 400 items directly relating to W. Pierrepont White's activities as president of the New York Mills Corporation, and other materials relating the the development of the factories and village of New York Mills, 1809-1913.

Interviews

Chrabas, Cecilia Powroznik. Interviewed by the authors, July 13, 1988.

Chrabas, Zenon. Interviewed by the authors, July 13, 1988.

Dziedzic, Michael. Interviewed by the authors, January 16, 1988.

Furgal, Stella. Interviewed by the authors, September 13, 1987.

Jones, Mary. Interviewed by Winifred S. Pula, 1975.

Kogut, Peter. Interviewed by the authors, July 1, 1988.

Kozak, Bertha Nowicki. Interviewed by the authors, June 13, 1987.

Krawiec, Stanley. Interviewed by the authors, October 11, 1987.

Kupiec, Josephine. Interviewed by Stella Furgal, November 8, 1987.

Kupiec, Stanley. Interviewed by the authors, August 8, 1987.

Madey, Pauline (Kozak). Interviewed by the authors, June 13, 1987.

Motyka, Leonard. Interviewed by the authors, January 7, 1989.

Nassif, Sadie. Interviewed by Stella Furgal, November 23, 1987.

Nowicki, Stephanie. Interviewed by the authors, October 31, 1987.

Piszcz, Joseph. Interviewed by Eugene and Michael Dziedzic, August 17, 1981.

Rogowski, John. Interviewed by Stella Furgal, November 19, 1987.

Rosinski, Richard. Interviewed by the authors, September 12, 1987.

Silcox, William. Speech in the New York Mills Public Library and interview by Eugene Dziedzic, Stella Furgal and others, September 20, 1988.

Szczych, Sophie. Interviewed by Stella Furgal, February 7, 1988.

Zima, Stanley. Interviewed by the authors, November 19, 1988.

Zurek, Stephen. Interviewed by the authors, May 25, 1989.

Published Documents

Annual Report of the Adjutant General of the State of New York for the Year 1912. Albany: J. B. Lyon Company, Printers, 1913.

Annual Report of the Bureau of Labor Statistics. Albany: Department of Labor, 1912.

Annual Report of the Bureau of Labor Statistics. Albany: Department of Labor, 1913.

Annual Report of the Bureau of Statistics of Labor, 1884. Albany: New York State Bureau of Labor, 1885.

Annual Report of the Industrial Commission for the Twelve Months Ended June 30, 1917. Albany: New York State Department of Labor, 1918.

"Changes in Wages and Hours in 1913." Albany: New York State Department of Labor Bulletin No. 64, Series on Wages and Hours No. 1, 1914.

"Court Decisions on Workmen's Compensation Law August, 1916-May, 1918." Albany: New York State Department of Labor, Bureau of Statistics and Information, Bulletin No. 87, Part I, June, 1918.

"Court Decisions on Workmen's Compensation Law August, 1916-June, 1919." Albany: New York State Department of Labor, Bureau of Statistics and Information, Bulletin No. 95 (Constituting Part II of No. 87), September, 1919.

"Dangers in Manufacture of Paris Green and Scheele's Green," Special Bulletin No. 83 of the New York State Department of Labor. Albany: The Industrial Commission, July, 1917.

"Directory of Trade Unions 1914." Albany: New York State Department of Labor, Bureau of Statistics and Information, Bulletin No. 63, Series on Labor Organization No. 2.

"Idleness or Organized Wage Earners in the First Half of 1914." Albany: New York State Department of Labor, Bureau of Statistics and Information, Bulletin No. 61, Series on Unemployment No. 3.

Konstytucya Pol. Hali Robotniczej Inkorporowanej w New York Mills, N. Y. New York Mills, NY: Drukiem J. Łabuz, 1913.

Preliminary Report of the Factory Investigating Commission, 1912, 3 Volumes. Albany: The Argus Company, Printers, 1912.

Proceedings of the Eleventh Annual Convention of the United Textile Workers of America. Published by the U.T.W.A., 1912.

Proceedings of the Nineteenth Annual Convention of the United Textile Workers of America. New York: Freytag Printing Co., 1919.

Proceedings of the Seventeenth Annual Convention of the United Textile Workers of America. New York: Freytag Printing Co., 1917.

Proceedings of the Sixteenth Annual Convention of the United Textile Workers of America. New York: Freytag Printing Co., 1916.

Proceedings of the Twelfth Annual Convention of the United Textile Workers of America. Published by the U.T.W.A., 1912.

"Report of the Bureau of Mediation and Arbitration for 1912," *New York Labor Bulletin*, Vol. XIV, No. 1 (June 1912).

"Statistics of Trade Unions in 1913." Albany: New York State Department of Labor, Bureau of Statistics and Information, Bulletin No. 60, Series on Labor Organization No. 1.

"Statistics of Trade Unions in 1914." Albany: New York State Department of Labor, Bureau of Statistics and Information, Bulletin No. 74.

"Strikes and Lockouts in 1912 and 1913." New York State Department of Labor Bulletin No. 66. Albany: Bureau of Mediation and Arbitration, 1913.

Third Biennial and Twenty-Seventh Annual Convention of the United Textile Workers of America. New York: U.T.W.A., 1928.

Twelfth Annual Report of the Commissioner of Labor for the Twelve Months Ended September 30, 1912. Albany: New York State Department of Labor, 1913.

Twelfth Biennial Convention, United Textile Workers of America, A. F. of L.

Twenty-Sixth Convention and Concert, Polish Singers Alliance of America, District 6. Utica, NY: n.p., 1958.

"Union Rates of Wages and Hours in 1913." Albany: New York State Department of Labor, Bulletin No. 65, Series on Wages and Hours No. 2, 1914.

Williams, John. "Annual Report of the Bureau of Labor Statistics," New York State Assembly Document No. 48C, March 17, 1913.

Williams, John. "Eighth Annual Report of the Commissioner of Labor," New York State Assembly Document No. 30A, January 18, 1909.

Williams, John. "Eleventh Annual Report of the Commissioner of Labor," New York State Assembly Document No. 28A, February 5, 1911.

Williams, John. "Ninth Annual Report of the Commissioner of Labor," New York State Assembly Document No. 30A, January 24, 1910.

Williams, John. "Twelfth Annual Report of the Commissioner of Labor," New York State Assembly Document No. 48A, March 17, 1913.

Dissertations, Theses, Reports and Other Unpublished Manuscripts

Bancroft, Everett Clair. "The Basis of Cotton Textiles — Raw Material," in "Textiles .... A Dynamic Industry," Textile Study Project, Department of Economics, Colgate University, September, 1951.

Bourke, Norman Francis. "A Study of Unionism in the Textile Industry of Utica, New York," M. S. Thesis, Cornell University, October, 1946.

Crook, Wilfrid H. "Inter- and Intra-Union Conflicts," in "Textiles .... A Dynamic Industry," Textile Study Project, Department of Economics, Colgate University, September, 1951.

Dziedzic, Eugene. "Ten Fingers: An Account of the Development of N. Y. Mills with an Emphasis on the Polish-American Experience in That Locale." Unpublished paper.

Fisler, Barbara C. "The Textile Industry in New York Mills: Development and Decay," July, 1968.

Indenture, Lot 13, Woodhull Tract, Oneida County, State of New York, in the possession of Eugene Dziedzic.

Jareckie, Stephen B. "An Architectural Survey of New York Mills From 1808 to 1908," M.A. Thesis, Syracuse University, June, 1961.

Kallas, Louis. "History of New York Mills." New York Mills High School, ca. 1940.

Kessler, William C. "An Outline History of the Textile Industry in the United States," in "Textiles .... A Dynamic Industry," Textile Study Project, Department of Economics, Colgate University, September, 1951.

Millson, Barbara. "Spatial Development of New York Mills." New York Mills, n.d.

Mortgage No. 1023, Polish Workingmen's Hall Association of New York Mills, Inc., July 17, 1914. In the possession of Ms. Bertha Solnica, New York Mills, N.Y.

"New York Mills History," n.d. Possession of the authors.

Savoie, Ernest J. "The New York Mills Company 1807-1914, A Study of Managerial Attitudes and Practices in Industrial Relations," M. S. Thesis, Cornell University, September, 1955.

Toczydlowski, Jeff and Jim Pawlak. "The History of New York Mills," May 16, 1975.

Van Horn, Schuyler. "The Little Falls Textile Strike of 1912," Independent Study Project, Hobart College, May 12, 1968.

Newspapers and Journals

American Federationist (American Federation of Labor).
Bulletin (New York State Industrial Commission).
Congressional Record (United States Congress).
County Courier-News (Clinton, NY).
Il Pensiero Italiano [Italian Thought] (Utica, NY).
La Luce [The Light] (Utica, NY).
Młotek Duchowny [The Spiritual Hammer] (Utica, NY).
Słowo Polskie [The Polish Word] (Utica, NY).
Telegram Codzienny.
The Textile Challenger (United Textile Workers of America, AFL).
The Textile Worker (United Textile Workers of America, AFL).
Utica Advocate (Utica NY).

Utica Daily Press (Utica, NY).
Utica Deutsche Zeitung [Utica German Newspaper] (Utica NY).
Utica Herald-Dispatch (Utica, NY).
Utica Observer (Utica, NY).
Utica Observer-Dispatch (Utica, NY).
Utica Saturday Globe (Utica, NY).
Utica Sunday Tribune (Utica, NY).

Published Sources

The American Story of Industrial and Labor Relations. Albany: New York State Joint Legislative Committee on Industrial and Labor Conditions, 1943.

Atlas of Oneida County New York. Philadelphia: D. G. Beers & Co., 1874.

Bodnar, John. "Immigration and Modernization: The Case of Slavic Peasants in Industrial America," *Journal of Social History*, pp. 44-71.

Briggs, John W. *An Italian Passage: Immigrants to Three American Cities, 1890-1930.* New Haven: Yale University Press, 1978.

Bruce, Dwight H., ed. *The Empire State in Three Centuries.* New York: The Century History Company, n.d. Multi-volume.

Canfield, W. W. and J. E. Clark. *Things Worth Knowing About Oneida County.* Utica, NY: Thomas J. Griffiths, 1909.

Chrypinski, Anna, ed. *Polish Customs.* Detroit: Friends of Polish Art, 1973.

Clarke, T. Wood. *Utica For a Century and a Half.* Utica, NY: Widtman Press, 1952.

Conk, Margo A. "Immigrant Workers in the City, 1870-1930: Agents of Growth or Threats to Democracy," *Social Science Quarterly*, Vol. 62, No. 4 (!981), pp. 704-720.

Cookinham, Henry J. *History of Oneida County, New York, From 1700 to the Present Time.* Chicago: S. J. Clarke Publishing Company, 1912. 2 Vols.

Davis, Susan G. "Old-Fashioned Polish Weddings in Utica, New York," *New York Folklore*, Vol. 4, No. 1-4 (Summer-Winter, 1978), pp. 89-102.

Davis, Susan G. "Utica's Polka Music Tradition," *New York Folklore*, Vol. 4, No. 1-4 (Summer-Winter 1978), pp. 103-124.

Davis, Susan G. "Women's Roles in a Company Town: New York Mills, 1900-1951," *New York Folklore*, Vol. 4, No. 1-4 (Summer-Winter, 1978), pp. 35-47.

Diamond Jubilee, 1896-1971, Holy Trinity Church, Utica, N.Y. Utica, NY: Holy Trinity Parish, 1971.

Diamond Jubilee, 1910-1985, St. Mary of Our Lady of Częstochowa Church, New York Mills, New York. New York Mills, NY: Published by the Parish, 1985.

Dubofsky, Melvin. "Organized Labor and the Immigrant in New York City, 1900-1918," *Labor History*, II (1961), pp. 182-201.

Dudajek, David. "For Whom the Bell Tolls," *County Courier-News* (Clinton, NY), December 17, 1975.

Dunn, Robert W. and Jack Hardy. *Labor and Textiles: A Study of Cotton and Wool Manufacturing.* New York: International Publishers.

Dziedzic, Eugene. "A Brief Account of the Polish Community in Utica," in *Uniquely ... Utica* (Utica, NY: City of Utica, 1982).

Dziedzic, Eugene. "A 'Happy Easter' in the Best Traditions of Their Religion," *Utica Observer-Dispatch*, March 26, 1978.

Dziedzic, Eugene. "Christmas Customs Part of a Beautiful Legacy," *Utica Observer-Dispatch*, December 24, 1978.

Fink, Gary M., ed. *Labor Unions.* Westport, CT: Greenwood Press, 1977.

Fish, Larry. "N.Y. Mills Finds Itself in Limbo," *Utica Observer Dispatch*, May 9, 1975, pp. 9-10.

Flick, Alexander C., ed. *History of the State of New York.* New York: Columbia University Press, 1934.

Fones-Wolf, Kenneth. "Revivalism and Craft Unionism in the Progressive Era: The Syracuse and Auburn Labor Forward Movements," *New York History*, October, 1982, pp. 389-416.

Galenson, Walter. *The CIO Challenge to the AFL: A History of the American Labor Movement, 1935-1941.* Cambridge: Harvard University Press, 1960.

Giergielewicz, Mieczysław and Ludwik Krzyżanowski. *Polish Civilization, Essays and Studies.* New York: New York University Press, 1979.

Golden Anniversary, St. Mary's Parish, 1910-1960. New York Mills, NY: Published by the Parish, 1960.

Goldstein, Elizabeth and Gail Green. "Pierogi- and Babka-Making at St. Mary's," *New York Folklore*, Vol. 4, No. 1-4 (Summer-Winter, 1978), pp. 71-79.

Gompers, Samuel. "Immigration Legislation Effected," *American Federationist*, Vol. XXIV, No. 3 (March 1917), pp. 189-195.

Gompers, Samuel. "Reasons for Immigration Restriction," *American Federationist*, Vol. XXIII, No. 4 (April 1916), pp. 253-256.

Graham, A. A. "The Un-Americanization of America," *American Federationist*, Vol. XVII, No. 4 (April, 1910), pp. 302-304.

Harris, Seymour E. *American Economic History.* New York: McGraw-Hill Book Company, Inc., 1961.

Hartman, Peter and Marc Tull. "Photographic Documentation of a Polish-American Community," *New York Folklore,* Vol. 4, No. 1-4 (Summer-Winter, 1978), pp. 21-34.

History of Oneida County, New York. Philadelphia, PA: Everts & Fariss, 1878.

Jones, Pomroy. *Annals and Recollections of Oneida County.* Rome, NY: Published by the Author, 1851.

Kelly, Joseph. "Company Houses Reminder of Old," *Utica Observer-Dispatch* (Utica, NY), January 18, 1976, p. 4B.

Kruszka, Wacław. *Historya Polska w Ameryce.* Milwaukee, WI: Drukiem Spółki Wydawniczej *Kuryera,* 1905-1908, 13 Volumes.

Lamb, Wallace. *Lamb's Sectional Histories of New York State.* Phoenix, N.Y.: Frank E. Richards, Publisher, n.d.

Maziarz, Robert. "Polish Customs in New York Mills, N. Y.," *New York Folklore,* pp. 302-307.

"Membership of the A. F. of L. 1881-1911," *American Federationist,* Vol. XIX, No. 1 (January 1912), pp. 54-55.

Moses, John G. *From Mt. Lebanon to the Mohawk Valley: The Story of Syro-Lebanese Americans in the Utica Area.* Utica, NY: Privately Printed, 1981.

New Century Atlas, Oneida County, New York. Philadelphia: Century Map Company, 1907.

O'Brien, David. *Faith and Friendship: Catholicism in the Diocese of Syracuse, 1886-1986.* Syracuse, NY: Diocese of Syracuse, 1987.

Pamiętnik Srebrnego Jubileuszu Parafji Rzymsko Katolickiej Matki Boskiej Częstochowskiej w New York Mills, N. Y. New York Mills, NY: St. Mary's Parish, 1935.

Pamiętnik z okazyi Poświęcenia Kościoła oraz Wykaz Ofiar Imiennych z lat 1912-1918 włącznie w Parafii M. B. Częstochowskiej w New York Mills, N.Y. Utica, NY: Drukiem Słowa Polskiego, 1918.

Pamiętnik Złotego Jubileuszu Towarzystwa Krakusów Polskich Pod Op. Kazimierza, Kr. przy Parafji M. B. Częstochowskiej. New York Mills, NY: St. Casimir's Society, 1961.

Pamiętnik Złotego Jubileuszu Tow. Najśw. Rodziny Nr. 459 Zjednoczenie P. R. K. w Ameryce. New York Mills, N.Y.: St. Mary's Parish, 1959.

Peterson, Florence. *Handbook of Labor Unions.* Washington, DC: American Council on Public Affairs, 1944.

Priddy, Al. "Controlling the Passions of Men — In Lawrence," *The Outlook,* October 19, 1912, pp. 343-345.

284   *United We Stand*

Pula, James S. "American Immigration Policy and the Dillingham Commission," *Polish American Studies*, Vol. XXXVII, No. 1 (Spring 1980), pp. 5-31.

Roberts, Harold S. *Roberts' Dictionary of Industrial Relations*. Washington, DC: BNA, Inc., 1966.

Rozanow, Zofia and Ewa Smulikowska, *The Cultural Heritage of Jasna Góra*. Warsaw: Interpress, 1979.

Snyder, Robert E. "Women, Wobblies, and Workers' Rights: The 1912 Textile Strike in Little Falls, New York," *New York History*, January, 1979, pp. 29-57.

Szkoła Matki Boskiej Częstochowskiej w New York Mills, N. Y. New York Mills, N.Y.: St. Mary's Parish, 1948.

Thuma, Linnie H. "Image and Imagination: How an Ethnic Community Sees Itself," *New York Folklore*, Vol. 4, No. 1-4 (Summer-Winter 1978), pp. 7-19.

Towpaths, Turnpikes and Towns. New Hartford, NY: Oneida County Board of Cooperative Educational Services, 1986.

Wager, Daniel E., ed. *Our County and Its People. A Descriptive Work on Oneida County, New York*. The Boston History Company, 1896.

Walaszek, Adam. *Polscy robotnicy, praca i związki zawodowe w Stanach Zjednoczonych Ameryki, 1880-1922*. Wrocław: Zakład Narodowy im. Ossolińskich Wydawnictwo, 1988.

Walsh, John J. *Vignettes of Old Utica*. Utica, NY: Utica Public Library, 1982.

Wepsiec, Jan. *Polish American Serial Publications 1842-1966, An Annotated Bibliography*. Chicago: 1968.

Wesser, Robert F. "Conflict and Compromise: The Workingmen's Compensation Movement in New York, 1890s-1913," *Labor History*, pp. 345-372.

Whitestown 1784-1984: Official Commemorative Book for the 200th Anniversary of the Settlement of Whitestown, New York. n.p., n. d.

Yabroff, Bernard and Ann J. Herlihy. "History of Work Stoppages in Textile Industries," *Monthly Labor Review*, April, 1953, pp. 367-371.

Złota Księga czyli pięć lat pracy dla Polski w Utica, N. Y. Utica, NY: Polish Community, 1919.

Index

In the following listing, Polish proper names are alphabetized as if the Polish letters were English to facilitate usage. Alternate forms of names are indicated where they were in common usage. Names listed in the acknowledgements, preface and appendices are not included in the index.

Dziziel, Josephine, 87

Erie Canal, 6
Ethridge, Mrs. John B., 134
Evans, Evelyn Morgan, 8

Falcons, see Polish Falcons Alliance
Federowski, Stanisław, 127, 220
Fedeschi, S., 195
Felician Sisters, see Sisters of St. Felix
Fijałkowski, Rev. Aleksander, attacked by socialist labor leader, 125-126; attempts to intercede for union, 63-64, 68; career of, 63; mentioned, 126, 127, 128, 140, 220; photo of, 80; position on 1912 strike, 79; position on 1916 strike, 159, 173 174, 194, 195; pressured by A. D. Juilliard Co., 102, 144; supported by parishioners, 144-145
Fila, Jan, 203
Finney, Rev. Charles G., 9
Fish, George, 43, 47, 52, 55, 59, 75, 104, 106, 107, 108, 112; attempts to settle 1912 strike, 71-72; resigns in dispute over company tactics, 143
Ford, Henry, 150
Fox, Frederick, 175
French Canadian workers, arrival of, 7, 13, 226; in 1912 strike, 66, 72, 79, 83, 100; in strike of 1916, 147, 162, 173, 177
Fuller, ---, district attorney, 169
Furgał, Stella, 19, 26, 40, 210, 224; photo of, 20
Furgał, Jan, 88, 128, 175, 220

Gadziała, Bridget, 87
Gadziała, Józef, 24
Gadziała, Michał, 87

Geissler, Fred, 153, 157
George, Ferris, 204
George, Joseph, 192
Gilkowski, Aleksander, 86
Gilmore, Sheriff, 18
Głód, Józef, 208
Głód, Wawrzyniec [Lawrence], 136
Gołąb, Franciszek, photo, 28
Gold, Thomas, 2
Golden, John, on 1916 strike, 215; supports Local 753, 55 56, 138, 141, 146, 161, 212
Gomólski, Jan, comments on New York Mills, 125; editorial support for Local 753, 53-54, 141; photo of, 139
Gompers, Samuel, 46, 142, 231, 233
Gondek, Antoni, 31
Goodness, Ira A., 193
Goodyear, S., 201, 204
Góralu Czy Ci Nie Żal, 131-132
Górecki, Piotr, 129
Graham, A. A., 45
Grant, H. J., 99
Grant, Madison, 15
Greczkowski, Jan, 221
Greene, Victor, 234
Guggenheim, Benjamin, 109

Hałat, Marek, 23, 208
Hałat, Rozalia, 23
Hałat, Zofia, 23
Handlin, Oscar, 232, 233
Hareves, Tamara, 232, 233
Harvey, William K., sheriff, 147, 156, 157, 159, 160, 168, 178, 185, 193, 195, 201, 203
Haskell, Benjamin, 217, 218
Hibbert, Albert, 62; sends letter in support of Local 753, 60
Hobbs, Alexander F., 152, 153, 157, 170, 171, 183, 184, 199, 213
Hodek, Marya, 23

Eugene E. Dziedzic (left) was born and raised in the Utica/New York Mills area. He was educated by the Felician Sisters at the St. Stanislaus Elementary School in Utica and graduated from New York Mills High School in 1963. After obtaining a B.S. degree from the State University of New York at Oswego in 1967, he earned an M.S. from Syracuse University in 1972. He has also done post-graduate work at Colgate University.

Mr. Dziedzic has been a Social Studies teacher at Whitesboro Senior High School since 1967. He has published several articles on ethnic oriented themes and is active in many civic organizations.

Mr. Dziedzic, his wife Nancy, and their sons Christopher and Matthew, reside in Deerfield, New York.

James S. Pula (right) graduated from New York Mills High School in 1964, obtained a B.A. in social sciences from the SUNY-Albany in 1968, an M.A. and Ph. D. in history from Purdue University in 1970 and 1972 respectively, and did additional postgraduate work at the University of Maryland and Harvard University.

Dr. Pula is editor of *Polish American Studies*, the scholarly journal of the Polish American Historical Association. He is a member of the Boards of Directors of both the Polish American Historical Association and the Polish Institute of Arts and Sciences of America, and has published numerous books, articles and reviews in the field of Polish American history.

Dr. Pula has a son Michael and a daughter Marcia.